'Canna unlocks the mysteries of achieving financial independence with easy-to-apply tips, hacks and advice for anyone, because the secrets to managing money are not just for briefcase-wielding men! Canna completely changed my relationship with money by following her simple advice and steps as I work towards my own number for financial freedom. I refer all my followers to her videos and posts because everyone deserves to be their own "SugarMamma!"' Chloe Morello, International Beauty YouTuber

'Canna Campbell helps demystify investing, adding simplicity, efficiency and effectiveness in a busy world drowning in excess information. She is straight to the point, inspiring and gets the reader on track with a valuable financial balance in their lives.' Lars Kroijer, International Hedge Fund Trader and author of *Money Mavericks and Confessions of a Hedge Fund Trader*

'Listening to Canna is crucial for me in today's financial world – a world I sometimes struggle to fully understand. She makes sure I make the right decisions.' Tom Williams, TV presenter

'Canna Campbell is the money-whispering single mum who can turn your finances around.' *MamaMia*

'Canna's books are a breath of fresh air in a market saturated with every conceivable alchemy relating to money. Straightforward, common sense and highly motivational.' Peter Thornhill, author of *Motivated Money*

Mindful Money

CANNA CAMPBELL

VIKING
an imprint of
PENGUIN BOOKS

VIKING

UK | USA | Canada | Ireland | Australia
India | New Zealand | South Africa | China

Viking is part of the Penguin Random House group of companies
whose addresses can be found at global.penguinrandomhouse.com.

First published by Viking in 2019

Graphs on pps 150 and 153 courtesy of Peter Thornhill.

The advice provided in this book is general advice only and does not take into account your
financial situation, objectives or needs. Before acting on this information, you should consider the
appropriateness of the advice, having regard to your own financial situation, objectives and needs.

Cover photography by Julie Adams
Cover design by James Rendall © Penguin Random House Australia Pty Ltd
Internal design and typesetting by Midland Typesetters, Australia
Printed and bound in Australia by Griffin Press, part of Ovato, an accredited
ISO AS/NZS 14001 Environmental Management Systems printer

 A catalogue record for this
book is available from the
National Library of Australia

ISBN 978 0 14379 432 5

penguin.com.au

This book is dedicated to anyone who yearned for something better, and wanted to do something about it

CONTENTS

INTRODUCTION

SugarMamma – Mindful Money

'The real source of wealth and capital in this new era is not material things – it is the human mind, the human spirit, the human imagination and our faith in the future.'
– Steve Forbes

Whether you picked up this book in a shop, read about it online, follow me on YouTube, or someone kindly gave it to you as a gift, it has come into your life for a timely reason – to offer you a richer and more mindful experience of the world. This is *your* moment, to learn that there is more to living than being weighed down by money stress. In refusing to accept this any longer, and deciding to make that powerful shift from this point forward, you have chosen to create a healthier, happier and more financially mindful life for yourself and your loved ones. In choosing authentic financial freedom, you will proactively and intentionally create more time, energy and flexibility for yourself.

There is a Buddhist saying: *When the student is ready, the teacher will appear.* I don't view myself as your teacher, more as your financial friend or mentor – someone who deeply cares about *your* financial future. I speak as a real person who has been there, who understands how hard and frustrating it can be, who knows the emotions and exhaustion, but who wants to see you thrive and succeed and believes you can do this **because I know you can**.

I am not here to boss you around, to make you feel ashamed or embarrassed, or to judge you, but rather to help you, inspire you, educate and empower you, and to give you the knowledge, tools and strategies to change your financial future for the better.

This book – the steps, strategies and investment advice – is for everyone, no matter your stage of life or where you live.

All you need to do to get started is find a quiet spot, grab a highlighter or pen, and relax. As you read, highlight, underline, and circle any sections that resonate with you. You can add your own crib notes in the margins, and I've provided workbook spaces throughout for you to fill in your own calculations and goals along the way. Your old toxic financial habits, attitudes and mindsets will be understood, forgiven and then put in the past, while you create new, healthier ones that drive results. This book will become your personal financial map, to guide you and to lead you to your destination. And you can re-read it as many times as you like or simply return to your favourite sections whenever you need a refreshment of inspiration, so that you are motivated to keep growing and staying on your path towards even greater money mindfulness.

Using my personal and professional experience and knowledge, I am going to take you through everything you need to know about creating mindful money habits and a financially secure future. Together we'll start small and simple, keeping it nice and easy, as we steadily build financial momentum. Along the way, I have included my personal tips – they've really helped me, and I'm confident they'll help you too.

By the end of this book, you will be so thankful that you invested the time to do this for yourself today, not later. And as you see your finances and cash flow improve and strengthen, you will be in awe of what your future promises for you. This is exciting, so allow yourself to get excited.

As you read through this book, you will quickly start to look at money in a different light, with greater confidence. Money will become your friend.

You will experience a financial light-bulb moment, and you'll never look back as you continue towards a new world of possibilities, freedom and well-earned rewards. And those rewards will be whatever you want them to be: weekends away, long holidays, adventures, experiences and treats. Best of all, you will enjoy these rewards guilt-free, because you know and respect the amount of work that has gone into making them happen.

It doesn't matter how old you are, what country you live in, how much you earn, how smart you are, whether your parents have money or not, how educated you are or even how much money you already have in savings. This is about being accountable, taking ownership and responsibility, setting goals for yourself and raising your bar to see how amazing you really are at creating the life that you want and proudly deserve.

This book has seventeen chapters, each focusing on a different area that you need to learn and understand, but they're all perfectly in sync with each other. I will take you through everything you need to help you strengthen and understand your pathway to financial wealth. I'll help you find your entry point to get you started, and show you the next steps to work towards until you are happily on your way.

I'll help you create your list of priorities so that we maximise your financial efficiency, and then I'll show you the tools, steps and strategies that will continue leading you forward to your own personal financial destination.

But one size doesn't fit all, so I encourage you to customise my recommendations, ideas and strategies to suit you, your goals and your financially evolving situation. This is a creative process; there are no aggressive or strict rules, percentages or deadlines to follow. As you go through this process, you will quickly learn what works best for your situation and personal goals, so listen to your gut and let it guide you.

A LITTLE BIT ABOUT ME

I am just like any normal person, I love to travel, love good food, have a weakness for beautiful handbags, and will never say no to a good bottle of bubbles. And investing in my health and fitness are important to me.

I also love experiences and connection: spending time with my son, Rocco, my partner, Tom, my two dogs, Giuseppe and Sofia, and of course my closest friends, with baby number 2 (nicknamed Apple by Rocco) arriving around the time this book will be published.

What also makes me feel happy is being able to help people around me. The ability to give back is part of my passion, and led to my free YouTube channel, SugarMamma.TV, which has over 450 videos and is watched around the world by over 115 000 subscribers and is growing every day as well as my website, SugarMamma.TV.

These are the things that make me feel authentically wealthy. By becoming more financially free, I gain greater time to enjoy these precious moments and people, and I can be present for them more often.

IF I CAN DO THIS, SO CAN YOU

Being dyslexic, and having auditory perception difficulty and a stutter, I was at the bottom of the class for almost every subject at school. I did the simplest type of maths on the school curriculum, and focused on creative subjects such as French, Drama, Photography and – my favourite subject – Business Studies, to get me through my final year of school.

But these learning difficulties taught me an extremely valuable skill. Managing my dyslexia taught me how to break letters, words, sentences and stories down into small and manageable parts. I was taught to look at things differently, and to develop creative ways to overcome the challenges in processing and understanding concepts that come to most people automatically. I taught myself how to look at problems from different angles and to make them fun and easy so that I would want to keep progressing. And I taught myself how to put my head down, focus, get motivated and work my backside off. These skills have contributed significantly to how and why I am here today.

While I was at school, I studied hard so that no matter what mark I got, I could honestly say that I had genuinely tried my best, and would have no regrets.

Fortunately, I ended up surprising my parents – and myself! – and got into a good university course. All of which actually meant nothing in the end! I had absolutely no idea what I might do with myself after I graduated, but I had faith that a sign would come my way – and it did. (Phew!)

My first job out of school, while studying at university, was working in a bar; I focused on good customer service throughout the long shifts and always walked away with tips in my pocket.

After my shift every Friday and Sunday night, I would come home at 3.30 a.m., stinking of house spirits, sweat and other people's cigarettes. Exhausted and with my brain still thumping in rhythm to the loud music that I'd been listening to for the last eight hours, I would throw my cash tips into the drawer of my bedside table, telling myself I'd 'deal with that later'.

About a year passed and my late-night cash deposit habit continued. I never thought much about the little piggy bank accumulating in my bedroom until one afternoon, looking for absolutely anything to distract me from studying for my upcoming econometrics exam, I decided to count all the gummy $5 and $10 notes that were by now overflowing from my bedside table drawer.

Shocked but pleasantly impressed by how quickly those $5 and $10 notes had added up, I decided to take my hard-earned tips to the bank. No, not to deposit them, like any sensible person would do, but to convert them into $100 notes as they were 'taking up too much room'! So, I popped up to the bank in my 1990 Holden Barina and converted them into fresh, clean, cool green $100 notes and promptly returned them to my safe and secure bedside table. (The first place any burglar will strike.)

Little did I know, apparently when you bank large amounts of cash, especially in small denominations, it signals potential drug money and laundering! So they asked me a few questions and took a copy of my driver's licence. The second thing I should point out is that I did this cash conversion at the bank nearest to my home – not my personal bank but my parents' bank, where my parents visit daily and are known personally.

So, upon my father's visit to the bank later that day, the same bank teller who served me decided to inform my father about my recent visit to the bank and my little bounty of cash. (Yes, a total privacy breach!)

My father came home ropeable! But he wasn't furious that I had such a large chunk of cash that wasn't being kept safe, rather that it was sitting there not earning any income or capital growth. The next day he took me to my personal bank, where my neat pile of $100 notes was deposited into my own account and then promptly withdrawn to be invested in my first parcel of shares.

It went in and out so quickly, but for a brief few seconds I got to see, for the first time in my life, those figures in my bank account, which I had never experienced before. It felt good – really good.

Initially, I was not impressed by my father's bossiness when it came to dealing with my hard-earned tips. But when I opened the mail to find my first dividend cheque (which is part of the business profits, paid to shareholders for being a part owner of the business), my mental money shift began.

I showed my father the cheque, not quite sure if it was really meant for me. 'What do I do with it?' I asked sheepishly.

'Well, Canna, it's yours. You can deposit it in your savings account, or reinvest it,' he told me.

'But I did nothing to earn it,' I said, feeling a sense of unworthiness.

He replied, 'Yes, it's called passive income: it is your money, working for you.'

My brain was freezing up with confusion – and I was nervous about sounding even more stupid if I asked another question. But, to be honest, I was also impressed that I hadn't had to stand behind a bar for eight hours with people screaming at me for rum and Cokes to earn the three digits written in black and white on the cheque in my hand.

Finally, I pushed myself to ask another question: 'So what should I do with it?'

My father sighed, but realised that if he didn't answer my question, there was no way I was going to leave him in peace. 'If you want to, you could actually use it to buy more shares, and then the dividends will grow slowly over time and get bigger.'

I curled up in my bedroom to mull over this idea. Could I potentially build this 'passive income' over time and get it to a point where my dividends covered my living expenses? And if I could, I would never need to work . . . Imagine that!

I could travel the world, donate time and money to charity, pay for good-quality food and education, and, best of all, have time and choice.

That was my personal *aha* moment.

Surely, if I had come this far without too much effort, I could keep going and build upon this amount. The excitement of this possibility burned inside of me and I wanted to really get into this and keep going.

And so I did.

I kept shopping for investments and building up my passive income. And soon I realised how important it was to me to show other people how to do this for themselves and help make their own lives financially easier. So I started working part time for a financial planning business, while studying full time at university for my Advanced Diploma of Financial Planning. I was busy, but it was worth it.

I read a wide range of books – some exceptionally boring, and others with embarrassingly stupid and extremely dangerous advice.

And I put my money where my mouth was, continuing to save hard and invest sensibly and regularly. I watched the growth of my investments and, more importantly, my passive income grow.

After working for a range of amazing financial planning businesses including a bank, I launched my own boutique financial planning business, SASS Financial, at age twenty-six.

I was completely naive at the time, but I'm grateful for that, as I may never have taken that leap otherwise. And SASS has gone from strength to strength, even through the challenges of the GFC. I managed to build an amazing business of special clients with important goals.

SugarMamma.TV was launched in early 2015, when I was home alone with Rocco. My financial planning client and friend, the influential beauty vlogger Chloe Morello, had just given me that much-needed push of encouragement to start my own YouTube channel. Her support, enthusiasm and genuine passion for female empowerment is incredible, and I owe her so much. Thank you, Chloe.

Life is full of stresses, deadlines, hardships, pressures, challenges, expectations and occasionally crises, so if you can take financial stress out of the equation, life should be that little bit easier for you. For example, sometimes I hear people say they have chosen not to have another child because 'they can't afford to', even though they would absolutely love to. Hearing this breaks my heart.

Similarly, financial pressure is a leading cause of divorce. And I am pretty sure that you would be pressed to find a doctor who would say that financial stress is good for physical and mental health.

For me, putting in a few hard yards now for long-term peace of mind is an invaluable investment. Not only financially, but also physically and emotionally.

Knowing that I don't have the distraction and drain of financial stress gives me a really good feeling. Knowing that I am on the right path to arrive at my destination on time – and that I have the flexibility to tweak and alter my adventure as I choose – feels empowering and responsible. Taking care of my financial future is one of the highest forms of self-love and self-respect I can practise.

I can be more focused at work, a more supportive and loving partner, a more fun and energetic mother, and a more reliable and supportive friend. And the financial freedom to take regular holidays and weekends away helps break up my year and recharge my batteries with quality connection time and the creation of memories.

So, I'm going to use this passion and determination to show you how to look after yourself financially, get out of toxic debt, create emergency savings and, most importantly, build your own passive income, giving you a richer life with more mindful money.

xCC

CHAPTER ONE

Authentic Financial Freedom

'Money loves clarity, so define what wealth means to you.'
– Denise Duffield Thomas, author and entrepreneur

Being a financial planner, I work intimately with people to help them achieve their financial goals and dreams, while also helping alleviate the stress and pressure that money can add to their lives. And these powerful conversations, where I get to really understand how people work, think and act around money, are where the best solutions are born.

I have seen so many different financial situations and listened to so many different stories, both good and bad. And, above all else, I've learnt that there are many misperceptions about money.

I meet people who appear to be living the good life: they have great clothes, impressive cars, dine at the newest restaurant, enjoy amazing holiday destinations. But as you peel back the layers, the reality is revealed: their lifestyle is funded by toxic debt. Frequently, they are living hand to mouth and only just surviving – most often, they are living in denial.

They may earn a large income, but their lifestyle has adjusted with every raise. They have increasingly higher rent or larger mortgages to pay, bigger car repayments, a greater desire for even more luxurious holidays . . . This is where our egos can become expensive, not just to our bank balances but to our souls.

For these people, holidays go on credit cards that are close to being maxed out, their cars are leased, and they rarely have much in their superannuation or retirement accounts, which are often scattered across different providers, eroding away in fees and the wrong investments. And there is definitely no emergency money or savings. They have no source of income other than their job, and an early retirement isn't sounding realistic unless something changes quickly.

They are slaves to their situation and choices.

This type of financial cycle is a toxic source of stress and anxiety for many. But it doesn't have to be this way. You can still have the things that are important to you, but with authenticity and gratitude.

My job is to help fix, improve or rebuild people's financial health by giving them the best advice for their situation and their goals, and, most importantly, educating them. And when they come out the other side and see the light, they say that their biggest regret is not doing this years ago.

The further along in life they are, the bigger the challenge; but on the flip side, the bigger and more valuable the potential growth – if, that is, they are ready for the shift. **Wealth creation is about education and mindset.**

I talk a lot about 'authentic wealth', and this is at the heart of what I want to help you create for yourself. To me, authentic wealth is not necessarily about being 'rich' or having lots of money. It is about having a happy, balanced life with a safe and secure financial situation which grows stronger and stronger each day. Where you can afford to be generous to the people you love and care about.

That sense of financial health and security comes from knowing that you have everything you need, and still spend less than you earn. Money that is left over is put towards further financial growth opportunities or for even greater financial security. Personal debt (if any) is paid off or reducing at record speeds – to your delight and relief. And all your other financial ducks are lined up correctly for you.

There are healthy cash savings set aside for emergencies, away from temptation, for your comfort and peace of mind. There is one superannuation or retirement account, invested correctly for your long-term goals. There are the right types of personal insurances in place for additional protection. And there is an established investment portfolio, providing a growing passive income stream, which you are free to add to if and when you feel inspired.

Most of the people I work with actually earn very modest salaries, and they still manage to build amazing portfolios and passive incomes that continue to grow organically year after year. These people are authentically wealthy, and authentically happy too.

They paid their mortgages off quickly as a priority; they built strong and consistent passive income, coming in from a variety of sources, which more than covers their living expenses. Their finances are well in order and they understand and respect the value of a dollar. And that appreciation breeds more financial abundance. **What you appreciate, appreciates!**

I have helped tens of thousands of everyday people achieve their dreams and gain complete financial freedom, and now it is our turn to **work together**.

Money certainly doesn't buy us happiness, but it buys us time and the option to do the things that make us happy, and helps create the life that we want. Taking away financial worry allows you to focus on what is really important to you and what makes you authentically happy – whether that be spending more of your time raising a family or caring for loved ones, turning your hobby into a small business (or even a big business), writing a book, starting a blog, working for a charity or travelling the world. Likewise, if something *doesn't* make you happy, you are financially free to move, get help, heal, change, fix, improve, quit, divorce or leave. The choice is completely yours, and you are free to change your mind along the way if you want or need to, because you have financial freedom. Here are some reasons financial freedom is an important goal:

- Financial freedom gives you the opportunity to live where you want when you want.
- Financial freedom gives you the comfort and space to focus on your health and wellbeing – mental, emotional and physical.
- Financial freedom gives you the luxury and indulgence of buying what you *really* want, when you want and how often you want.
- Financial freedom gives you the option to have as many children as your heart (and body) likes – without being financially stressed while raising them.
- Financial freedom gives you the time to spend with family and friends. Breakfast, lunch or dinner, anytime and anywhere.
- Financial freedom allows you to give your time and money unconditionally to charities, and to feel good about it.
- Financial freedom gives you the option to be able to help family and friends out when and if they need it; whether it is

to help them start up a business or do a course; reduce a friend's financial stresses; or help pay for lifesaving surgery or treatment for a friend or even a friend's pet.

- Financial freedom allows you the opportunity to take time off from your job to venture into something that you have always dreamed of, or to make a change in jobs even if it means lower pay.
- Financial freedom gives you the option to go part time or even retire early.

Basically, financial freedom gives you the ability to turn your dreams into your reality.

THE KEY: PASSIVE INCOME

The key to being financially free is having enough passive income to cover your living expenses and, if possible, have a little extra for a rainy day.

'Passive income' is what I like to call income that you earn while you sleep at night. It is your money working for you, instead of you working for your money. And it works for you by providing you with an income that you do not physically have to work for.

I am not talking about pyramid marketing, option trading software programs or get-rich-quick schemes. I am talking real financial assets and financial security by following practical and realistic steps.

Some examples of passive income are rental income from an investment property, dividends from shares or managed funds, interest from a savings account, or even royalties from books, music or videos.

In fact, you probably earn some form of passive income already – you just may not realise it yet!

If you look at your bank account statements, sometimes you see an 'interest credit' of, say, $1.05 – an amount of money paid to you by your bank, based on a percentage of your total balance for a certain period of time. That is an example of passive income. You have not physically, mentally or emotionally done anything to earn that interest in your account, no matter how big or how small your balance. We just need to turn up the volume on this passive income for you, so that over time it grows to $10.54 per month or even $10 540 per month.

One of the best aspects of earning passive income is that it does not require you to put on your work clothes, travel on packed public transport and then spend half of your waking day working to make someone else financially wealthy. Passive income *works for you*, day and night, weekends, public holidays, rain, hail or shine.

The first thing you need to understand about passive income is that you create it from owning assets. Not the car parked in your driveway – that's a liability, as it requires a constant flow of money to keep it (petrol, rego, insurance, and so on), let alone drive it. A real asset is something that generates an income stream all of its own and grows in value over time. If you want to earn more money and give yourself a pay rise, it's very easy – you simply buy more passive income sources or build on your existing passive income sources. And I am about to show you how to do this for yourself.

Some examples of passive income sources are:
- interest on cash savings or term deposits
- dividends – my favourite!
- rent for residential, commercial, industrial or rural investment properties

But before we jump to building these passive income sources, there are some important thought processes for you to go through.

DEFINE YOUR FREEDOM

First, you need to work out exactly what financial freedom looks like to you. Developing a crystal-clear vision of what is important to you is an essential step in this wealth creation journey.

If you can't visualise what you want, you won't have a destination to focus on. It's kind of like steering a ship – if you don't know where you want to head, you will keep drifting or going around in circles. How can you expect to actually get anywhere, let alone in the most efficient, safe and enjoyable way? **Without a destination, the journey will be pointless.**

Your definition of freedom is completely up to you and what your true, authentic self desires. You certainly do not need to justify your needs to anyone, including yourself. Whether you want a first-class lifestyle, or a lifestyle filled with simple pleasures, that is your business. As long as you are comfortable and confident with owning your definition and vision, you deserve everything that you can create for yourself.

Sit down and ask yourself the following questions:

What do I love doing?
What is important to me?
What would a perfect day look like for me?
What do I want to achieve in my lifetime?
What do I want to bring into my world?

Here are some of my answers and those of my clients' to help get you going . . .

WHAT DO YOU LOVE DOING?

- **Travelling** – going on adventures to new places and returning to special locations.
- **Exercising** – going hiking, strengthening my body and mind. Yoga early in the morning, cycling around the beaches or going for a surf during the day, golf on late afternoons.
- **Spending time with pets** – taking my dog to the park, riding my horse, curling up on the sofa with my cat.
- **Reading or listening to podcasts** – learning new things about the world and other people's experiences through their words.
- **Spending time with the people I love** – giving them my time and energy without distractions.
- **Learning** – discovering new skills and building my existing skills, such as taking up a new hobby or language, or improving a skill like cooking.
- **Contributing** – helping to make something better or being a part of the solution, such as working with disadvantaged people, endangered or abandoned animals or an environmental cause.
- **Creating** – using my artistic skills, cooking, photography, interior design and even fashion.

WHAT IS IMPORTANT TO YOU?

- Being there for my family and friends
- Not needing to worry about money
- Having the freedom to spend money on things I like, without guilt
- Being able to invest in my mental and physical health

- Being able to have breaks away to recharge
- Being part of my community
- Having time to catch up with my friends
- Having time to work on my creative interests
- Having time to work on building my career or business
- Enjoying my time without feeling guilty or watching the clock

What would a perfect day look like for you?

- Going for an early morning walk or sleeping in
- Going out to a restaurant or having a big cook-up at home
- Seeing a concert, play or ballet
- Studying for a new course
- Working on a hobby or new business idea
- Reading a good book or watching a movie
- Catching up with friends over breakfast
- Having a romantic dinner
- Spending time away with my family
- Enjoying new experiences
- Having a great workout at the gym without worrying about time

What do you want to achieve in your lifetime?

- Live in another country
- Learn another language
- Start my own business
- Have a healthy, happy family
- Build a healthier mind and body
- Form great friendships
- Travel internationally
- Help a charity or cause; make a difference

WHAT DO YOU WANT TO BRING INTO YOUR WORLD?

- **Security** – if an unexpected bill comes in I can pay it promptly without financial stress, and I can accept any financial challenge.
- **Spontaneity** – if a great opportunity unexpectedly presents itself, I have the financial freedom to give it a go without worrying about it negatively affecting my financial situation.
- **Independence** – I'm not reliant on others for my financial wellbeing and freedom, and I don't need to ask permission for financial decisions.
- **Generosity** – I can help out any family member or friend who is in need, whether that be financially or simply through giving my time and support without any conditions.
- **Gratitude** – I have more mindfulness, respect and appreciation when making a special purchase, guilt-free.
- **Freedom** – to make my own decisions without relying on someone, asking permission, justifying or even compromising.

Now it's your turn!

What do you love doing?

_____

_____

_____

_____

_____

What is important to you?

_____

_____

_____

_____

_____

What would a perfect day look like for you?

_____

_____

_____

_____

_____

What do you want to achieve in your lifetime?

_____

_____

_____

_____

_____

What do you want to bring into your world?

_____

_____

_____

_____

_____

Notice how none of these points are actually about finances? Sure, some of them require money, but, at the heart of it, it is all about what makes us feel happy, whole and connected.

By understanding what makes us happy, we can set a goal to start working towards. This gives us the determination to keep going, no matter what challenges come our way, because we know that it will be worth it.

BE THE PERSON YOU NEED TO BE

After you have worked out the vision of your future and completed the previous section, you need to consider the *person* that you need to be to achieve this new way of life.

If you want to attract and hold wealth, you need to tap into some additional characteristics that will help you achieve financial freedom.

Almost everyone I meet wants to have more money – it's probably why you picked up this book! And there is absolutely nothing wrong with that. However, while most people want more money in their life, only a select few (like you!) will actually put the right foundations in place and keep going with the journey to get the maximum emotional fulfilment and personal growth from this.

I hear people say, 'Next year I will start investing – right now I'm just enjoying myself, life is too short.' But often they've been saying that for more than a few years and, yes, life is short – so perhaps it is time to cut the crap and actually do what you have been promising yourself for so long.

Successful people are proactive people.

In order to achieve your goals, you need to adopt certain characteristics that will help trigger change within you. You need to tune in and take on these attitudes and approaches. To help give each characteristic depth and meaning, I think of people I know or know of, who I admire or am inspired by, who also hold these values, and I write down their name or initials to remind me on an emotional level of what that characteristic should look like.

If I ever struggle to think of someone, I simply think of movie characters, singers or entrepreneurs that possess these traits. Just the thought of these people is enough to tune into their energy, passion and mindset.

Personally, I draw upon the following characteristics to help me achieve my goal of complete financial freedom:

organised	**motivated**
in control	**inspired**
responsible	**open-minded**
focused	**appreciative**
aware	**happy**
calm	**determined**
resilient	**excited**
respectful	**self-disciplined**

Have you noticed that none of these characteristics are actually skills? They are all mindsets. Learn how to use the power of your mindset, and you will become that much more effective in achieving all your goals, financial and otherwise.

What traits do you need to develop to be able to achieve your own vision of financial freedom?

_____

_____

_____

_____

_____

HONOUR YOURSELF

One of my favourite quotes is from Gail Devers, an American athlete who, despite some serious health issues, won three Olympic medals.

> Keep your dreams alive. Understand to achieve anything requires faith and belief in yourself, vision, hard work, determination and dedication. Remember all things are possible for those who believe.

This wealth creation process is not going to be easy, nor will it happen overnight. But I guarantee you will feel a powerful shift each day that you work on your game plan, and you see your progress because we will track it against one big but simple goal.

And I promise to make it as simple as possible and show you how to achieve your financial goal in the quickest, savviest way – but it will definitely take commitment, hard work, self-discipline and healthy financial habits and time. So prepare yourself!

At times this process can feel exhausting, frustrating and simply too slow. But when we hit challenges, it is proof that we are creating the life that we are asking for. **And from challenges comes growth.**

However, if you do find your energy levels flat-lining, or you're feeling frustrated, it's important that you do whatever you need to do to recharge those batteries. This may be rewarding yourself with something nice, taking a weekend break or even getting a good night's sleep. Whatever works for you. Just stop and take a moment for yourself, to rebuild your energy and your self-belief. Or as my son Rocco likes to say, 'fill your bucket'.

Also, when times are tough, it's important to focus on the blessings that come from these challenging moments. What are your new realisations? What are you discovering about yourself? How are you growing? Some of our most profound strengths are born out of darkness. These might include:

Awareness
Control
Sense of direction
Sense of purpose
Respect of balance and responsibility
Change in motivation
Increase in determination
Strengthening of commitment

PERSONAL INSIGHT FROM CC:

It took me over six years to save the deposit for my first home. And as painfully slow and frustrating as it was, it made me appreciate how long it takes to save and how quickly you can spend those savings if you're not careful. When I finally purchased my first home, I was so grateful of the discipline that I built over time and so proud of how dedicated I was to making my dream happen. I appreciated my accomplishments so much more than I would if I had been given or won the money. I felt like I really grew as a person, maturing more and becoming more grounded.

After my parents watched me save for such a long time and remain so dedicated to my goal of buying my first home (which I still own today – it is rented out, contributing to my passive income), they contributed some money to put towards my deposit. Since then I've offered to pay them back, but they have refused, saying it was an unconditional gift; I am so grateful for this, and hope to honour them by doing the same for my children, grandchildren and even great-grandchildren, but only after I have seen their own sacrifice and hard work (see Chapter fourteen).

When I help coach people out of credit card debt, their attitude has often transformed so much by the time the debt is finally paid off that they are almost a new person in the way that they look at money in their lives. They are so much more respectful and appreciative of how they use and manage money.

They have come back from the dark side, leaving all the blame and guilt behind, because it was turned into lessons and blessing, allowing them to make peace within themselves. Proud of all their hard work, they have obtained the wisdom not to jeopardise their financial health ever again. They look back at the money mindfulness they have gained as a valuable lesson that they will carry forward forever and treasure.

What will you appreciate in this process?

_____

_____

_____

_____

_____

_____

What will you learn about yourself from this process and how will you grow?

_____

_____

_____

_____

_____

_____

How will you show appreciation of this process to yourself? (These are your rewards or 'bucket fillers'.)

_____

_____

_____

_____

_____

_____

POINTS TO REMEMBER:

- Your success is dependent on what you _do_ with what you earn.
- Passive income is money that you earn from your money working for you.
- The more passive income you have, the more financial freedom you have.
- Having enough passive income to cover your living expenses is the key to being financially free.
- Invest in (buy and build) long-term passive income and capital growth sources.

- Work out your personal definition of financial freedom.
- Define the situation that you are working to achieve for yourself.
- Being able to clearly explain to yourself what you are working towards will give you motivation and commitment to the journey.
- Make yourself accountable and responsible and commit to this.
- Leave the blame, shame and guilt behind. We are paving a fresh new path.
- Believe in yourself – have a powerful headspace and mindset.
- Identify the characteristics, strengths and values that you want to embody.
- Draw on the characteristics of people you admire to help you strengthen your own attitudes and approaches.
- Regularly remind yourself of the blessings and lessons of what you have learnt so far.
- Know how to refill your bucket – including budget-friendly strategies.
- Look for the lesson and growth you will gain from this journey. Your financial future is exciting now.

CHAPTER TWO

Your Number

'When your clarity meets your conviction and you apply action to the equation, your world will begin to transform before your eyes.' – Lisa Nichols, motivational speaker and author

Most of us have heard about the SMART goal principles – your goals should be Specific, Measurable, Attainable, Relevant and Timely. And we can tick off all these points in one very efficient swoop by working out your defining number.

How much money do you need per year to enjoy a comfortable lifestyle in accordance with the needs, tastes and desires that *you* appreciate and value?

This number will be the focal point of your financial motivation. Live it, breathe it, love it and, most importantly, do it.

This is the number that you should hold in your head as you drift off to sleep. It should spring into your mind the moment you wake up in the morning. You can hold on to this number for sanity in difficult times.

It is your light at the end of the tunnel, knowing that there's a bigger and better plan for you. Each dollar that you put towards this goal takes you one step closer to passing the finish line and grabbing your prize: true financial freedom and independence.

Let's work out *your* number.

YOUR NUMBER

To get started, let's calculate what your current living expenses are so that we know they are accurate and honest. Then we can add in or even take away your expenses for your ideal lifestyle, which we established as we worked through Chapter one.

First, look at your household living expenses. Start with the basics: food, gas, electricity, insurance, internet, clothing, and rent or mortgage payments. All the essential expenses that you must be able to cover as a minimum. **Round all these expenses up to the nearest $10 or $100, or simply add 10%.** We do this as a buffer to cover rising expenses.

Then move on to the optionals: gym, additional lifestyle clothing, takeaway and dining out, gifts, hobbies, beauty and self-care services, and social activities. **Again, round all these expenses up to the nearest $10 or $100, or simply add 10%.**

Then include the average amount that you spend on holidays and weekends away per year. Say you normally go on one international holiday per year at a cost of $7000 including airfares, accommodation and spending money, and you tend to have one domestic holiday per year at a cost of $2000, and then you have two weekends away at an average cost of $500 each. This means that you would spend approximately $10 000 per year on travel and adventures.

The final and most sensible expense to add to your living expenses is a regular investment plan. This is so that you can keep building your passive income, even when you are financially inde-pendent and living off this income comfortably. This helps ensure that your financial security continues to grow. This is a set amount of money that you put aside on a regular basis to put towards your investment portfolio's continued growth opportunities.

Ideally I recommend that you factor a minimum 10% of your total living expenses towards new investment into your portfolio, helping your financial security and choice strengthen further.

For example, if you discover that your total rounded-up living expenses come to $50 000 per year, you then need to allocate an extra $5000 per year (10% of $50 000) towards buying and investing in more passive income streams – either building upon your existing investment or adding new ones.

This means that you must allocate at least $420 per month into your budget for regular investing plans. This is not negotiable – it is essential for your long-term financial freedom, and it's the only rule in this entire book that I strongly recommend you follow.

To make working out your number a lot faster, easier and fun, you can use my Sugar Budget app from the Apple App Store – it will not only prompt you for these expenses, but also give you cash-flow instructions on how to manage your living expenses, which we will go through in Chapter four. Plus, because your budget is on your phone and easily accessible, you can quickly update and check it, which means that you'll always be on top of your cash flow and living expenses and stop any sneaky new expenses sliding into your budget without your permission.

Alternatively, I have a budget template you can access for free when you subscribe to the SugarMamma.TV website. And of course, there is a wide range of apps available, such as ASIC's Money Smart Track My Spend, Pocketbook and Money Brilliant, which are also free.

Whether you use the Sugar Budget app, the free budget template or your own budgeting system, your expenses and budget **must be written down** – and written down where you can quickly and easily access them. No more budgets in your head, or on a loose piece of paper. This is time to get serious and really understand the nature of your expenses, goals and values.

But you must check your budget on a regular basis, at least once a month. If you're in a relationship where you have combined living expenses, you must check them together. New expenses always creep in, which is fine, but you must decide if they can stay and what needs to be adjusted in your budget so that your cash flow remains under control and you aren't jeopardising your financial goals.

Once you have worked out what it costs you to live – in this example, $55 000 – you then need to factor in tax. So work out how much gross income you need to earn to net $55 000 *after* tax.

Our tax rates vary each year and are different for each country, so you will need to check your current tax rates (there are lots of tax

---

CHEAT TIP FROM CC:

It's amazing how easily we forget about or downplay our expenses, especially ones that only pop up once a year or so, such as those new tyres or a prang on our car above our excess, an unexpected trip to a specialist or someone close to us celebrating a special upcoming birthday or anniversary. Refer to your bank transactions or credit card statements so that you know your numbers are true and accurate and ask yourself what possible one-off expenses could realistically come your way, then factor them in.

calculators available for free online) or simply ask your accountant. But income tax has to be paid by everyone, regardless of whether we earned our income via passive income or slogging it out at work. It helps pay for the police that protect us, the hospitals that help us get better, the roads that we drive on, and many other benefits. So we must add income tax on top of this number to give us our final formal number.

So in this example, rounding everything up to be conservative, netting $55 000 per annum after tax would mean that we need to allocate $16 000 p.a. in tax according to the Australian Taxation Office's income tax calculator at the time of writing. Therefore our number would be $71 000 p.a. ($55 000 + $16 000).

And remember, this is to be passive income – income that you do not need to physically earn. It is simply your money working for you, rather than you working for money. And if you build this passive income properly, on a rock-solid foundation, it should continue – and, even better, keep growing – year on year. So, technically, your passive income will grow to the point it exceeds your living expenses.

Now *that* is authentic financial freedom.

The next step is to go back and look at your *ideal* lifestyle from Chapter one and work out how much that will cost, now that you have a grounded idea of what your *current* lifestyle costs.

We would rather overestimate our living expenses, and have a little extra left over as a pleasant surprise, than fall short and be bitterly disappointed.

Does your ideal lifestyle include more travel? Will you be spending more on education? Will you want more luxury? Or maybe you plan to give more to charity? You need to research what these will cost and add them to your number. It's not necessary to work it out to the exact dollar, but do some research into the estimated expense and then round it up to the nearest $1000 or even $10 000 to be safe.

Perhaps your ideal lifestyle looks like it will be cheaper than what you currently need to spend. You may want to move to a different town or even country where the cost of living is better value for money and taxes are lower. Or you might realise that you simply don't need as many expenses in your life as you currently have, or even that you are prepared to let go of some of your expenses and lifestyle if it means you will be financially free sooner. This could mean that your passive income number is much lower and potentially easier and quicker to achieve.

It intrigues me when I do this exercise with clients and see people choosing between certain lifestyles or an earlier retirement. Those 'essential' budget requirements, such as designer clothes, expensive restaurants and cars, often can't compete with the thought of not only retiring earlier but knowing the goal will be easier and more enjoyable to achieve. People start to see what is worth the investment of their effort, and reduce or cut out some of those 'essentials'.

And then, of course, you may be happy in your job and your life, but would simply like to create passive income to give you the benefit of more time. Perhaps you dream of cutting down to part-time work, studying part time or taking longer and more frequent holidays without creating financial jeopardy in your life.

The important point is to have a number – something concrete that you can set down and actively start working towards with motivation and direction.

We all have different desires, values and sources of inspiration. So listen to what excites you, what feels liberating, what resonates inside you, and honour that. This is your new financial journey, and simply knowing your number is enlightening – **and we have only just begun.**

What are my total annual expenses?
$_____ **p.a.**

To show you how different people's desires and journeys can vary, in the pages that follow I'll share the situations of a range of everyday people to illustrate their personal motivations for wanting to build up their passive incomes. These stories and situations may help you work out what you want from your financial future.

HONEY

Honey is twenty-four and has a good job in marketing. She loves staying fit and healthy with regular yoga and Pilates classes. She values buying fresh, healthy food from the local markets even if it costs more, because she likes supporting local businesses and purchasing consciously.

Her weekends are spent catching up with friends, often in new restaurants and busy bars. She likes to spend money on clothes and beauty treatments, but equally hangs out for an overseas summer holiday every year. She rents a share house with a group of friends in a fashionable inner-city area, where they share the household expenses.

What drives Honey is being financially independent, knowing that she decides how she spends and uses money and never needs to rely on another person to help her financially.

Honey's next dream and goal that she is working on is to create some freedom with her work, so that she can change to part-time work (three days per week) by age forty, and start her own business or raise a family. Either way, she wants to be on her way to being financially free by age forty. She wants to ensure that she is planting the right financial seeds early in life that will pay off over time, so that her money is working for her as quickly as possible and so that achieving financial independence is realistic.

Honey goes through her budget and works out that her rounded-up living expenses come to a total of $44 390 per year.

We then add 10% ($4439 p.a.) for her additional regular investment plan for a total of $48 829 p.a. (I always recommend rounding everything up to be safe and savvy, so we will call it $50 000 p.a.).

If Honey can build a net passive income after tax of $50 000, she can afford to cover all the important living expenses that mean something to her – without getting out of bed. She has complete financial freedom.

Right now in Australia, if Honey wants a net (after tax) income of $50 000 p.a., she will need to allow for $13 000 p.a. in income tax, making her number $63 000 p.a.

So as soon as Honey's gross passive income exceeds $63 000, she has the choice to quit her job, or reduce to part time, start her own business, or step into more casual consulting/freelancing work. Plus she has the comfort of knowing that she has prioritised at least $4400 p.a. in the budget that she can contribute towards her portfolio to help her investments continue to grow.

Honey's number is $63 000 p.a.

BEN

Ben is twenty-nine years old and works in mining, earning a good salary. However, he does long hours underground, and he is often under a lot of pressure from the corporate politics of the company he works for.

While he loves that he is not stuck behind a computer all day, he dreams of throwing it all in as soon as possible, moving to South America or somewhere similarly off the beaten track, volunteering to help build schools and homes with his carpentry skills, and surfing on the weekends.

After doing his research, he works out his number will only be $30 000 p.a. gross in passive income to give him this freedom. As the cost of living and taxes are lower in any of the countries that he is considering moving to, he doesn't need as much as Honey, but he has also ensured that at least $3000 p.a. is available to ensure that he can continue contributing to his passive income stream through his regular investment plan factored into his budget.

As a bonus, Ben knows that should he decide to return to Australia, he will still have $30 000 gross income p.a. This gives him the option of taking a different career path that may not pay as much as his previous job, but allows for more career satisfaction or even working part time.

Further still, should Ben decide that his dream isn't turning out to be quite what he thought it would be, or if he achieves what he wanted from his sabbatical and then wants to return to the corporate world, he has a surplus cash flow of $30 000 every year that he can put towards further wealth creation opportunities, giving him even more financial security and independence.

AMANDA

Amanda is thirty-eight, a single mother with two young children. She has just gone through a messy divorce. She is about to get her settlement after the sale of the family home and legal fees are paid out, which leaves her with just over $120 000, plus her superannuation.

She is an account manager earning a good income and enjoys her job. There are future promotions ahead of her and she is always meeting new people in her travels.

She has moved into a rental property and is happy to continue renting for at least the next ten years while she gets her children settled into a routine and focuses on rebuilding her life, particularly around her financial security. One day she would like to buy a home, but she would much prefer to prioritise building a passive income first, which will give her the financial independence that she values, and then she will re-consider buying a home only if the numbers stack up.

From watching the dangerous financial behaviour of some people in her past, such as borrowing large amounts of money and taking big risks that backfired with expensive financial and emotional consequences, Amanda does not want to take on any form of debt for the time being, but instead wants to slowly and steadily rebuild what she has left after walking away from her marriage.

She is great at managing her family budget and cash flow, and her goals are quite simple: she wants the option of being able to retire at age sixty-five and has worked out that by that time, her two young boys will have moved out of home, freeing up her cash flow. After doing her desired budget and checking it against her current budget she works out her number is $80 000 p.a., which includes our 10% rule for continued regular investment and income tax.

This will give Amanda enough money for rent, travel and the occasional special gift for her boys to help them along the way, when she thinks the time is right. In the future, when the boys are grown up, she would like to be in a strong enough financial position to help them out if they need it, but only after she has seen them help themselves first.

THE HOWARDS

Kim and Paul Howard are a couple in their early forties. They have two young children, ages one and three, a mortgage of just under $500 000, some super and a handful of shares that Kim was granted years ago when she worked for a bank as part of its employee share plan and Paul has some left over 'speckies' that he bought years ago, on the advice of a hot tip from a friend that flopped.

In their twenties they both did lots of international travel and had many adventures, but since then haven't had many holidays other than interstate trips on school breaks. Their weekends are spent cleaning and fixing things around the house, rushing to school sports and catching up on work emails and deadlines.

They don't have an official budget that they follow, but simply buy what they need or want without too much hesitation. They feel like they should and could be doing much better with their money but just don't know where to start.

On the plus side they don't have any credit card debt. Their $20 000 emergency money sitting in a separate savings account and their super are the only financial assets that they own.

They constantly feel like they are treading water with their mortgage never reducing and no money ever left over at the end of the month. Literally seeing their bank accounts close to $0 balance in time for payday.

When their children are old enough to appreciate an overseas trip, the Howards would love to be able to take them to visit some of the amazing destinations that they explored when they were younger, but the go-go-go pressure of city life, especially with children, the bills and long working hours makes it expensive and hard to squeeze in the time, leaving them exhausted and frustrated. This results in nothing ever happening or changing for them, no matter how much they voice their concerns and complaints.

Kim and Paul both enjoy their jobs and have made a good group of friends in their community, but they would like more time together as a family. They sit down to discuss their dreams, their goals and their fears.

After calmly and respectfully listening and hearing each other, together they decide that being able to each cut back their work by at least one day per week would allow them to slow down and enjoy more moments as a family. Little things like starting work later, being at the school gate at 3.30 p.m. and going on an international holiday every year is what reignites a spark and passion in them.

They work out that they need a passive income of $20 000 a year to cover the combined reduction in their salaries from shortening their working hours, and another $15 000 p.a. to pay for weekends away and family holidays. They have rounded everything up to the nearest $1000 and allowed for the 10% rule for future continued investment ($20 000 reduction in salary + $15 000 international holidays + $3500 continued new investing). When factoring in income tax, this means they need to generate an annual gross passive income of $50 000.

So their figures look like this:

$20 000 salary replacement
$15 000 annual holidays
$3500 continued investing
$11 500[1] income tax
$50 000

As the kids get older and more independent they may not want to travel with their parents, but Kim and Paul can actually still continue on benefiting from their number, either by increasing the number of holidays, the duration of their holiday or even their level of luxury – as long as they have their passive income of $50 000 p.a.

Honey, Ben, Amanda and the Howards have all made the decision to start building their passive income sources *now*. They can all begin shopping for investment assets that not only produce this essential long-term passive income, but also help ensure this income continues indefinitely; there's more to come on this in Chapter seven, so keep reading.

To help get there, they each need to use a combination of different tools and strategies that suit them, their comfort levels and goals, which I'll be sharing and explaining further along. And they also need to keep an eye on inflation, which I will also cover later. What is important right now is for you to work out your number.

Before you jump into working out your number, please keep in mind that the bigger your expenses, the bigger the portfolio you need to build. So if you want or need big expenses, it may take longer or

---

1   To be conservative, the income tax for Kim and Paul has been based on one income to one person, so in fact they may need less if they share tax equally across two marginal tax rates. However, they will need to watch additional tax payable on their total income as their passive income grows before cutting back to part-time work.

require a more aggressive approach to get to where you want to be. This is absolutely fine as long as you understand and accept it.

Your number = current desired passive income:

My number is
$_____ **p.a.**

Use this number to be your anchor and your motivation. Use it to encourage yourself to work smarter, not harder, and stay centred. And use it to eliminate mindless and squander-lust spending: each time you consider buying something that you don't really value, think of how you could be adding that money towards your passive income goal, getting you one valuable step closer towards your number.

NEXT STEP: SNAP SHOT SUCCESS

After you have worked out your number, we need to work out where you currently stand financially and what passive income you may already have.

This is how and where we will **track, monitor and grow** your success, which also helps us set important mini goals to work on (coming up shortly). **It is really important that you do this**.

Each time your financial situation changes, update your financial diary, workbook or journal – whatever your preferred tracking method is. Sometimes a simple note in your phone is sufficient – just make sure that you review it regularly and update it when achievements have been made. Even if you only add a small amount of money to your savings, investment portfolio or towards paying off your debts, make sure you **record it and track it, and add the date**. Every little bit counts, and it will feel euphoric seeing your hard work actually coming to fruition, and how far you have come. Making the process so much more enjoyable and worthwhile.

The feeling is not too dissimilar to being on a new diet plan – it can feel dull, boring and limiting, until you get on the scale and see the kilos dropping. Your shift in perspective changes and you can see that it is totally worth it and you want to keep going.

This is why it is so important that you track your progress, so that you are forced to see how far you have come and over what period of time. **Progress feeds success.** It fuels your motivation and pride as you see even the smallest successes as signs that you are on the right path, so that you remain committed, engaged and excited to create more progress. Progress towards success, i.e. **your passive income, your number**.

Honey's journal looks like this:

Date: 01/07/2019
My number = $63 000
My financial snapshot

Assets:
Cash savings: $10 000 (ready to start investing)
Emergency savings: $5000 (held in a savings account)
Superannuation: $23 500
Shares: $5600 (gifted from my grandfather)

Liabilities:
Credit card: $0
HECS: $0

My gross wealth: $44 100
My net wealth: $44 100

Your turn:

Date:
My number =
My financial snapshot

Assets:

_____

_____

_____

_____

Liabilities:

_____

_____

_____

_____

My gross wealth: $_____

My net wealth: $_____

CHEAT TIP FROM CC:

I keep my passive income diary and financial balance sheet both in my mobile phone and on my laptop (on the cloud). By keeping them in both places, I have access to the top-level summary on my phone any time I need inspiration, reassurance and motivation, while I also have the more detailed numbers and visual graphs that I can check on my computer. I update and check both regularly, every time something changes or improves.

Attending to this, which only takes a few minutes, fuels me with more energy and focus and inspires me to continue. I recommend you do the same yourself so that you can see and feel your progress.

As I work through my mini goals, I give myself rewards along the way. For mini goals it might be something like a hot bath, massage or even taking myself out to lunch, and then for the accumulation of lots of mini goals, (usually by the end of the year) I allow myself one special treat for all my discipline (usually a new handbag, or amazing pair of shoes!). I enjoy my treat with pride and without guilt, take a moment to reflect and look at that progress in my Snapshot diary, and then get excited about the new goals that I am going to set for myself, quickly getting back on the job putting my energy into my next mini goal.

So celebrate your achievements and success along the way. Do small, special things for yourself now and then and then maybe something a bit more substantial for the end of the year (not necessarily expensive!).

SET ME TO SUCCESS . . .

Now that you have an idea of what your number is, and a firm understanding of where you stand right now financially, we can start setting mini manageable goals that will lead you in the right direction towards successfully achieving your number and, in turn, your other financial goals.

Just like when I'm doing The $1000 Project, I have a 'big picture goal' to start with. I then build mini goals ($1000 at a time) around the one big goal (this is my number). That allows me to put 100% of my energy and focus on what I can do in the immediate term (i.e. within the next few weeks or months) to keep me on track and progressing towards my big goal, rather than paralysed with fear and feeling overwhelmed.

As you read through this book, write down some mini short-term goals that you can do right now. If you aren't ready yet to start working on your number, and you have other financial goals that you want to focus on, you should still do this for the goals that you want to achieve right now. They should be realistic mini monthly goals that are directly aligned to what you need and want. For example:

- Reduce credit card debt from $10 000 to $9000 by 30 March.
- Increase passive income from $250 p.a. to $300 p.a. by 30 August.
- Have $5000 in my emergency savings account by the end of January.
- Have $30 000 in my deposit savings account for my first home purchase by 1 December.
- Have my student loan down from $28 000 to $26 000 by 1 August.
- Buy $3000 worth of shares by 30 September.

Your goals must be defined with numbers, rather than vague notes like 'pay off credit card'. You must detail the exact amount, such as 'reduce my credit card loan by $4000 from $8000', to show the difference, so you are reminded how far you've come and to feel inspired to keep going. And you must also have a firm deadline – not 'in a month's time', but rather 'by 31 March' – that falls within the next few weeks or few months so that you are triggered into short-term action. I recommend this because by having a solid and short-term deadline, you will realise as each day goes by that time is ticking, and you will be more accountable and motivated to work to achieve your goal, rather than pushing it further into the future.

As Honey is ready to start building her number today, she makes short-term mini goals, which are purely focused around her number. She sets the date and the new passive income she wants to be earning by a certain date.

Have a look at this:

Date: 01/07/2019
Current passive income: $280 p.a. (dividends from shares)

Mini goal
Deadline: 01/08/2019
New passive income: $780 p.a. (from new investment portfolio)

Honey knows what to put her focus and energy into. She has kept it short term, simple and easy to follow, which should make it easy to achieve so that she can set the next mini goal, taking her closer and closer to her number, which is her big picture.

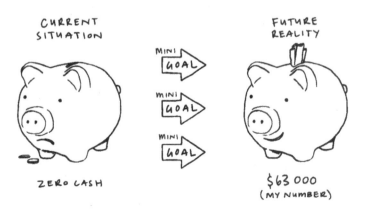

This is something you can very easily do for yourself.

Date: / /
Current passive income: $

Mini goal
Deadline: / /
New passive income: $

I recommend you read your mini goals and your big goals both morning and night. This way you wake up with determination and direction, and you fall asleep with the comfort of knowing that you are working and focusing on the right strategy to help your dreams become your reality. Also, new ideas and inspiration may come to you as you drift off to sleep.

As you achieve your goals through the month, start thinking about the new goals that you want to set for yourself next month. If you achieve these current goals quite quickly and with relative ease, maybe you could set something a little more ambitious? Remember that financial growth isn't just about money, but has a strong underlying element of personal growth – and when we are growing, we are alive.

If you find yourself not quite achieving your goal, but know that you have made a serious attempt, that's okay. We can't always expect to nail our goals ten times out of ten. You can adjust the goal and make it your next month's goal. This way, your eyes remain on the prize and you have another good go, with more experience.

I occasionally fall short of my personal monthly financial goals. Sometimes it is my fault, and other times life gets in the way. But I never give up – I accept it, try to learn from what went wrong so that I can be better prepared or know what changes I need to make, and then I go for it again. This is about self-love and respect, not beating ourselves up.

CHEAT TIP FROM CC:

Making yourself accountable for your financial goals is a great way to put some healthy pressure on yourself. A lot of people from the debt-free community post their monthly financial goals and results on Instagram, so everyone can witness what they're working towards. It allows others to comment, give support and share tips to help along the way.

I have a private members-only Facebook group called The $ugar Tribe, where we share our monthly financial goals (mine included). We encourage each other, cheer each other up when we fall short and celebrate each other's success. Anyone is welcome to join as long as you are serious about your financial goals. The details can be found on SugarMamma.TV.

In the next chapter we will invest some time, energy and care into readying your money mindset. I want you to be mentally and emotionally prepared as you embark on this financial journey so that this time your results are game-changing. This includes having the right headspace and strength so that you don't repeat old habits, self-destructive patterns or let other people hold you back. It is possibly one of the most important but also most confronting chapters in this book; it helps you do the internal work first, which will make the external work easier and more effective, with bigger and better results for you to revel in.

POINTS TO REMEMBER:

- Work out your living expenses, including your lifestyle costs.
- Work out the cost of your ideal cost of living – factor in travel, living expenses, upgrading of appliances and cars, charity – everything that is important to you and which you value.
- Factor in a minimum 10% for regular ongoing investment; if you want, add more.
- Add income tax based on your country's current tax rates.
- Round that number up to either the nearest $1000 or $10000.
- See your number and imprint it into your brain!
- Start your financial snapshot – this is particularly great for tracking your debt reduction.
- Start your passive income diary. Write down your number, then today's date = $0 passive income. Every time you do something that builds your passive income, update your notes. Even if it is only by $1, it is $1 more than you had yesterday!
- Set monthly mini goals around your number, defined with amounts and deadlines.
- If you aren't ready to start working on your number yet, use this approach to achieve your other financial goals.
- Read your goals morning and night.
- As the month goes by, and you are achieving your goals (or not), set new ones. Raise your bar each time and watch your financial muscle strengthen.
- Remember, progress fuels success.

CHAPTER THREE

Money Mindset

'The single most powerful asset we all have is our mind. If it is trained well, it can create enormous wealth seemingly instantaneously.' – Robert Kiyosaki, author of *Rich Dad Poor Dad*

I have realised over my years as a financial planner that financial well-being is not just about the numbers. In fact, the numbers are the easy part. Rather, it is about mental application: a firm commitment to the end goal, mindset change and acceptance of some sacrifice.

That's why this finance book is different from the rest.

I'm not offering a quick fix, but rather a long-lasting change to keep building your financial health and wealth. It's a change for good, beginning from the inside: always the best place to start for lasting change and serious improvement.

This won't be something that you try for a few months before giving in or forgetting. This time, you'll immediately see and feel the benefits from changing and improving the way you think about money and wealth. And then you'll keep progressing, raising your bar at every step.

But first you need to do the essential internal groundwork. Prioritising, reprogramming and nurturing the right mindset and self-awareness are some of the most important steps to building a solid foundation for great success.

Money is emotional. We all have mental blocks and self-imposed limitations, incorrect ideas or misunderstood messages, triggers and, of course, dangerous moments of self-destruction. They can be subtle, or they can be strong. And when these self-imposed blocks aren't analysed and challenged, they can hold us back.

The good news is the only place these blocks really exist is within our own heads. They can be overcome if we are willing to do the work. But first we must be able to identify and explore these blocks so that we can understand them, which gives us keys to then reprogram them to create goodness in our lives. Just think: if these negative thoughts, feelings and actions can create so much destruction, imagine how much greatness and happiness they can create when switched to the other direction.

The sooner you tackle this type of reflection and self-analysis, being as open and honest with yourself as you can, the fewer setbacks you will have. And when challenges do come your way (which they will, as they do for everyone as they are a part of life), you will recover more quickly and be back on your feet again sooner.

Sometimes it can be a little uncomfortable to uncover these blocks and incorrect self-beliefs. But **this discomfort shows you are on the right path** and making deep life-changing improvements. You can choose to see it as a sign to keep going and keep doing the work on yourself.

It's not dissimilar to embarking on a new health and fitness plan, with an objective to lose weight or improve your diet. If you don't do the mental and emotional work, taking the time to understand yourself, your body image history, your weight-loss setbacks, your eating triggers – all of which represent blocks in one form or another – you set yourself up for a longer, harder and more demanding journey towards achieving your health goal.

But if you pause and reflect before you begin, you invest valuable time and self care in yourself. If you can understand how your mind works, and what self-destructive, toxic and incorrect messages, patterns, ideas, misinterpretations and theories you have picked up, you can look at them constructively and rationally and then break them down, adjust them or even remove them, and start clearing the path ahead of you.

Often when I meet a new client and listen to them talk about their financial situation – what's working, what isn't, what they are worried about, what they'd like to achieve – I learn so much more about them just by listening to their choice of language and tone, rather than the facts and figures.

In listening to these stories and situations, I hear both good and bad attitudes, approaches and perspectives. Sure, sometimes we experience bad luck, but it's our attitude to the situation and the responsibility we take for it that determines the emotional effect of the outcome. We can either remain a victim stuck in anger, resentment, bitterness or sadness, or we can grow to become stronger and wiser.

I frequently hear excuses and misunderstandings at the heart of these obstacles: 'If I get a second job, I will be taxed at 50%'; 'My time is too precious to be thinking about money'; 'I'll have to wait until I earn more'; 'Wealthy people are often greedy or have ripped people off'; 'You have to be intelligent to be wealthy'; 'I work in a low-paying industry, I'll never be able to earn good money'; 'It takes money to make money, so unless someone gives me money, there is no point'; 'It's so much tougher to make good money in this day and age'.

If you have these attitudes, you need to challenge them, often by confronting some factual information to help kick you into action. For example, let's consider the 'idea' that if you take a second job, you will be taxed at 50%. It's not true. Your second job might be taxed at the highest rate, but you'll get that tax back as a refund when you lodge your tax return. You pay no more tax when you have a second job that what you would pay in tax if you earned the same total income from the one job. So that excuse is fundamentally incorrect.

And the claim that someone doesn't have time to focus on their finances really makes me laugh. No one is suggesting that we work around the clock to get ahead financially. Just a few extra hours here and there can make a huge difference, and not merely financially. Can you imagine sitting down to a meal with your family and friends, knowing that all your bills for the month have been paid? Do you think you'll be more present? Are you likely to have more energy and even time to spend with them?

When I sit down to dinner with Tom and Rocco, I can enjoy every second connecting with both of them, enjoying our quality time without financial distractions. Knowing that I don't have to worry about lack of money frees me up to focus on the special things that money cannot buy. So if you catch yourself using this particular excuse, it's time to realise that small sacrifices to gain financial control can give you more headspace to become a healthier, happier person.

Then there's the 'I'll wait until I am earning more money to start investing' excuse. Exactly how much do you plan to earn before you start investing or taking your finances seriously? What salary do you need to reach to start taking your finances seriously? Trust me, if you take your finances seriously from the start, you will never regret it. This is because when we get a pay rise, our living standards often go up with it – we either start buying more expensive versions of the same things, or simply *more* of the same things. We shift from Tony Biancos to Christian Louboutins, upgrade our computers and gadgets, and go on more frequent holidays or more expensive holidays, not to mention upgrading our cars. And stepping back from this more indulgent lifestyle can be hard and painful.

Know that there's never going to be a better time than now. Even if you can only save $1 right now, it is helping build a new habit. That new habit is a powerful one, and its power will keep growing as you persist with it.

'I work in x industry and the pay will never go above $x p.a.' Okay, but what if you scaled your skill? What if you turned your skill, knowledge and insight into a book, a workshop, a course or a product that could be of value to lots of people all at the same time without too much more effort? Such as an online workshop where you can help thousands of people at the same time? I recently met a childcare educator whose sister had set up a school camp for the kids in her local area and made a whopping $50 000 profit for the two-week program.

'It's too tough out there to make money, not like it used to be.' Again, wrong! There are more ways of making money than ever before: we buy apps, we buy software programs, we employ help with everything from building flatpack furniture to walking our dogs. People even sell ghosts in a jar on eBay! Everyone can do something to make money.

When you catch yourself in these destructive mindsets, look for the external evidence to prove yourself wrong, then be positive and kind to yourself – even if you have to google stories of self-made millionaires. These stories will shut down that toxic mindset immediately.

I could go on debunking these notions all day, but I'm sure you get the idea. Before we move on, though, try writing down your beliefs about money. Seeing them written down may make you laugh at how ridiculous they are, which will immediately set them free. Then rewrite them with an honest, realistic but positive attitude, removing the excuses.

Here's one of mine: 'It's too slow to make money – I'll be a hundred years old before I get to retire.'

I can switch this to: 'Sure, time is one of the most important elements to building stable wealth, but there are lots of things that I am doing today to help speed up the process and ensure that I am working as efficiently as possible, which I am. Plus you never know what exciting opportunities may be just around the corner.'

Notice how I'm not bullying myself for being disheartened? I am acknowledging the way I feel with compassion, but adjusting my attitude to be more courageous, upbeat, real and open to opportunities. This makes my energy change and I feel more willing to work towards my goals.

If you struggle with this, there are two powerful questions to ask yourself (even if you don't have children). The first is: **'Would I want my own child to think like this?'**

Assuming your immediate answer is no, stop and think why you are letting yourself think this.

The second powerful question to ask yourself is: **'What has this self-limiting mindset cost me? And what will it cost me in the future if I keep this attitude going?'**

Your turn:

My beliefs about money _____

_____

_____

The second level of financial block is our language – the way we talk to ourselves about our relationship with money and wealth.

So often I hear 'I'm no good with money', or 'I am great at making money but can't stop spending it all', or 'It's impossible for me to get ahead financially'. These comments are charged with negative energy, and I can guarantee very little change or improvement will come from that headspace.

When you are completely honest with yourself and look around for examples that contradict the ideas you have clung to, these blocks will start to crack and crumble.

Take 'I'm no good with money' – that may have been the case in the past, but it doesn't need to remain true. Just by reading this book you have chosen to develop new awareness and knowledge, so this message is no longer correct. If you go on Instagram and search #debtfreecommunity, you'll see hundreds of thousands of people changing their financial future by getting out of debt, building savings, achieving their goals and building passive income. It's inspiring, to say the least! It's time to reframe through honest self-talk: 'I used to be bad with money, but things have changed and I am actually getting back in control of my money. Every day I have a chance to bring about improvement.'

The comment 'I am great at making money but can't stop spending it all' is a total contradiction. If you're great at earning money, you just need to use those same skills to earn and create savings. Press delete and replace that thinking with: 'I am one of those lucky people who is great at earning money, so now I use that skill to put more into savings accounts/investment accounts/retirement accounts – it's like spending my money on my future financial health.'

Notice how I am using the **present tense**? I say 'I am' rather than 'I will'. By changing your language and self-talk to present tense you make the changes and improvements immediate, which means you see and experience results sooner.

Some people actually enjoy playing the victim or pitying themselves when it comes to money, even to the point of making fun of themselves to others. This is a form of self-deprecation or self-bullying, and it does no good if you want to change your financial future. If you know you're guilty of this, stop it right now – you are smarter and way more powerful than that. Ask yourself, would you find this attractive or inspiring if you heard someone talk like this? Shift your energy to positive changes and head in a new direction.

Next time you tell people what you're saving for or what the goal is that you're working towards, watch their attitude towards you shift and improve. Not only will you take yourself more seriously but so will others, and you'll most likely end up inspiring them along the way. How good will that feel?

The idea that 'it's impossible to get ahead financially' is probably one of the biggest blocks of all, as this way of thinking will keep you stuck in the same situation without even trying. And it's a load of crap! I personally know plenty of everyday people who have got ahead financially on very humble incomes. It definitely won't be easy, but no one is expecting you to become a millionaire overnight. You get ahead financially by taking one step at a time, working efficiently, being mindful and exploring new options as they arise.

So when you catch yourself thinking like this, change it to something that is kind, positive and comes from a place of self-love: 'Sure, things are a little tight right now, but the future will be different as I am becoming so much more knowledgeable about money and cash flow. And while I can only afford to put a small amount towards my financial goals, it still counts and it still helps. It will only get better from here.'

When you catch yourself speaking poorly of your finances, ask yourself, 'How and what would I say to my best friend about this?' It's likely your language will change to being kind, loving and supportive. If you can take back your power and show yourself some self-respect, your energy will change. Immediately the future will seem so much less depressing, you'll get a little inkling that you can do this, and you'll realise that your future does not define your past.

Best of all, as the restrictive energy dissolves and gives way to a more secure, grounded and positive feeling, you'll start to move to a space where you no longer repel money but instead are open to it, which will attract more ideas, inspiration and opportunities.

Write down your negative ways of speaking about yourself and your financial situation, and then rewrite each idea from a positive, empowering and uplifting perspective – and watch your self-worth flourish.

I'll even help get you started:

'I don't earn enough.'
I am focusing on solutions and ways that I can increase my income or even earn some extra money from a side hustle. Plus it won't always be like this.

'It's impossible to budget and live a normal life.'
I am working through my expenses, finding little savings here and there, which add up to impressive new savings.

'It's too hard to live in this city/state/country and have a life and still save.'
It's not about trying to do everything; it's all about balance and appreciating what I can do and what I can experience.

Rewrite the previous, negative self-talk you identified and then flip it into a positive, loving approach.

NEGATIVE ⟶ POSITIVE

_____ _____
_____ _____
_____ _____
_____ _____
_____ _____

The next level of block is belief. There's no point in telling yourself and others that you're improving your financial future if you don't genuinely believe it.

I know, this is easier said than done, but you break it down. All you need is a small amount to start with, which you can build over time by adding to it each day. It then goes from complicated to simple.

To help develop your sense of self-belief and faith, look at even the smallest financial gains that you've made. Simple things like paying for coffee with cash instead of credit. Or paying back a family member the $20 that you borrowed. Or the small amount of savings that you currently have.

Write down your top ten proudest financial moments.

1. _____
2. _____
3. _____
4. _____
5. _____
6. _____
7. _____
8. _____
9. _____
10. _____

How do you feel now? Even if you only have the tiniest bit of belief and faith in yourself, I bet it's slightly bigger than what it was before you wrote these down.

You've realised you're better with money than you thought. You don't feel so disheartened about it. You don't feel so useless. You realise that you have a chance of achieving your financial goals.

Keep building this list, and when setbacks happen re-read your notes to give yourself the faith to hang in there and push forward.

BACK TO YOUR ROOTS

Many of our beliefs, messages and habits around money and wealth come from our childhood. If our key family members had unhealthy habits with money, we often copy them in our own adult lives. However, we do have a choice. Even if the most influential figures in your childhood were horrendous with money, you can actually use that energy to channel you in the opposite direction.

Some of my most motivated clients came from financially toxic backgrounds, with parents who had spending addictions, were drowning in debt, suffered from gambling problems, never had enough discipline to put a little money aside from each pay cheque, and basically wallowed in financial misery. Instead of mimicking their parents' habits, though, these clients use their experiences as a way to fuel their desire to create a much more financially harmonious lifestyle. They work out what they want to create for themselves and what they want to leave out.

The key is to look at the emotional impact of the habits and attitudes you've witnessed in those key influential people (parents, aunts, uncles, grandparents, family friends, neighbours and so on). For example, if you grew up with parents who were always in debt, the emotional impact would have most likely weighed them down, possibly causing tension in the household, and meaning that the family may have had to go without certain necessities.

Without dwelling on the negative, use what you didn't like emotionally to identify what you want to create in your world, and focus on creating that for yourself. As Napoleon Hill famously said, 'We become what we think about.' Turn these negative experiences into positive guides by using this as motivation to do things differently – to do better. It's a form of self-healing.

Write down some good and bad experiences that you have witnessed both as a child and as an adult. Then write down the emotions you experienced and witnessed. Look for the advice, lesson or wisdom at the heart of these moments and use them to help define what you want. Try to come from a positive and kind approach.

Even if you had a happy, healthy childhood, there will still be valuable lessons and messages to pick out that you can carry forward in your own life. If, for example, your parents were very generous or spontaneous, and you really loved that about them growing up, stopping and acknowledging that is just as valuable.

Think about the first time that the idea of money or even an emotion associated with money entered your life. What do you remember? What did you feel? What did you believe at the time? Was it good or bad?

Remember, you can choose to keep any good aspects that are important to you in order to build on them and keep them in the positive form.

As a child, money was _____

_____ and money felt _____

_____

Write down five positive things that this experience has now brought to your attention:

1. _____
2. _____
3. _____
4. _____
5. _____

As an example:

Experience or memory: Tense family moment due to lack of money / excessive debts / financial misfortune

Emotions from experience: Anxiety, embarrassment, guilt, neglect, shame

Switch: *I am creating a life for myself and my loved ones where financial security is a priority. And to me this means having emergency money always set aside, and I make responsible financial decisions around spending, saving and investing.*

See how you can use a negative experience to generate a positive path for yourself?

It does take work, though, and it can be extremely confronting. But if you can do this work, it could be one of your most powerful sources of motivation and inspiration, which will serve you well in any challenging moments or if temptation arises.

Use this section to list memories, the emotion they evoke, and how you can flip that into a positive approach.

Experience/Memory	Emotion	Switch
_____	_____	_____
_____	_____	_____
_____	_____	_____
_____	_____	_____
_____	_____	_____
_____	_____	_____
_____	_____	_____
_____	_____	_____
_____	_____	_____
_____	_____	_____

SELF-WORTH

Ask yourself: 'Am I worthy of being wealthy?' Do you genuinely believe that you deserve to be wealthy or have financial freedom? How does thinking about money and your finances *feel* in your body? Comfortable and freeing, or guilty and shameful? Sit with the feeling even as you enjoy or challenge it.

If discomfort arises within you, explore it, question it and prove it wrong. You deserve to be financially free. And I know that as you start to become financially free, you will start giving back simultaneously. You will give people more time, more presence, more charity, more inspiration, more education. The world needs more wealthy people like you!

Write down what positive aspects and benefits greater financial freedom brings you. Here are some examples to get you started:

I can employ more help in running my home or business, which gives another person an opportunity to improve their lives.

I can buy higher quality food and education for my family so that they are healthier and can be of more value to the world.

I can explore the world through travel, spending money in different towns and supporting other communities and businesses.

Your turn:

_____
_____
_____
_____
_____
_____
_____
_____

After doing these exercises you should feel more comfortable with the idea of greater financial freedom, and also experience a deeper sense of self-worth, knowing that you are deserving of more financial abundance in your life.

Now that you have done the work and cleared a lot of conscious and subconscious blocks, you need to keep being aware of this so that you can prevent new blocks, while discovering and removing old ones.

Always treat a financial mental block with love and respect, as it was planted innocently as a form of self-protection. It is now your time to turn it into a blessing that guides you to a happier, healthier place.

POINTS TO REMEMBER:

- Any self-imposed limitations, excuses and justifications are only held in your head and can be easily removed.
- The quicker you start catching them out and learning how to adjust them with self-love and kindness, the quicker you will see results, not just financially but in the way that you look at and carry yourself.
- Your mindset and attitude should aim to be courageous and loving.
- Look to your past, and note what you want to change and what you want to take forward into your financial future.
- Focus on what you want to create, not what you want to avoid.
- Dare to question your beliefs and opinions about money – debate them, look to contradict them.
- Watch your language – never talk about yourself in a deprecating way. Talk to yourself as you would talk to your best friend.
- Regularly re-read your financial accomplishments and add to them when you can!
- Ensure your language and self-talk is positive and in the **present tense**.
- Channel any previous negativity from your past to help you define and create what you want to build for yourself.
- Regularly ask yourself how you feel about being worthy of wealth. Your answer will vary depending on what's going on for you, but it's a great thermometer to show what self-worth work you need to do.
- As your experiences grow, continue to invest in your mindset.

CHAPTER FOUR

Your Banking Ritual

'Habits are like financial capital — forming one today is an investment that will automatically give out returns for years to come.' – Shawn Anchor, author of *The Happiness Adventure*

Now that we have cleared all the mental and emotional financial blocks, we'll get started on some practical steps. The hardest part is over!

I'm going to show you how to manage your cash flow. It will be easy and simple, I promise. Furthermore, it will be enjoyable, because you'll quickly find how good it feels to know, understand and be in control of your finances, rather than letting them control you. When you can manage your cash flow properly, saving, investing and building wealth is easy.

The secret to successful cash-flow management and easy wealth creation is consistency, foresight and, most importantly, habit.

When we fall off our financial path, it is often because either an unexpected expense pops up out of the blue or we 'accidentally' forget about that large annual bill that's suddenly due. These moments can feel like a financial kick in the guts and most of us reach for a credit card to fix the problem, because we don't have the right amount of cash set aside in advance. But this bandaid solution can do more harm than good, and things quickly spiral more out of control.

For most of us, our income is consistent but our expenses aren't. Our net pay is the same each week/fortnight/month, but we have cheap months and expensive months. The festive season is a classic example of an expensive month. When you accept this, you **learn to stockpile your finances in preparation for those expensive months**.

Counterintuitively, often it is the cheap months that can set us up for failure. They create a false sense of security, allowing us to spend any spare cash on something not in our budget, only to discover later that we actually needed it for an important expense down the track or just around the corner.

But when we know what larger expenses are coming up (and have been preparing in advance) and have the comfort of emergency money set aside, we feel calm, prepared and maybe even proud.

This is what I am going to show you to create for yourself. You're going to be so in control of your finances that no bill will ever want to mess with you. And because it's so simple, you'll want to do your cash-flow banking the moment you get paid, because you will immediately see and feel how well it's working for you. This will be your new financial ritual.

Step 1: Put down the credit card. Even if you are responsible with your credit card and always pay it off in full each month, I want you to have a little credit detox. Spending with credit is a zombie transaction. The 'I'll deal with it later' or 'it's only $40' attitude when we mindlessly swipe, tap or wave our cards is not the same as the feeling of spending cash. Spending cash makes us more alert and present, and forces us to stop and question the value and necessity of what we're buying. Sometimes this reality check will show that the new dress/shoes/gadget isn't worth having $300 less in our savings account after all.

So enjoy a month's holiday from the card, even if it's simply to see how your spending reduces as you discover more about what you love, value, use and appreciate. Kind of like a financial detox.

Advanced level: If you are seriously motivated, you could make this thirty-day credit card–free detox purely cash-based. This means paying for everything in cash. It will involve regular trips to the ATM, but it definitely gives you a huge wake-up call as to the speed with which you can spend money. You could also split your spending between cash and debit card if you like.

Step 2: Have an everyday bank account with a linked debit card, and make sure it is with a bank that allows you easy access to ATMs near your home or work, so that you don't waste money on withdrawal fees. Research the most competitive fees, interest rates and organisations that allow you to have multiple linked internet-based savings accounts (ideally at no extra cost and no monthly costs) that pay a competitive interest rate. You don't have to go overboard in your research and give yourself analysis paralysis – just pick the bank you like most and is best value for what you want, sign up and move on. Your time is worth more!

When you log in to your bank account, I want you to be able to view your entire cash-flow situation on the one screen. You need to quickly see all your savings accounts and review all your transactions to ensure that you are sticking to your budget. No logging in and out of different apps and internet banking sites to check different accounts, and definitely no 'out of sight, out of mind' savings accounts. More often than not, these accounts get lost in our own cyberspace, where 'out of sight' ends up being some random account with $20 in it somewhere and you have no idea how or where to find the log-in details.

You are big enough and motivated enough now to have the self-discipline to stick to your budget. You won't blow your emergency savings on silly impulse purchases, because you know the regret is not worth it, and you will get more pleasure seeing your accounts in order and full. Which in turn allows you to then diligently and responsibly work towards your other important financial goals and more excitingly . . . your number.

CHEAT TIP FROM CC:

If you already have a home loan or an investment property loan, this is the bank you should use for all your new bank accounts. That way all your accounts and loans are grouped together within the one bank and app. *Mindful Money* is about efficiency in a busy modern world, so I want you to be able to log in to your accounts and see your entire cash flow situation within the one screen. (If you have personal loans or car loans that are not with a bank or financial institution that offers everyday banking, this rule doesn't apply. Keep these loans where they are and have your cash accounts with your preferred institution, but all grouped together within the one bank and one app.)

You should nickname your internet banking account 'Everyday account'. This nickname is important: it reminds you of the purpose of the account and helps keep you focused.

All your daily, weekly, fortnightly and monthly expenses should come from your Everyday bank account. Grabbing coffee or lunch at work? Use your debit card. Buying a new outfit to wear on the weekend, assuming it is within your budget? Use your debit card. And this should be the only account that has a linked debit card; the others I describe below should only be internet-based, so that if you want to access that money, you have to log in and mindfully transfer it to your linked Everyday account, so that you at least earn some interest in the meantime.

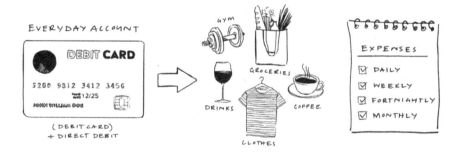

This Everyday account is where your salary is deposited, and where most of your expenses are withdrawn from. All your monthly memberships and subscriptions come out of this Everyday account via automatic direct debit. It should always have money in it, right up until payday. And I will show you how to make this happen.

Step 3: Open a linked internet-based savings account with the same bank (remember, all savings accounts are with the one provider). Nickname this one 'Life + $X Emergency Money account'. This is where your quarterly, biannual and annual expenses come from. For example, Christmas presents and other special occasion gifts, rego, strata or owners' corporation fees and utilities. It should also include a set amount of money for emergencies, such as unexpected medical expenses, dental bills, car trouble or family emergencies. Use the term X in the nickname, but update it once you know what your emergency money number is. For example, 'Life + $10 000 Emergency Money' in Honey's case.

WORKING OUT YOUR EMERGENCY MONEY NUMBER

When it comes to knowing what is the 'right' amount of emergency money, everyone is different, and there is no one-size-fits-all answer. You need to look at what is realistic and necessary in your life, and what will be an efficient use of your money. So have a think about what lump sum of money for emergencies would help you feel more secure, and write it down.

CHEAT TIP FROM CC:

Think about what emergency could realistically happen to you, and work out its cost. Do you have elderly parents overseas? Do you have young children? Do you have a medical condition, or does someone in your family have a medical condition? Is one of your pets susceptible to certain illnesses or conditions that pet insurance won't cover? Is your home in a high risk area of danger? Do you have much sick leave or annual leave saved up? Sit down and work out the costs you would incur in an emergency; for example, flights, accommodation, time off work or medical expenses.

For me, being self-employed (so no annual leave or sick leave) meant I needed an emergency amount of $32 000. This would cover any short-term gap on my insurance policies and provide more than three months' worth of living expenses, including my mortgage repayments. Seeing this number in my bank account gives me a much better quality night's sleep.

Step 4: Open a third internet-based account and give it the nickname of a lifestyle goal: perhaps a holiday, or a new car, or a new laptop or camera. Make sure the nickname clearly identifies the goal. This account will give you a sense of balance and sanity, as this is where you get to reward yourself, guilt-free. Again, this account should be with the same bank, and all of your accounts should be viewable online.

Step 5: Open a fourth internet-based account, this one given a nickname in line with your financial goal, such as 'Deposit for First

Home' or 'Deposit for Investment Property', or 'Money to Invest for the Future'. Use this account to start building your passive income for your magic number.

THE DRIP FEED

If you are not on a salary, but get paid irregularly because you are self-employed, or work on a freelance, commission-based or even seasonal basis, you can still follow this advice, however, we need to make one simple alteration, which is adding an extra account called your 'Drip Feed account'. This is where you have all your pay deposited and then you 'drip feed' yourself a consistent flat dollar amount each month (or fortnight if you need), which is transferred from the drip feed account into your everyday account, just like a salaried person gets paid.

As mentioned above, the key to good (and easy!) budgeting is **consistency and habit**. So by using this Drip Feed account, you are no longer having the stress and anxiety of juggling irregular pay and irregular expenses, but are creating consistency by paying yourself a base salary. This makes it far easier to manage your expenses by following the above instructions.

Managing your budget with a close eye is even more important if you are on an irregular income as you must ensure that you do not pay yourself too much out of your Drip Feed account and run it dry, i.e. spending more than you are earning. You are better off withdrawing an amount that covers your budget closely and not too much more. If you find your Drip Feed account is accumulating at a faster rate, you can look to give yourself a pay rise by increasing your monthly amount, or perhaps pay yourself a bonus every quarter to put towards some or all of your goals. This is something that I do myself as I am self-employed, and it makes life so much easier!

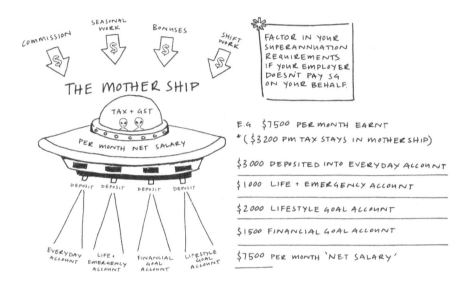

HOW TO USE THESE ACCOUNTS TO INCREASE YOUR FINANCIAL EFFICIENCY AND EASE

Now to fill these accounts. Every time you get paid, you need to add money to each of these four accounts. To know how much to allocate to each of them, start by grabbing your list of living expenses from Chapter two. Look at each of your expenses and figure out their frequency and due date.

EASY EVERY DAY

The easiest expenses to see are the daily, weekly and monthly expenses. These might include food, gym memberships, mobile phones, rent/mortgage payments, health insurance, etc. Add all these expenses up, and it will give you the total number that you need to allocate to your everyday account to get you through the month.

CHEAT TIP FROM CC:

When your expenses are consistently the same each month with no large irregular expenses, managing your cash flow is so much easier. I try to make as many bills monthly as possible, even if they aren't issued monthly. So for my quarterly bills, I will actually pay them like they are monthly bills. For example, my water bill is on average $190 per quarter, so each month I will transfer $65 ($190/3 = $63.33), kind of like pre-paying it and putting my account in credit. That way I am always on top of my bills and if I am slightly short, I can easily fix up the difference without too much financial stress.

Every time you get paid, you immediately allocate this amount to your everyday account as a priority. This will keep your head above water with most of your regular payments and expenses.

LIFE + $X EMERGENCY FOR A GOOD NIGHT'S SLEEP

Next is to add up those quarterly, biannual and annual expenses and divide the total by the frequency that you get paid during the year. So say that your total quarterly, biannual and annual expenses come to $7000 per year and you get paid fortnightly, you would divide by 26 ($7000/26 = $269; rounded up = $300). So every fortnight that you get paid, you must transfer $300 into your Life + $X Emergency account. If this was monthly it would be $583, rounded up to $590 per month.

CHEAT TIP FROM CC:

The Sugar Budget app, which can be downloaded from the Apple Store, helps you manage your budget and show you how to do your cash-flow allocations to these accounts. Plus you can mark upcoming expenses in the Sugar Budget calendar. Alternatively, when you subscribe to my weekly newsletter, The Sugar Hit, you can get a free Excel budget template which will prompt you to add up these expenses and get you started. You can save this document and work from it on a regular basis.

But you also need to allocate money towards your emergency amount. It is important that you don't forget this, and I recommend, if possible, trying to prioritise building this account up rather than adding too much to your other lifestyle and financial goal account as this is the account that acts as your financial float account. It keeps you out of trouble and in control of your cash flow and expenses, and prevents you from turning to a credit card as a quick-fix solution.

Say that you worked out your living expenses to be $3000 per month, and you decide that $10 000 would be a wise and responsible amount to have in cash for emergency use. To save up for this, you would need to allocate $385 per fortnight ($10 000/26 = $385) for the next twelve months. Or, if you are paid monthly, $835.

And remember, as soon as you know what your emergency money goal is, make sure that you replace the $X in the nickname of the 'Life + $10 000 Emergency account'. As the account balance grows, you don't want to get lulled into a false sense of security when looking at a big bank balance number and be tempted to go shopping or book an expensive holiday.

Once you have built up your emergency money amount ($10 000), those payments of $385 per fortnight or $835 per month can be redirected and distributed into the other two accounts – your lifestyle goal account and your financial goal account. But if you ever need to tap into those emergency funds, even just $700 of your $10 000, for example, you should aim to replace and repay that money as soon as possible.

CHEAT TIP FROM CC:

If you have a mortgage, I recommend having your emergency money sitting against your mortgage, with the redraw facility switched on. This will save you thousands of dollars in interest and time against your home loan, as the emergency money is offsetting your mortgage by the same amount, while your repayments remain the same.

I will explain this in more detail shortly, but if you have a mortgage, you can separate your life amount from your emergency money, with your second account simply being your 'Life' account, serving the purpose of stockpiling your cash savings for those quarterly, biannual and annual expenses. You can either put this lump sum against your mortgage, **after ensuring the redraw facility is switched on**, or put the emergency money in an offset account against your home loan.

Either option will have the same effect financially, however, I prefer to have it against my home loan via a redraw rather than an offset as I find seeing that lump sum gives me a false sense of security and I can find myself getting lazy with my mortgage reduction goals. Having it against my home loan via a redraw and seeing my emergency money coming off my home loan inspires me to keep paying the mortgage off as fast as possible. So my $32 000 emergency money sits against my mortgage, but with the redraw facility switched on.

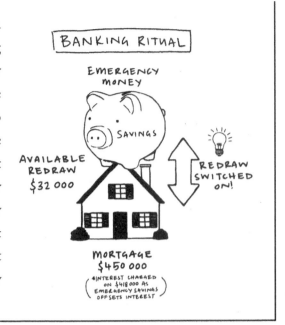

Your Life + $X Emergency account will be the hardest and possibly the slowest to build up – you could, for example, get hit with a financial snowstorm of quarterly bills before you get a chance to save enough in this account. If this happens, try to find some short-term savings or extra cash earnings (see the next chapters!) to help pay these bills now. And when they're sorted out, know that you will have a small financial respite to be able to build your Life + $X Emergency account again and be ready for the next round of quarterly bills.

The second-last account that you need to add to is your lifestyle goal account. Work out the cost of this lifestyle goal and when you want to achieve it by. Say, for example, you want to take an $8000 holiday at the end of the year, you would then work out how many paydays there are between now and then and divide the cost by that number. If there are fifteen more pay cycles between now and the end of the year, $8000/15 = $533 (rounded up = $540) per fort-night needs to be allocated towards this account.

Even if you don't have any major lifestyle goals, I still recommend having this account with a nominal goal, even if it's just used to help pay for rewards and treats for yourself to keep your energy levels up.

Also, if you want to achieve your lifestyle goal sooner, keep reading – I will help you find ways to gain extra savings and extra income in the next chapters. But make sure that you are always honest with yourself – if you are trying to live beyond your means, be prepared to have a heartfelt chat with yourself.

The last account to be contributed to every month is the financial goal account. This is where I want you to deposit whatever is left after your four other cash-flow allocations. This account could be for the deposit for your first home or, what I recommend, money to invest to build your number! Just make sure it is clearly nicknamed and add to it when you can.

The next chapter will show you how to grow this regular deposit, and then Chapter six will show you how to get started on building your number, which is your passive income for authentic financial freedom. So keep reading – the best is yet to come!

Let's work through an example using these guidelines. If your net pay is $5500 per month, you will allocate your money as follows:

$2780 – Everyday
$1420 – ($585 – Life savings + $835 – Emergency savings)
$500 – Holiday

This would leave $800 per month that you can now put into the financial goal account.

So total cash-flow instructions are:

Everyday account	$2780 p.m.
Life + Emergency account	$1420 p.m.
Holiday savings account	$500 p.m.
Financial goal account	$800
	$5000 TOTAL

By getting this money out of your Everyday account, you cannot spend it. You know that if you dare transfer money out of your other accounts, you will only be disrespecting the work that you have already done and making it harder to get back on the right path.

If something exciting or tempting pops up that is technically not within your budget, I'm not saying that you can't or shouldn't have it. But know that you will need to find or create some savings or extra money to cover this new expense so that it doesn't damage all the great work you've done. Set up your accounts and complete the worksheet below to help you work out your cash-flow allocation.

DAILY, WEEKLY, FORTNIGHTLY & MONTHLY EXPENSES

DAILY EXPENSES:

Coffees
Weekday lunches
Groceries

MONTHLY EXPENSES:

Gym
Phone
Internet

Memberships
Personal services (nails, hair etc.)

QUARTERLY EXPENSES:

Water   Electricity

Gas   Strata/owners' corporation fees

ANNUAL EXPENSES:

Christmas presents

Rego

CTP (compulsory third-party insurance)

My emergency 'sleep well at night' number is $_____

CREDIT CARDS

If you have to have a credit card, ideally have only one or a maximum of two credit cards. This makes it easier to keep them under control with a watchful eye. I recommend treating your credit card like your debit card. This means that when you use it, you immediately transfer the cash from either your Everyday account or your Life + $X Emergency account. That way you are not in credit card debt for a single second, but you still get to use them to your advantage.

Technically, yes, you are missing out on earning interest on the savings in your bank account, however, the mental and emotional benefit is that you are not running the risk of forgetting what you have charged to your card during the month, with it dangerously adding up. This also removes the temptation to spend the cash innocently sitting in your bank accounts, which actually needs to go towards paying off the card.

And with all your accounts and cards viewed within the one app on your phone, this quick transfer from your cash account to your credit card takes only a few seconds.

Another important point is make sure that your one and only card has no annual card fee or a competitive annual fee that you can justify with a good benefits program. For example, your credit card may have an annual fee of a couple of hundred dollars, but if it comes with free comprehensive travel insurance, which saves you over $300 every time you travel, plus gives you a great frequent flyer program that saves you on airfares and upgrades, it may be worth the expense.

CHEAT TIP FROM CC:

I have one credit card but it comes in the form of two cards, sharing one limit and one bill. My annual fee is waived each year. And I only use it for larger transactions to maximise reward points. For transactions under $100, I always use my debit card.

One card is a Mastercard, the other is American Express, issued by my bank, where I hold all my accounts and loans together. The American Express has no international fees, which is perfect for when I'm travelling and don't want to carry cash, and I earn double the points than with the Mastercard. However, not everywhere accepts American Express (or if they do, sometimes they charge a ridiculous fee to use it), so then I use my Mastercard.

My points roll over automatically to my linked frequent flyer program and add up quickly. I use these points to help pay for my personal flights or upgrades – it's saved me tens of thousands of dollars and helped pay for many holidays.

This banking ritual may take a few months to get used to and that is perfectly normal. As I said earlier, if you need to tweak these rituals to make sure they work better for you, go for it, as long as you are not getting into debt and feel more in control of your cash flow. Once you have fine-tuned this banking ritual, you will really enjoy the simplicity of it and value paying your bills on time. And, as your wealth grows, these habits will increasingly help you build more financial harmony and your money mindfulness will grow.

POINTS TO REMEMBER:

- Create your banking ritual – occasionally you may need to tweak it to suit your changing lifestyle, but always come back to the foundations of your cash-flow intentions.
- Check your account balances and transactions on a daily basis – this is great for identifying any fraud issues, and it also keeps you informed and ahead of your upcoming expenses.
- Regularly check that you are sticking to your budget and that your budget is realistic. I check my account transactions every night.
- All your accounts and loans should be with the one bank. You want to be able to log on to internet banking and see an immediate snapshot of your savings and loans.
- Try to have the bulk of your bills due on a monthly basis to make cash-flow management easier. You can even call your utilities providers and ask them to send your bills monthly. If they don't offer this, just pay them in credit each month like I do with my water bill.
- Round your expenses upwards when doing your numbers to be conservative.

- Don't forget to add an amount for emergency money within your Life + $X Emergency account's nickname. Things happen in life and we are not invincible, so it's important to have a safety net.

- If you have to have a credit card, only allow yourself one or two as an absolute maximum and transfer the payment from your Everyday or Life + $X Emergency account as soon as you use it (or even beforehand).

- Even if you can only afford to put $1 into your financial goal account, that is okay. Creating the habit is the most important principle here! And I will help you build this up.

- Once you have done all this, take a moment to stop and realise how good it feels to know how much more aware you are of your living expenses and cash-flow responsibilities. You are actually getting back in control of your finances and financial future, and this is only going to get better.

CHAPTER FIVE

Successful Savings

'The habit of saving is itself an education; it fosters every virtue, teaches self-denial, cultivates the sense of order, trains to forethought, and so broadens the mind.' – T. T. Munger

Once you have finalised your budget and worked out your banking ritual, it's time to look at ways to build more financial success for you beyond your current situation.

There are two approaches we're going to look at in this book. The first one we will cover in this chapter, which is to review your current living expenses and find ways to *save* you more money within your existing budget, so that you can proactively free up and allocate these savings to your other accounts and financial goals.

The second approach, which we will cover in the next chapter, is to look at ways to help you *earn* more money, which are unlimited and far more exciting. But we must first pay respect to developing the ability to save and the skill to exercise self-control.

These two activities combined will set you on the right path for your financial journey, and allow you to make progress a lot faster and feel more efficient. Plus you will enjoy having a greater understanding of your living expenses and knowing that your cash flow is more mindful with no financial waste.

The most important thing to remember is that you must pro-actively reallocate these newfound savings or earnings towards your financial goals to make them count. If you don't do this, your newly created bounty will quickly be spent on something else, most likely on something that is not particularly valuable to you, and those savings will evaporate. For example, say you need a new pair of jeans, and the ones that you have been saving up for suddenly go on sale for $50 less. Technically you have saved $50, but unless you bank the savings by transferring it into one of your separate accounts, that $50 will end up being spent on something else and will literally evaporate within a short period of time. **So make sure you get your newfound savings immediately out of temptation's way and put them to good use.** I'll show you how to do this in this chapter.

As we begin to focus on finding new savings, the first step is to review your current living expenses to see what needs to be done to find better balance and to help you understand what you **love, value, use and appreciate** (my money mantra).

BALANCED BUDGET CONUNDRUM

Often when we are trying to improve our financial situation, we immediately get bogged down in cutting down or completely cutting out certain expenses. We start from a place of scarcity but we can only go so far while living frugally.

At times this is necessary – although hopefully only temporary – but when we deprive ourselves too frequently and too aggressively of the pleasures that help us value ourselves and our lives, it can feel like we are punishing ourselves. The end result can often be a financial blowout or throwing in the towel completely. Then we find ourselves in the same challenging financial situation we started in – or even worse.

This book is not about becoming penny-pinching and tight with money. Instead, I really believe you need to start from a place of self-love and respect. Respect and appreciate the flow of money, and only spend money on what you **love, value, use and appreciate**.

Give yourself permission to reach for balance, and allow yourself those sanity expenses (manicures, sporting events, concerts) *within reason* – those treats that make you feel authentically happy. If you do this, you are far more likely to stick to your budget. In fact, you'll no longer view it as a budget but rather as a safe and healthy boundary to spend and play within, keeping you away from trouble. It will allow you to honour yourself and your needs, while still successfully achieving your personal and financial goals.

WHAT YOU NEED TO DO

Go through every single expense in your budget and ask yourself if you love, value, use and appreciate each one. Take your time and be honest with yourself. If you can genuinely say yes and know in your heart that it is a non-negotiable, it can stay. But you also have to be aware of living within your means, so watch out for too many yeses – remember, fewer expenses means more money towards your goals and achieving those goals sooner.

As you go through your budget and look at each expense, remember where you want to see yourself in the future and what is a priority for you. Working out what can stay and what can go becomes a lot less painful when you can see a sacrifice is worth the benefit. It also helps you to clarify precisely who it is you value spending your hard earned money on.

CHEAT TIP FROM CC:

Honour your expenses (within reason), particularly costs associated with your health and wellbeing. Try to keep these in your budget if you need them – as long as the accumulative cost isn't excessive. Maybe the thrice-weekly yoga sessions, massages, personal training and acupuncture treatments need to be rationalised a bit more, or stretched out over a month rather than a week. Always come back to asking yourself how much value or benefit does each expense add?

The same goes for beauty treatments. What beauty treatments make you truly feel beautiful inside and out? Honour those but maybe for all the other expenses that are just add-ons, stretch them out so that they are not as often or save them for special occasions. Even learning how to do a few treatments yourself (such as home facials), in-between the professional ones can help save you hundreds of dollars per year.

For example, takeaway dinners three times a week might not be worth missing a seven-day family holiday for. The daily takeaway coffee and bacon-and-egg roll isn't worth delaying retirement for five years. That new designer dress isn't worth the credit-card debt that is going to haunt you, and the stress attached to that. Through this process, we gain a valuable sense of perspective as well as a greater understanding of our values.

Ask yourself: is this expense worth jeopardising the financial goal that you are so excited about?

There are going to be expenses that you discover are your non-negotiables, and this is absolutely fine as this is your value system staying true to you and your needs. A common example of this is having a regular cleaner, as many people feel the time and energy this frees up is a worthwhile investment. If you need to go on a tight budget, and this expense is important to you, maybe consider other areas where you can cut back so that you can comfortably fit this in your budget.

For other expenses that need to stay, look at ways to reduce them, either in cost or frequency. For example, if you love pay TV – are there different, more cost-effective packages that you could downsize to? Or more competitive offerings elsewhere? If you value a home-delivered dinner after you've had a long, hard day, can you cut back to only having it once a week? I guarantee you will end up appreciating these luxuries even more when they are not in excess.

I also highly recommend jumping on the phone and asking what other options are available. When service providers hear that customers are thinking of leaving, a lot of them will pull out all stops to keep you as a customer in some capacity. You don't want to use empty threats, of course, but it doesn't hurt to ask what other options exist. You never know what special offers they have coming up that might be worth your time, especially if they are a company that values loyalty. And if they can't help because you're already on the best deal, you can take comfort knowing that you have done your best and are in fact getting good value for money.

To help you uncover as many saving opportunities as possible, I've suggested in the following pages areas where you can find ideas to help save money. However, choosing where to save money is very personal, and will vary from person to person. I have focused on the main big-ticket expenses to help get you started in your savings discovery, and then you're free to explore further.

UTILITIES

Use government comparison websites, such as Energy Made Easy (energymadeeasy.gov.au), to research your utilities providers as these are independent and not swayed by commission or sponsorships, and they show you all the market competition. By having an accurate view of all the options available to you, you can see if your power and gas providers are the best value for money. If not, call them or go to their websites and see what offers they have available. If another provider looks like they could be better value for money, give them a call and then go back to your current provider and see if they can beat the offer.

You should do this every year to avoid having the rates automatically put up after a twelve-month promotion ends. Changing utilities providers is quick and easy – the phone call is definitely worth your time. Plus you never know what better offer may be presented to you once your old provider realises that you're willing to leave.

INSURANCE

Cutting back or even cutting out insurance should be one of the last financial haircuts you make. Part of sleeping well at night is knowing that you, your family, your family's health and your personal belongings are properly protected. But if you feel that the premiums are getting out of hand, call your provider and ask what can be done to help manage the premiums first. Things like increasing your excess, installing additional security, shopping around can make a difference. Again, use government websites such as Private Health (privatehealth.gov.au) or North Queensland Home Insurance (nqhomeinsurance.gov.au), or Choice (choice.com.au), which is independent and member-run. Look at the add-ons and the extended list of coverage included – it may not all be necessary for your situation. And always be careful of the differences in policies, waiting periods, definitions and exclusions. Changing to a cheaper policy that doesn't properly cover you is not worth it. So check carefully and compare before changing anything.

CLOTHES, SHOES AND ACCESSORIES

There are only so many clothes that you can wear! Start to think about quality over quantity and creating your own signature style. This will help stop those expensive 'what was I thinking?' purchases. And this approach shouldn't just be limited to you, but applied to all members of the family (kids' clothes are adorable, but they can really add up – plus they wear them out and grow out of them so quickly).

With so many great platforms for the second-hand economy, you can even buy current-season clothes for a fraction of the original price. I have personally saved thousands of dollars by doing this. Check out any 'buy, sell, swap' social media groups dedicated to your favourite designers and see what they have on offer. My favourite groups on Facebook are: High End (an amazing mix of designer groups), Buy Sell Swap Scanlan Theodore, Buy Sell Swap Zimmermann and Dion Lee. There are also local 'buy, sell, swap' groups that are easy to find and join. And on top of this you have Poshmark, eBay, Gumtree, Vestiaire Collective, The Real Real and the Grace Tales–approved Retykle, a website for second-hand designer children's clothes – it's now fashionable to buy pre-loved! Also, don't forget your local second-hand consignment stores and charity shops.

CHEAT TIP FROM CC:

I had the pleasure of visiting The Salvation Army's flagship store in Tempe and filming three videos for my YouTube channel with eco-stylist Faye De Lanty. She shows not only how to shop for pre-loved clothes but also how to style them, and actually built me a capsule wardrobe for less than $250. Check out my YouTube channel to watch these videos, they are so helpful!

This will also reduce your environmental footprint, and you'll create a healthier, more respectful relationship with your wardrobe. You'll want to take extra care of each item and get your dollars-per-wear down.

Here are four more tips to slim down your wardrobe excess:

1. Unsubscribe from all email newsletters from clothing stores – this will not only save you money but also be a lot less distracting and you will get more work done!

2. Become a fussy but loyal shopper – pick three to five stores that you genuinely love going into or spending time visiting their website. You will find identifying your style so much easier and matching clothes to make different outfits a quicker process because of their consistent styles, colour palettes, cuts and fabrics.

3. Invest in quality – think about your dollar-per-wear and how items will wash and age. Look at the stitching, the durability of the fabric. If you really love an item, you'll want it to last a long time.

4. Develop a signature style – think of the fashion icons whose styles transcend trends and remain universally chic (Grace Kelly, Jackie O, Audrey Hepburn). Spend time discovering what looks resonate with you and build your wardrobe around them. With time and care, you'll find that your wardrobe will work harmoniously.

LOANS

Okay, this can be a very powerful way to save money, but it must be done with incredible care and control. If you can do this wisely, it will save you a tonne of money and, even better, a tonne of time. Which will make you and me both very happy and proud.

If you have a loan – a mortgage, personal loan, car loan, etc. – I recommend shopping around to see what better offers exist. Don't head into your bank; find a local independent mortgage broker. Someone who isn't paid by the bank to sell you that specific bank's products, but rather someone who will actually shop around for you to get the best rate for your needs, not their commission.

You can often find competitive mortgage rates online through your own research and independent comparison websites. You can quickly view a wide range of different loan providers and see their rates, which is a great starting point. If you get stuck or feel uneasy, ask trusted family and friends for a recommended mortgage broker that works with a wide range of different providers, so that you are not being 'sold' their only commission-paying product. Check that they have been doing this for at least five years or longer so that you know they are experienced at getting you the best rate and package and can handle your application correctly and with speed.

Good mortgage brokers are well known and respected within their local communities. Just make sure that you follow my next steps by giving the mortgage broker these instructions.

Once you've found a reputable mortgage broker or found a new loan provider that you want to refinance your loan with, explain your situation and your financial goals. You need to tell them that you're looking to not just save on your interest rate, **but to pay your mortgage/loan off as fast as possible!**

Often when people refinance their loans (which is what we are potentially doing here), the bank will restart the loan period. **We must avoid this!** For example, if you're six and a half years into your thirty-year home loan and you refinance your mortgage, most banks will restart your loan clock, which means that it'll now take thirty-six and a half years to pay off your home. You do not want to be in your sixties, let alone your seventies, still paying off your home! I can't stress this enough!

If the bank can offer a more competitive interest rate than what you are currently paying, you *must insist* that the loan term remains the same! So if you are six and a half years into your home loan, which was originally set as a thirty-year term, your new home loan term would be twenty-three and a half years or less. Don't be tricked or tempted by the new smaller repayments. They have just re-stretched your loan. Stick to your current loan term, or even better, shorten it if you can increase your repayments.

You should also ask the bank to keep your repayments the same as what they previously were (or, as mentioned above, increase them if your budget permits). Remember how we said at the start of this chapter that we would make our newfound savings count? Well, this is exactly what I'm talking about. These savings that are now being put towards your loans (such as your home loan) will save you thousands, if not tens of thousands, and take years off your home loan, meaning that you will own your home a lot sooner than you ever imagined.

CHEAT TIP FROM CC:

If you don't feel comfortable asking for a recommendation or don't know anyone, I can recommend my personal mortgage broker to you. He has looked after me and my clients for almost eight years and always finds incredible savings and gives straight-up honest and wise advice; he helps people across Australia. You can contact me through my website (sugarmamma.tv/contact/) for his details.

FOOD

Food is one of the biggest expenses for young growing families. But boy, do we waste a lot! One third of the food produced in the world gets lost or wasted, which amounts to US$680 billion. As well as throwing money away, this causes so much destruction to our environment, wasting nearly a quarter of our water supply and releasing toxic methane gas from rotting food in landfill. Not to mention the wasted resources from transportation, production, packaging, etc.

The good news is that there are heaps of things you can do to help save money on food – which don't involve fasting or starving yourself! These tips do involve a little effort and organisation, but seeing your bank balance sitting higher than it normally would in a given week will give you the motivation to keep going.

Here are thirteen tips to save money on food, all of which I do personally!

1. Food plan with your calendar – work out what meals you're going to make for each night of the week, and make sure you have all the ingredients to cover you. Check your fridge and pantry before shopping so that you don't double up and waste money.

2. Shop online – one of the benefits of shopping online is you can see the total cost of your shopping basket adding up as you go. You can then work out what to take out and what to keep if you're on a tight budget. Trying to do this in-store can be difficult and even embarrassing (unless you're great at maths or comfortable walking around a supermarket with a calculator). Standing at the checkout and then suddenly asking the assistant to remove some items from your bags can be a little humbling when people are waiting in the line behind you!

3. Meal prep – having food and ingredients pre-prepared so that you can come home from work and quickly put a meal together is a great way to avoid those 'I'm too tired to cook tonight' excuses. (Yes, I am completely guilty of this sometimes.) For example, you can meal prep spaghetti bolognese, casseroles, soups and curries.

4. Takeaway/home delivery – sometimes there are nights where home delivery is actually better for you as it doesn't take a toll on your energy levels and quality time with your family. However, make sure you only order what you need (my family is often guilty of our eyes being bigger than our appetites and over-ordering). And order meals that can be used to supplement meals the following day (for example, a roast chicken's leftovers can be turned into chicken sandwiches).

5. 'Eat up the bits' – this is what my mother always would say as she made up a smorgasbord of salads, cold meats

and cheeses from leftovers. You can easily make a healthy omelette or frittata or – Tom's favourite – a colourful poke bowl salad. Waste not, want not.

6. Local markets – if you have access to local markets, this is a fantastic way to support the little guys. In fact, most of Australia's economy is made up of small businesses, so this isn't just helpful for saving money, it's good for our country's financial health. You can access fresher food and meet the people who produce it. However, be mindful that local markets aren't necessarily cheaper all the time, so do your research.

7. Prepared meal boxes – I used to do this a lot and still come back to using these services, such as Marley Spoon or even Odyssey Lean, when my workload ramps up and I'm worried that I'll resort to unhealthy quick meals. These boxes are delivered to your door with all the ingredients and instructions (and sometimes meals) ready to make your meals for the week. They are well-priced, nutritious and generally leave no food wastage and most of the packaging is reusable or recyclable. The range of meals crosses many cuisines, inspiring you to learn and cook more as your culinary skills improve. (I'm a terrible cook, and these services have saved me many dinner negotiations with Rocco, as well as the mental load of planning a meal.) And most of these services have fantastic introductory offers to tempt you to try them out.

8. A little bit goes a long way – this is a very personal decision, but sometimes investing in a higher-quality product can actually be cheaper over the long run. For example, when I pay a higher price for chocolate, it's more satisfying and I find I consume less (kilojoules included!),

whereas when I buy a family-size block of cheaper chocolate, the whole thing is gone within a day. (Okay, an hour.) This analogy can be used for a variety of other products, including cheeses, clothes, cleaning products and baking ingredients. And make sure you also compare the prices per weight of different options. Most supermarkets display the price per kilo, gram, litre or millilitre. Taking the time to check between the different products can save you a lot of money.

9. Go green – think of the environment when it comes to your food, and it will save you money as well. You can buy pre-grown herb gardens from most outdoor home centres, which is perfect for when you only need a sprig of rosemary rather than the expensive full bunch from the supermarket. Invest in some reusable glass containers (the plastic ones have limited lives and end up in landfill eventually, while the glass ones are recyclable and better for your health). I highly recommend reading Anita Van Dyke's book, *A Zero Waste Life*. It's full of great ideas.

10. Take your lunch to work or school. Even if you only do this one day a week, these savings really add up and you tend to eat better. A saving of $20 per week adds up to more than $1000 remaining in your bank account in a year. The trick is to have some quality Tupperware containers to keep your food fresh and prepare the night before, so that you can't come up with excuses in the morning. This is where keeping some leftovers from the night before can come in really handy. As Tom likes to say, 'Cook once, eat twice.'

11. Cleaning products – your old stained T-shirts or pyjama pants can be cut up and used as cleaning cloths, and there are myriad cleaning products that you can make at home

really easily for less than $1, from household ingredients like vinegar or bicarb soda blended with essential oils. There are thousands of recipes online. This has cut my cleaning products bill down dramatically and I now have fewer chemicals in my home.

12. Use your freezer – it's a time capsule. If you shop in bulk, put your food in the freezer so that your savings can go the distance. Even that half-eaten bag of chips or Twisties can be put in the freezer (actually, they come out even crunchier!). You can freeze bread, meat, herbs (frozen in water with olive oil), berries, boiled eggs, etc. This will also help with planning your meal prep, as you'll be more likely to have the ingredients you need readily on hand.

13. Know your supermarket – ask the staff at your local supermarket what days of the week new deliveries arrive. They can often tell you what days of the week or times of the day certain food typically starts to get discounted. And shop outside peak hours. You're more likely to see the specials that often get blocked from view when it is busy, and you will zoom down those quiet aisles, saving time as well as money.

HOLIDAYS AND TRAVEL

This is the one expense that I would never recommend you cut out. Getting a break is incredibly important for your mental and emotional wellbeing and is an investment in yourself.

When we go on holidays, we get a valuable, eye-opening insight into other places in our own country and the world, and how other people live. We learn about customs and cultures and become more open-minded and adventurous. We often bond with the people we meet in our travels, creating new friendships and connections with people on the other side of the world. And, best of all, we create memories that last a lifetime. To me, travel seems a worthwhile investment in yourself.

And you don't have to deprive yourself of this just because of your financial goals or stresses. Balance is the key, along with some smart planning and preparation.

Here is my advice:

- **Have a separate, dedicated savings account nicknamed 'Holiday Savings'** – this could be your lifestyle account. (It is for me!) There is a comfort and confidence that comes from logging in to your internet banking on a bad day and seeing this account there – even if it only has $1 in it – because you can see your intention and your goal. I recommend paying for all your holiday expenses with money that you have saved up first, including airfares, accommodation, experiences and excursions. It is particularly important that you get your spending money from the remainder of what you have saved. For my own holidays, I pay upfront for as many expenses as I can and then transfer my savings onto my credit card so I can enjoy my spending money without racking up any debt. Doing this will allow you to enjoy your holiday guilt-free and come home jet-lag and debt-lag-free, ready to start saving for your next holiday.

- **Join a frequent-flyer program** – research the different options, understand how they work and how to maximise their rewards and their loopholes. Know when the promotions for double points run, what offers they have with their partner programs, how to make the most of your membership. Monitor your account so that you're correctly collecting your points and have accumulated enough in time each year when your membership renews. Once you have picked the right one for you (normally your main domestic carrier or your preferred airline), fly with them loyally. Sometimes this may cost you more in the short term, but when you see the loyalty points add up, which you can then use to help pay for flights or upgrades, those costs are worth it.

CHEAT TIP FROM CC:

I have been a frequent flyer with my favourite airline for over fifteen years, even though I am not someone who flies regularly. I always make an effort to fly with this airline or any of the linked partner airlines so that I can maximise my points and keep my status up. The points quickly accumulate, especially as my only credit card is linked to the frequent flyer account and I also use my membership with their other partner-preferred businesses, such as hotels, supermarkets, car hire, bottle shops, restaurants, and even online shopping malls. I went through the fine print of the program and know how to ensure that it works for me. And whenever I've had an issue and have called them, they've found a fair solution for me, as they acknowledge how long I've been a loyal customer.

As a result of my loyalty, at times I've been able to fly at no charge (except for taxes), or have been able to use my points for free upgrades. Each upgrade or flight has been worth at least $1000; sometimes savings in a single trip have added up to $10 000 when Tom and I fly together and get upgraded together.* Sometimes my flights will be more expensive at the time, but I know that in the end I'll come out ahead.

And my frequent flyer program has the side benefit of allowing access to airport lounges, where I can have a shower or eat a decent meal or have a good cup of coffee to break up a long flight. Not to mention extra luggage allowance, priority check-in and seat allocation!

*Tom and I are members of the same frequent flyer program so that between us we always have points. Tom flies a lot for work, so he has managed to maximise and cap out the loyalty program across two different programs, which gives him further flexibility and can save even more on travel.

- **Plan ahead** – the longer you can plan in advance, the more you will save. This is particularly worthwhile if you want to use your points for long international flights and need to book other people on the same flights (such as booking a family holiday). If you're struggling to find available free seats when using your points, consider different routes. I know people who take their family skiing to the USA, but fly via Hong Kong on frequent flyer points. The stopover in Hong Kong allows them to enjoy an additional destination and gently get over the jet lag. And lots of hotels offer great discounts when you book in advance and online. But always take out travel insurance in case something unexpected forces you to change your plans, or, worse, you end up in hospital or have to come home early. The moment something goes wrong, it is too late. Never compromise on travel insurance, but remember some credit cards offer travel insurance, which needs to be activated before you travel and ensure that it is comprehensive, with all your travel companions covered.

- **Research** – consider a variety of destinations and speak to people in similar situations to yours who have been there. The newly married loved-up couple may highly recommend the tropical island, but your three kids may go stir-crazy – or make you go stir-crazy. Also, look at different accommodation options. Staying ten minutes out of the city or town can sometimes be worth it because it may reduce the cost, as long as you factor in the cost of transport.

- **Volunteer** – build schools and towns in Haiti, teach English at a school in Indonesia, protect endangered animals in Africa, or collect data in Madagascar. There are so many extraordinary experiences on offer!

- **WWOOFing** – volunteering through World Wide Opportunities On Organic Farms is a great way to travel and earn money or have your food and accommodation covered. This network of organisations offers anything from picking grapes in France to working on a farm in New Zealand.

- **Find package deals** – there are incredible packages available online and in the travel section of the weekend papers. When travelling as a family, consider packages that include food and drinks as this can allow you to return home without a financial weight gain. However, if travelling solo or as a couple, those optional breakfast add-ons can be expensive, especially when you may be able to support the local cafe around the corner for half the price. (Tom and I learnt the hard way – we once managed to spend $200 on a cup of coffee and a stale croissant!)

- **House-swap or house-sit** – there are heaps of websites that help match trustworthy people with others who need their homes looked after while they're away. Maybe you'll need to water the plants or walk the pet dog, but the savings can be incredible, and it will give you a more authentic experience. This will often give you access to kitchen and laundry facilities as well, meaning you can save a tonne of money. If you have young children, you'll most likely turn up to a home with a lot of your needs met: providing cots, kids' beds, toys, highchairs and so on. So you can enjoy packing a lot lighter! This can also work on the flip side – there have actually been times where I've profited from travelling, through renting out my home as a short-term holiday lease.

- **Stay local** – just because it's holiday season, doesn't mean you have to buy into the pressure of going away. Being a tourist in your own town has so many unrealised benefits. You can try new restaurants and cafes, learn about the history of the town, support the community, discover new parks and beaches. You gain a new appreciation for your town and it can cost next to nothing.

But remember, we want these newfound savings and mindful money habits to actually count, so that you can see and feel the benefits of going without these expenses. As you go through your budget, extracting all that is extravagant, excessive and unnecessary, make sure you redirect those new savings into your other accounts, so those savings are captured and can accumulate, and so you can proactively decide where you would like the savings to go, such as towards your financial goals. For example, after going through your budget you decide that you will take your own lunch to work three times per week (saving you, say, $50 per week), you cut your weekend spending money by another $50, and you save another $30 per quarter on your utilities bills. You're saving a whopping $5320 per annum!

So to ensure that this amount doesn't get eaten up or transferred to a new expense, you need to get on the front foot and update and increase your banking ritual to include these savings, so that they go straight into either of your other two savings accounts.

Using the same example of a person clearing $5500 per month after tax, they could now change their banking ritual to look like this:

$2380 p.m. – Everyday account ($400 p.m. less from lunch money savings and weekend money savings)

$1420 p.m. – Life + $X Emergency account

$700 p.m. – Holiday savings in the lifestyle account (an extra $200 p.m. here)

$1000 p.m. – Financial goal account (an extra $200 p.m. here)

See how these new savings are being redirected to help achieve the lifestyle goal of a bigger and better holiday sooner, as well as more money put towards financial goals such as starting an investment portfolio? We are now making these savings really count and work for you. And seeing and feeling this happen is incredibly inspiring, often leaving us to question where we can find more savings.

In this example, we have found just a couple of expenses to cut – imagine what else you could reduce or remove! And what you could do with the money now that you know your banking ritual! Want to achieve that goal sooner? Or maybe even make your goal bigger?

It is up to you how you would like to 'share the love' between your savings accounts, but I recommend prioritising building the Life + $X Emergency account first. It's safest to quickly stockpile any savings you can into this account, as those larger upfront bills may be just around the corner; the last thing you need is to find yourself short, especially when you are feeling so motivated.

CHEAT TIP FROM CC:

I always dedicate a specific amount to my lifestyle account (which is nicknamed 'Holiday Money account') and to my financial goal account (which is nicknamed 'Savings to Invest account'). However, as I get closer to my holiday, sometimes I slightly alter the amounts being allocated so that I always have enough money to go on holiday (I never want to come home with debt from packing too light financially), and then once I am back on deck, I catch up on my financial goals account. It's important to be flexible!

Furthermore, this account also holds your emergency money – if you don't have the full amount in this account yet, make this the main 'account receiver' of your newfound funds until you get there. Once you've built that up, you can split the amount between your lifestyle account and your financial goal account in whatever way feels right. There is no one-size-fits-all formula or strict percentage systems you must follow – this is *your* life and *your* money. Work out what is right for your situation.

But my advice is, when working out that split for your particular situation, be honest with yourself about what feels like the right thing to do for your long-term success and financial goals. And as I said in the above tip, adjust it as you need: some months 50/50 between the accounts, and then sometimes 30/70 lifestyle to financial, or vice versa. Just as long as you put something in both accounts each time you get paid, you can honestly say to yourself that you're doing your best.

And most importantly of all, the moment you have to dip into your Life + $X Emergency account, whether it be for $100 or $10 000, you must replace that money as soon as possible. Even if it means having to slow down on contributing to your lifestyle and financial goal accounts. Just because we experience one emergency doesn't mean we will be immune from another one. So safeguard your finances and rebuild that safety net. And any time you do have to tuck into that emergency account for a second mishap, realise how much easier it is to cope and how glad, proud and relieved you were to have this account in the first place. Being financially responsible feels good.

Once you have worked out how best to allocate your new savings, write down your updated banking ritual, and continue to allocate and manage your money the moment you get paid. And take a second to acknowledge your new financially responsible habits and how they make you feel (proud, excited, more grown-up!). This is only going to grow from here! Doing the budget was actually the toughest part of all, so the worst is over.

CHEAT TIPS FROM CC:

Here are some other little things my family does that really help free up our budget so we can put the cash savings towards more holidays and more financial security:

- Bulk-billing medical centre – my doctor (who is the best!) bulk bills and this saves me a fortune. Also if I ever have to see a specialist, or get tests done or X-rays, I always ask to be given a referral to a place that bulk bills where possible.
- Dental – my private health insurance provides access to free dental work through their dental clinic. I haven't paid for a trip to the dentist in years, and that includes fluoride treatments, X-rays, cleaning, etc.

- Taking lunch to work – Tom and I often make a packed lunch using leftovers, or I come home during the day to eat lunch. Sometimes something cheap like scrambled eggs is perfect to fill a hole, and it's quick to make too.

- Minimalism – I have been incorporating this lifestyle movement of consciously choosing to consume less and remove the excess in my life for more than five years. Not only has it created more 'space' in my savings and budget, but it has also had an emotional benefit because I have fewer distractions, more energy, and more time. There are lots of videos on my YouTube channel all about how to incorporate this incredibly powerful way of living into your life.

- Hand-me-downs – I like to swap or borrow clothes from my girlfriends. I also accept with open arms hand-me-downs for Rocco, and I always pass on his clothes when he grows out of them. There is something so lovely about seeing the clothes that your child used to wear on a younger child – it takes you down memory lane!

- Layby – every now and again I will see something that I absolutely love which isn't in my budget. However, I know it is something that I will love, value, use and appreciate. This is when I use layby. I will put a deposit on it so that I know that I won't miss out on it if it sells out, and then use the money earning tips (coming up in the next chapter) to pay that item off until I can bring it home. There is something really exciting about the delayed gratification and the build-up of excitement when you make that final payment, almost like you are claiming your prize and know there is no debt being created from doing this.

- Playdates and sharing babysitters – my girlfriend Georgie and I always help each other out with babysitting. We regularly take turns looking after the kids instead of booking a babysitter when our workloads and deadlines ramp up. Sometimes this is just for an hour or two, and sometimes it is for one day a week after school pickup. It saves us paying for a babysitter and the kids entertain each other. And in turn, we all feel more connected to our community.

- Entertaining at home – both Tom and I prefer to entertain family and friends in our home rather than in restaurants and bars. Being on a budget doesn't mean that you have to become a social hermit. Invite people over to your place and suggest that each person brings something with them, such as a bottle of wine, a nice salad or dessert. This also saves on babysitters – and often the kids wear each other out!

- Multi-purpose gym – I would love to use many of the free workouts online via YouTube or work out in my local park or beach, but I seem to have a much better workout in a physical gym. The gym that I belong to offers a wide range of different classes and programs, has a pool, spa, sauna and even a kids' club – and it is one of the cheapest gyms in Sydney. I used to find myself running around the whole city, going to hot yoga here, then swimming there, and gym class somewhere else. Having them all in the one place and part of the one membership saves me so much time, money and energy.

POINTS TO REMEMBER:

- Stop and question each expense, asking yourself, 'Do I love, value, use or appreciate this expense?' If not, look to reduce or remove it.
- Get on the phone and call your providers (health, insurance, utilities), asking what can be done to help reduce your premiums and bills. It is more expensive for a business to find a new customer than it is to retain one at a slightly lower rate.
- Make your savings truly count and ensure that you capture any savings you create by updating your banking ritual and proactively putting them in your accounts.
- Savings created should go to building up your Life + $X Emergency account first, then they can be split between your lifestyle and financial goal accounts.
- Keep your sanity – those expenses that keep you happy and healthy, like gym memberships (as long as you use them!) and travel, should stay. Just as long as they aren't excessive!
- Consider stretching out some of your lifestyle luxuries so that they're less frequent. E.g. an $80 haircut could be every 10–12 weeks instead of 6–8 weeks.
- Look at your loyalty programs, including those offered by supermarkets, airlines and credit cards. Check that they work for you and your needs.
- Invest some time getting to understand your frequent flyer program so that you know the loopholes and register for special offers. Travel is a big expense for most people, so any savings here can really help.
- Regularly review your budget – I will say this throughout the book, but new expenses will always try to creep into your accounts. Just make sure that if they do, they have your upfront approval.

CHAPTER SIX

Extra Cash to Cash In

Often when we need to deal with a financial crisis or achieve a financial goal, the first step is to rein in our expenses. To cut back, cut out, ration, deprive. And then so many of us simply stop there, thinking that's all we can do. But trying to fix financial problems or achieve financial success with limited resources makes any challenge even more difficult and disheartening.

The other solution is to try to earn some extra money. This can be put towards the financial crisis or financial goal, to alleviate the stress or achieve the objective faster and more efficiently.

Building money isn't nearly as draining or as restrictive as having to scrimp, save and cull your budget. It's no longer about going without, but about adding in. Its energy is free-flowing and expansive, as you can come from a place of abundance rather than scarcity and deprivation. Suddenly, possibilities and solutions are unlimited – whereas there is only so much you can do with a limited budget. You'll find yourself being open to ideas, opportunities and inspiration, and this will fuel more energy and empowerment.

But most importantly, when you find and do these things to bring in some extra cash, you must make that money count. As with those savings created from our budgets in the previous chapters, any extra money that you find, make, hustle, create or earn must be put towards one of your goals. Even if it's only $1.

By proactively putting your newfound cash into one of your goal accounts, you are making it count and mindfully honouring the work you did to create it. This is a big part of being mindful with money.

Have you ever made some extra cash unexpectedly – maybe through selling an unwanted item, being offered a fun paid project to work on, winning a competition, or being given an extra shift at work – and realised how easy and worthwhile it was, and wondered how you could do it again to create the same outcome?

So many opportunities exist around us to hustle up some extra cash. It's just a matter of working out what you can do and what you are prepared to do.

A few years ago, I created a fun financial challenge for myself called The $1000 Project, in which I welcomed others to join me. It was born out of my passion and determination to show people that by being more mindful with money, we can easily make a real difference to our financial situation and our future.

While other people use The $1000 Project to help pay off debt and save for home deposits, holidays and even weddings, I wanted to go one step further and show people that by applying these ideas, we can also build passive income through regular investing. And I realised the best way to show people was to lead by example. So I did.

I announced this challenge on my YouTube channel, SugarMamma.TV, and set about finding ways to save money, hustle money, etc. But I focused on manifesting just $1000 at a time. While I had a big financial goal, I concentrated on what I could do to create $1000 right then and there. To me, $1000 was enough money to make an impact but not an intimidating amount. It was approachable, and therefore achievable.

Everything I did to help come up with my next $1000, I shared on my YouTube channel, and on my blog – from market research on washing powders to tasting crackers and testing apps, from selling furniture and clothes on Gumtree and eBay to taking on extra work that I could do over weekends. I created fun financial challenges like Frugal February and Manifesting March and adopted a more minimalistic approach in my consumption.

You name it, I did it. And over the course of twelve months, I saved and invested $32 000, and built a passive income of over $1650 p.a. After a short break I realised that I was missing the sense of financial progress, and started again with Round 2. This time I saved $36 000 over thirteen months. The $1000 Project is still going today, with Round 4 about to commence, and the passive income is almost $5000 p.a. and growing every day.

The $1000 Project has become a mini movement, with people joining from around the world and doing their own versions of this financial challenge, such as The €500 Project or The £200 Project. I get photos from Italy to Iceland of people showing me their growing bank accounts or their side hustle. Seeing, hearing and reading people's excitement only inspires me tenfold, which is why The $1000 Project continues to grow with more and more people getting on board every day.

One thing each person doing The $1000 Project has in common is that every time we see our account balance increase, and realise the powerful impact of our efforts to bring in extra cash and financial abundance, it fuels our desire to see what we can do to create our next $1000.

The challenge has had such an effect that new businesses born from these side hustles have become full-time gigs! These people turned things that they loved doing, making and sharing into mini businesses, which allowed them to get out of debt quickly, build savings and start investing in passive income streams. And doing this extra work never felt painful, as it stemmed from their own personal passions.

CHEAT TIP FROM CC:

Anyone can do The $1000 Project. You can use it to help get through short-term financial challenges or for big-picture financial goals. It is fun, empowering and you will be amazed by what you achieve.

If you tag @SugarMammaTV and #the1000dollarproject or #mymindfulmoneynumber, we will follow you back. Your image will help inspire others with their own financial goals.

Read inspiring stories of people who have followed The $1000 Project, such as three sisters in Scotland who started a Scone Box business out of their café, or The Wedding Sitter, who established an at-event childcare service.

Here are just some of the inspiring things that people are doing to earn some extra cash to put towards their own financial goals:

- **Babysitting** – often doubles as a saving as well, as you aren't out spending money! Find work on websites such as jugglestreet.com.au or Facebook groups for local parents and babysitters.
- **Walking dogs and pet-sitting** – a great way to get some fresh air and exercise at the same time as making money. There are lots of websites, but madpaws.com.au has a great reputation.

- **Selling through markets** – grab a group of friends and take unwanted clothes and homewares to the local markets. Usually the cost of a stall and insurance is minimal and it can be divided among your group of friends. Contact your local council to ask where they are held and how often.
- **Transcribing** – whether it's police reports or simple dictation, this can be done in the comfort of your own home. There are heaps of websites that you can register online with for work.
- **Proofreading** – as above, and is perfect if you have a good eye for detail, grammar and spelling!
- **Translating** – if you speak another language fluently, you can find work similar to transcribing but also translating it into another language. This is particularly valuable as we become more globalised.
- **Data entry** – virtual office work is so easy to do, a minimal skill set is needed and in many circumstances it can be done remotely.
- **Testing products and services** – receive free products and be paid to test them in your own home in return for valuable and appreciated feedback. See, for example, usertesting.com and pineconeresearch.com.
- **Starting a weekend kids' club** – have a fun theme that includes getting back to nature by using parks and bushland, so it can be educational as well.
- **Writing** – got a talent for writing? You can be paid to create content by writing copy, such as for blogs, emails, articles, even advertisements. Check out websites like au.copify.com.
- **Growing bonsai trees or propagating valuable plants** – this doesn't involve too much energy or cost, and you can sell them online, with local pickups.

- **Growing fruit and vegetables** – to sell or turn into products that can be sold.
- **Renting out your home** – for photoshoots, commercials, TV series or even movies. It doesn't need to be big and glamorous – location agents need a wide variety of homes to shoot in, and they can pay anywhere from $800 to $2000! Check out bighouse.com.au.
- **Testing apps and websites** – trial apps and websites before they're launched and provide feedback to the designers.
- **Preparing home-cooked meals for people** – earn money while making life easier for busy families and allowing them to eat healthily. You can even do this while preparing your own meals for the week.
- **Keeping company** – enjoy getting to know the people in your community? You can be paid to spend time with people who are lonely, unwell and would like a home visitor. Websites such as homecareheroes.com.au pay you by the hour and do all the relevant security checks.
- **Photography** – turn your hobby into a business by promoting your skills for portraits, special functions, websites and more. You can even sell your beautifully captured images via stock photo library websites such as Shutterstock (shutterstock.com), Getty, Almany and Foap (foap.com) with 15–20% commission per download.
- **Selling your unwanted goods** – remember this is tax-free cash. My favourite is Gumtree for quick cash and for items that can't really be posted. I also love eBay.
- **Helping people declutter** – so many people want to organise their homes but don't know where to start, and will happily pay people to do it for them. You can even help them list

their unwanted items online and offer a flat hourly fee or a percentage of the sale price.

- **Becoming an Uber driver** – any driver you meet will tell you how much they can save and how much the extra cash helps.
- **Advertising your practical skills on Airtasker** – IT, handyperson work, and so on.
- **Cleaning homes** – or even helping with housekeeping, from doing the grocery shopping to running errands such as picking up dry-cleaning.
- **Tutoring children** – even the basics like reading and writing skills to maths and science. For languages you can go to websites such as preply.com, where they connect you with eager-to-learn students you can teach via Skype!
- **Writing an ebook** – if you know how to do something really well, you could write an ebook on the subject and sell it online for a flat nominal fee. This works well for resources that teach people a certain skill over a period of time. Being online it is really scalable.
- **Asking for a pay rise** – find out what new promotions are coming up, ask if there are new projects that you can be a part of or what additional training you can do to make yourself more valuable. Maybe even come up with a bonus or commission structure if certain business KPIs are achieved. Or maybe it's simply time to find a new, better-paying job.
- **Become a secret shopper** – if you have a good eye for detail, companies will pay for your honest feedback on your shopping experiences.
- **Starting a YouTube channel or blog** – it takes a while to earn income, but if you have great content and engagement it builds up over time.

- **Participating in market research** – surveys, taste testing and talking about products and services. Check out Bread & Butter, Your Source, eCash, Farron Research, Chat 4 Cash – just to name a few. These often pay in gift vouchers, but you can still make it count by using the voucher to pay for something you need and transferring the equivalent into your goal account. I've done work for Farron Research many times, and they have always paid well and promptly.

- **Teaching a skill** – such as make-up lessons, cooking classes, photography lessons. You can run your own private course or connect with an institution or educational facility. Websites such as Teachable.com show you not only how to create an e-course but also how to market it and sell it. I know quite a few successful entrepreneurs who now do this as a full-time job, and they're doing extremely well. But remember, your content must be valuable and scalable, meaning that it can reach a wide range of people without much effort or cost.

- **Renting out your car, garage, storage, belongings** – you can use platforms such as Designerex (designerex.com.au) to rent dresses and handbags, and there are even businesses that rent kids' equipment (such as prams, travel cots and toys) to families on holiday to save them having to lug it all around on their travels.

- **House-sitting** – care for people's homes, gardens and pets while they're away.

- **Social media** – if you have a high a level of engagement (this is not necessarily a high number of followers) on social media, your account may become a mini business itself, as people are paying attention to what you post about. You can list your accounts with selling platforms (such as The Right Fit Brand

Ambassdor World or IMG) to be paid by brands to help promote their products or services. You must always disclose that it is a paid sponsored ad, but it can help commercialise your following and you get to work with brands you genuinely love and use. You can also use affiliate links. If visitors to your site purchase particular items from your recommendation you earn commission. I personally know some people who make more money from affiliate links than they do from their salaries.

- **Running social media** – some emerging companies and brands need people to help run their social media for them while they work on demanding projects. Offer to help people with their posts and developing their accounts as a side business.

- **Renting out your IT expertise** – are you a bit of an IT expert? Well, there are people (like me) who always seem to get themselves stuck when it comes to using their gadgets. Join websites such as Experts Exchange (experts-exchange.com), where you get paid to give online support.

- **Utilising your inner poet or songwriter** – perhaps you're a bit of a poet or songwriter, or even fancy yourself as a jingle creator? Or maybe you can sing. Websites like Music Xray (musicxray.com) and Oatmeal Studios (oatmealstudios.com) can pay you for these talents.

- **Harnessing your love of music** – Slicethepie (slicethepie.com) will pay you to listen to music of upcoming talent and share your opinion before companies sign with them.

- **Earning cashback on your own shopping** – you can join websites like Cashrewards (cashrewards.com.au) for free, and when you shop online you earn cashback on your own shopping. I use Cashrewards to help me with my $1000 Project;

it covers grocery shopping, clothing, wine, and even big-ticket items such as appliances, holidays, insurance and utilities – and it is so easy. The cashback quickly adds up and after a certain period of time (usually three months to ensure products aren't returned), the money is deposited into your bank account. Cashrewards has paid Australians over $50 million in cashback; it also has a guarantee and supports the Starlight Foundation. But make sure you switch on your notifications, as there are amazing bonus rewards and special offers that can sometimes double your cashback.

- **Paid medical trials** – be part of modern-day medical practice where you help detect, prevent, or find cures to illnesses and diseases. These trials are generally well paid, with medical monitoring, and the companies often look for people from a wide variety of backgrounds – both healthy and suffering from conditions.

- **Designing websites and logos** – really creative, even just for a hobby? You can get paid to create designs, websites and logos through websites such as Fiverr (fiverr.com) and Upwork (upwork.com).

- **Sharing your expertise** – extremely knowledgeable in a certain field like law, medicine, mechanics? Well, people with particular questions will pay to be able to pick your brain online and ask you questions. You can register with websites like Just Answer (justanswer.com).

- **Reselling** – I've met lots of people who will buy certain brands of clothes and bed linens in clearance sales and then resell them online for a profit. Some even scour local op shops for luxury designer labels and sell them for an impressive quick profit. You can call yourself an eco-stylist!

- **Being an extra in a movie or on a TV show** – websites like StarNow (starnow.com) are always looking for people who can be extras. You may even get to meet a few celebrities along the way.
- **Making arts and crafts** – from jewellery to kids' toys, from costumes to soaps and candles, you can sell your wares by having your own market stall or online shop, or via websites such as Etsy.

Some of these ideas may take a bit of time to get off the ground (getting yourself out there, promoting your product or service by social media, working out rates, marketing etc.), and you may have to work late into the night or over the weekend, but keep at it and don't expect success overnight. If you have something to offer that's of value, word will spread. And help spread it yourself! Ask people to recommend you if you're serious about growing your side hustle.

You may think your time is worth more than spending it on earning an extra couple of hundred dollars each week. But when you think that that $200 per week is over $10 000 a year extra in your pocket and could be the difference that sees you achieving your number five years sooner or enjoying retirement or part-time work much earlier than expected, your attitude and perspective can quickly change.

Also, that $200 extra per week may save you tens of thousands off your home loan. It may pay for those annual holidays or help you finally get rid of that credit card debt and build your emergency money. That little bit of extra effort goes a really long way, and over time can put you miles further along financially than if you do nothing.

Now it's your turn to think up some ideas to earn some extra cash. Take a few minutes to write down ten things that you *can* do and *would be happy to* do today as your side hustle.

1. _____
2. _____
3. _____
4. _____
5. _____
6. _____
7. _____
8. _____
9. _____
10. _____

ONE PERSON'S TRASH, ANOTHER PERSON'S TREASURE

According to a recent Gumtree report into the second-hand economy, researchers discovered that Australian families have over twenty-five unwanted items in their home, worth in excess of $4200. So if your home is feeling a little cluttered, look to make some quick cash and get down to listing these items online by using the easy-to-use apps that are out there. Take lots of photos (include labels, boxes, receipts and warranties if you have them, as they can help you get a better price), describe the condition, explain why you are selling the item and do your research into similar items being sold second-hand so you know the value of what you're selling and what competitive price to set.

You can sell old laptops, mobile phones, appliances, serveware, glassware, artwork, furniture, sporting equipment, toys, clothes . . . pretty much anything. One person's trash is another's treasure!

Try to avoid getting trapped in the thought of how much you paid for the items that you are selling. Letting go of the items you no longer love, value, use or appreciate is about freeing up space in your life for more energy and new opportunities for a better future. The cash that you make will be put towards not only achieving your goals, but achieving them faster. This in turn will help improve your sense of self-worth and empower you to do more and see what else you can do. Also, by selling your items the flow-on effect allows others the opportunities to buy these goods at a price that they may not have been able to afford brand new. Then there is the environmental consideration – not dumping your items means less landfill, less pollution and less environmental destruction. So rethink your council clean-up day – selling your still-functional items is highly responsible on many different levels.

As you work through your own list of things that you'd be happy to do to earn some extra and appreciated cash, I recommend starting with the easiest idea first – the sooner you see the cash in your hand, the more you'll feel inspired and want to keep going. And a new idea or inspiration (or even a new business) may be born out of your progress.

Also, tell people that you're looking to make some extra cash and what it is for. When people hear you want to help yourself and improve your situation, they'll want to see you succeed. When I tell people that I'm doing The $1000 Project, they give me the best ideas and even sometimes opportunities I would never have thought of myself.

Never be ashamed of having to do something to create some extra cash in your life. It's actually inspiring to others and shows that you aren't settling for an average life, but instead aspiring to something better. In fact, I bet you'll inspire the people you tell about your goal, mission or project. They may just end up joining you!

And you don't need to flog yourself 24/7 to make additional income. We are human – we all have responsibilities, time constraints, commitments and our own sense of balance to maintain. Use these earning options when the time is right for you. You have the freedom to use these solutions if and when you want.

But remember, as mentioned above, the only (very important and strict!) rule is that **you must deposit any money you earn from your side hustle into one of your accounts as soon as you make it**. Otherwise it will evaporate as you unthinkingly spend it or allow it to be absorbed into your other expenses. I guarantee it. So bank it immediately into one of your key accounts, following the same banking ritual as outlined in Chapter four.

And while you work out which account you should be adding to, first add it to your Life + $X Emergency account. Then you can decide how you would like to split the remaining amount between your lifestyle and financial goal accounts. But if you're seriously motivated to get ahead financially, you are always encouraged to put your extra earnings – after you have built up your emergency money – into your financial goal account, and that's what we'll be really focusing on for the rest of this book.

CHEAT TIP FROM CC:

When I'm doing The $1000 Project and am on track to achieve my goals, I occasionally allow for a little reward and spend a small amount of that extra cash on myself. These are usually only minor treats, but they're so motivating – it might be a massage or a pedicure, or going to my favourite cafe or restaurant, or even a nice bottle of bubbles. Just enough to refill my emotional and energetic bucket and help me to feel inspired to keep going.

POINTS TO REMEMBER:

- Look for ways to earn, hustle, manifest and work for extra cash to put towards your goals. This will help speed up your success and allow you to move on to new and more exciting financial goals.

- All extra cash created must be put into one of your accounts, going towards your goals. The number-one priority is to build up your Life + $X Emergency account so that you never need to get into debt again.

- Be open-minded about the different ways to earn extra cash – sometimes my best ideas have been born out of the craziest ideas.

- If you don't know what your financial goal or lifestyle goal is, that's okay – just make sure money is going into these accounts so that you already have money there when your idea hits you.

- Don't fall into the trap of holding on to unwanted stuff that you don't use just because you paid so much for it. In selling these items, you're not only helping yourself achieve your own financial goals, but you're helping someone else buy something that they may not have been able to afford brand new. Plus by not dumping your unwanted items, you are helping reduce landfill and environmental destruction.

CHAPTER SEVEN

Your Sweet Spot

'That difference between ordinary and extraordinary is that little extra.' – Jimmy Johnson, American football coach

Your sense of awareness and motivation towards your financial future should now be shifting, even if it is only a little bit. Any financial stress that you were previously carrying should be starting to melt away as you find that there are simple and easy solutions and strategies to start today to make your life easier and get you back on track. In fact, you may even start to light up at the thought of the exciting opportunities that surround you as you begin to create a financially secure and harmonious life for yourself and family.

To keep us on track, we must always remember that financial security is based around your ability to earn passive income. The ability to earn an income without having to actually do anything is the key to becoming financially free. Any time that you are feeling deflated, come back to your notes and goals in the workbook section on page 20, re-read them and remind yourself of what you are building **and why**. Even a quick reminder of the value and benefits you are creating can quickly reinject some excitement and motivation into your world.

How much passive income you want to build and in what timeframe is completely up to you, **and your number and timeframe may change as your life and goals evolve, which is completely normal**. But it's important that you know exactly how to do this for yourself and that you start as soon as possible – even if it's only with $1. The point is, your journey towards financial freedom has begun and the only way is up from this point forward, starting now.

Building these income sources does take time and effort, but it isn't complicated and there are lots of things you can do to make it easy and fun. This is what I hope to show you from this page forward, so that you feel empowered to start straight away, even before you finish reading this book.

Let's go back to the example of Amanda in Chapter two, whose number is $80000 per annum and who wants to retire at age sixty-five.

Regardless of the amount of passive income that she needs to earn to cover her living expenses, her passive income must keep up with inflation at the very least, so that she can remain financially independent indefinitely. And by indefinitely I mean forever, unlike the popular Financial Independence Retire Early (FIRE) movement, which is based on a capital number eroding over time eventually to zero, forcing you to start from scratch at a much older age. With the possible depletion of that capital happening at a concerning speed due to inflation over the long run, this can be a huge financial killer that a lot of people only consider for the short run. What we are building are passive incomes that only get bigger with time.

That $80000 p.a. that Amanda wants in passive income in today's dollars is actually going to be just under $156000 in twenty-seven years' time when she is sixty-five if we assume an average inflation rate of 2.5% p.a. That is almost double her passive income number, so we need to work twice as efficiently to get there in time.

But remember, we have been safe and wise, and built into her budget the non-negotiable, ongoing investment plan of 10% p.a. with the original $80 000 passive income requirement for new and continued investing back into her portfolios, with this monthly amount also growing with inflation.

By using her time wisely (as in starting today) and investing intelligently, choosing quality investments that are cost effective, tax efficient and, most importantly, two-dimensional, with growing passive income based off growing values, this goal is realistic for Amanda.

And fortunately, there is something called the 'sweet spot', where a bit of extra effort can improve your situation exponentially, especially when you combine the two powerful investment dimensions. See Amanda's example below.

POWERFUL PARETO

After Amanda works out her game plan (coming in Chapter ten), she decides to simply increase her ongoing regular investment to 20% p.a. but keep everything else the same, and her numbers change spectacularly.

Just by increasing her regular contributions to 20%, Amanda can retire on a passive income of $184 500 p.a. which is the equivalent of $92 451 p.a. in today's dollars (assuming inflation is 2.5% p.a. compounded annually and her dividends grow on average at 5% over the long run). Her wealth will only continue to grow, with her portfolio being worth $6 400 000 (equivalent of $1 969 000 in today's dollars) in her mid-eighties, and it will still pay her that growing passive income of $489 000 p.a. (equivalent of $149 000 p.a. in today's dollars).

How many retirees do you know who actually get wealthier during retirement?

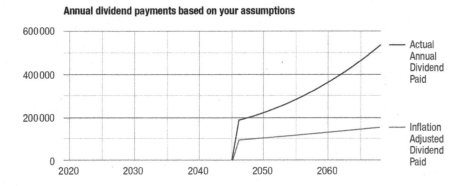

Annual dividend payments based on your assumptions

Because Amanda is experiencing the important and powerful **combination of income and long-term capital growth**, the capital growth on the portfolio is helping fund her passive income, which is not only keeping up with inflation, but exceeding it. And even with all the withdrawals in spending her passive income, it never erodes away or even goes backwards in value, like a waterfall that never dries out. This is because the income is growing with the capital growth, exceeding inflation, giving her more spending power. Which is why it's so important that your long-term investment assets have both capital growth and income characteristics; there'll be more to come on this shortly.

Is that a good enough incentive to invest that 20% today to create even greater financial security that should last the rest of your life? This 'sweet spot' will make your life even more liberating. And when you know what your sweet spot is, **you can decide if it's worth your extra effort**.

Simply write down what you have to start with to build your number and how much you can contribute towards building your number on a regular basis. You can play around with the

---

CHEAT TIP FROM CC:

To work out your minimum required ongoing contribution to your game plan to build your passive income, head to SugarMamma.TV, where under the Money tab you will find a range of really helpful calculators, including one called Sweet Spot Dividend Growth Calculator.

---

initial starting amount and the ongoing contribution amount and see how much indefinite freedom you can create for yourself. You will be amazed what you can create for yourself. If you can only contribute a small amount upfront and ongoing, that's okay because we can build on this over time.

Amanda has an exciting choice to make: if she wants to never have to worry about running out of money and ensure her financial security and independence only strengthen, giving her even more freedom and greater ability to give back and help others, she can add that extra 20%. But only if she wants to. And if she wants to stick with her goal, without the 20% extra effort, that is absolutely fine. She will still reach her goal of $80 000 p.a. in today's dollars, it will still keep up with inflation and it will never run out.

She has the choice to add further financial security and wealth if she feels like. It is her choice. And sure, there will be times or phases in her life where she may not necessarily be able to do the full 20% p.a. but there may also be times where she can do more than 20% p.a. The important point is that she knows what she needs to do and she has a choice.

And you can have this choice too.

Write down your different financial freedom sweet spots:

ACHIEVE YOUR NUMBER:

Indefinite financial freedom: starting amount $_____!
Indefinite financial freedom: ongoing amount $_____!

Gives me: $_____ p.a. and lasts forever

EXCEED YOUR NUMBER WITH 20% SWEET SPOT SUCCESS:

Indefinite financial freedom: starting amount $_____!
Indefinite financial freedom: ongoing amount with extra ongoing effort $_____!

Gives me: $_____ p.a. and lasts forever, making even greater financial security.

So now let's look at the investment tools, strategies and vehicles we need to make your number happen. To get us started, we need to know and understand these four financial friends which have a powerful effect when combined together:

- compounding interest
- time
- two-dimensional assets: capital growth and income
- regular investment

Let's have a look at how these work now.

COMPOUNDING INTEREST

Compounding interest is the growth that results from the interest that you earned being added to the principal sum or deposit. It comes from reinvesting interest income, rather than spending it.

Compounding interest is a really easy and effortless way to build wealth. This is why I always recommend reinvesting interest or income as you work towards your number.

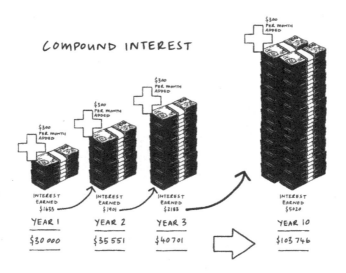

COMPOUND INTEREST

$300 PER MONTH ADDED

INTEREST EARNED $1655 — INTEREST EARNED $1901 — INTEREST EARNED $2183 — INTEREST EARNED $5020

YEAR 1   YEAR 2   YEAR 3   YEAR 10

$30 000 $35 551 $40 701 $103 746

Have a look at this example:

You have $30 000 saved up and decide that you'd like to invest it. You also have $300 per month, which you would also like to add to this initial investment. You continue to do so religiously over the course of ten years. Assuming this investment earns on average 6% p.a. and no money is ever withdrawn or spent during this period – all interest/income is reinvested (that is to say, no money is ever withdrawn but always placed back in the investment for further growth opportunities) – you would end up with over $103 000 at the end of the ten-year period.

However, when you look at that total amount of $103 000, this was not 'saved'; technically, $66 000 was saved through the deposit ($30 000) and regular contributions ($36 000). But through compounding interest over the ten years, an additional $37 746 was accumulated.

This $37 745 is compounding interest in action – an example of passive income, and money working for you.

You can use this to your advantage by initially going harder. If we doubled the initial deposit to $60 000, but kept the same regular investment plan of $300 per month and the same interest rate, you'd more than double your wealth by using the larger initial deposit of $60 000 to generate over $62 000 in interest. This is the effect of compounding interest, and it's really powerful for helping you achieve your number sooner.

TIME

The sooner you start investing and putting money aside to achieve your number, the easier and less stressful it's going to be. This is because you give compounding interest more time to work for you. So it's never too early to start investing, but it's never too late to start, either. As long as you have time ahead of you, and as long as you are, if possible, prepared to put in that extra 20% that Amanda commits to.

CHEAT TIP FROM CC:

If you don't feel as if you have time to reach your number, there are amazing things that you can do to make up for lost time. I'll be covering this subject in the following chapters, so keep reading!

If we take the same example above using the initial deposit of $30 000 and add an extra five years with the same regular contributions of $18 000, stretching it to fifteen years, we gain an additional $76 868!

So now you know this, you should feel motivated to start investing today. In fact, you can start right now!

The sooner you start investing, the sooner you can kick back financially. But remember how much time helps make a difference in our three previous examples? **And time doesn't actually require any effort or energy!**

TWO-DIMENSIONAL ASSETS

To achieve your number sooner, you need to buy two-dimensional assets. These are assets that produce not just income but capital growth as well. And it is because of these two powerful ingredients that Amanda's money will grow so efficiently and last for so long, even though she's drawing an income bigger than her portfolio is actually making.

Her passive income is still growing each year thanks to the capital growth, because the new annual income is based on the growing value of the asset, i.e. capital growth. And her passive income is even exceeding inflation each year, giving her more and more financial freedom.

Two-dimensional assets are typically:
- domestic and international shares – because they pay dividends (income) and grow in value (capital growth)
- property – because it pays rent (income) and grows in value (capital growth).

Examples of one-dimensional assets are:
- savings accounts
- term deposits
- fixed interest, such as bonds, when held to the end of their term.

All three produce income *only* through an interest payment without actually growing in value from capital growth. That $10 000 in a term deposit that pays you 3% p.a. ($300) is still going to be worth $10 000 in five years' time with the exception of the interest that it has paid to you.

An investment asset that only produces income is fine for your short-term needs, where you need the money in less than seven years, but over the long run, if the value of that income doesn't grow and exceed inflation, you will be going backwards. I will explain this in more detail in Chapter ten and in the following pages. But the reason the one-dimensional asset isn't efficient for long-term financial goals is because cash has no capital growth element. It simply pays income. The way to avoid this is to invest in assets that can continue to produce these two essential characteristics (capital growth *and* income) for a very long time.

You want your income growing year after year with the capital growth, ideally exceeding inflation, so that your passive income is always ahead of your living expenses. When you have this ingredient in your investment portfolio, it makes achieving the sweet spot a lot easier as the income grows with the capital growth.

REGULAR INVESTMENT

One of the most important reasons to write a budget and review your living expenses is to help free up or create some extra cash for yourself.

While some of this cash can go towards your lifestyle goal account, you must ensure that another portion goes towards your financial future. The more you can commit through regular investment, the quicker, easier and more enjoyable your wealth creation process will be.

The secret behind this is habit. It should be like cleaning your teeth morning and night: you don't actually think too much about doing this; you simply do it and it's done. Regular investing is the same – make it a habit, routine or ritual, and it frees up your mental space.

As you can see in the example below, if you double your regular investment from $300 per month to $600 p.m., your total interest grows to over $50 000, compared with the $37 000 in interest at only $300 p.m.

CHEAT TIP FROM CC:

Whenever I have received a pay rise, I have simultaneously adjusted my financial habits. I work out my new after-tax pay, and use the increase to adjust my mortgage repayment or regular investment plan accordingly – with a small upgrade for my lifestyle.

Say my net monthly pay increased by $450 p.m. after tax. I would either increase my mortgage repayment or my regular investment plan by $400 p.m., and then allow $50 for more fun in my monthly budget. Or I would split the $450 between the two, so $225 towards each goal. I decide what I want to do at the time, depending on my goals, but I love the choice and flexibility I have and the knowledge of how much this is going to make a difference.

The reason I do this so deliberately is because often when we get more money, our lifestyle goes up in proportion with our pay rise. We simply spend more. We buy more of the things that we like buying, or we buy more expensive versions of those things. And three months later, we're back to struggling with cash, wondering where all this new money is going. By being proactive when pay rises come, however, you can really make them count.

Now let me show you what happens when we combine all four financial friends! We kick off with a larger amount to get us started, we increase our regular investment plan, we increase our time, but we keep the return the same. Our total interest earnt from our money working for us is more than $150 000.

Now that you understand these four financial friends, I want to show you how to invest and in what. As you now know, the types of investments that we need to be looking at are growth assets, such as:

- international shares
- domestic shares
- property

Typically these have long-term capital growth (even though they can bounce around like yo-yos over the short to medium term), while they pay a passive income through dividends or rent.

In the next two chapters I will show you how to build a diversified investment portfolio, using a variety of different strategies that incorporate these four financial friends. But you should see the value and importance of these two-dimensional investment assets and how they can help you achieve your number now.

CASH

Cash and fixed-interest investments such as savings accounts and term deposits are most definitely an important safety net for your finances, and one that I will recommend as part of your strategy once we've gained some headwind in building up to your number (see my two-year sleep well strategy coming up soon). In the meantime, however, cash isn't going to be the most helpful financial asset in helping build your long-term wealth.

Don't get me wrong, cash is definitely king for all your short- to medium-term expenses and goals – it's the perfect way to save for your holiday, a new car or even the deposit on your home, because there's very little short- to medium-term risk or volatility with your savings account balance bouncing around like a yo-yo. You never want to be in a situation where you're forced to sell your investments when the value is temporarily down; it will mean crystallising a loss on your portfolio and you may end up without enough money to pay for that expense or goal.

So if your goals or expenses are to be achieved within the next **seven years**, such as savings for a home deposit, holiday, wedding or starting a family, keep that money in cash. Do not be tempted to invest it, as investing requires a long-term timeframe of at least **ten years**. I will explain why this is in more detail in the next few chapters, but unless you are prepared to invest and hold an investment for ten years or more, I would urge you to keep your money in cash, through a high-interest online savings account or term deposit.

But in the meantime, understanding and incorporating growth-inclined strategies will bring you greater long-term value and be a far more efficient way to accumulate wealth.

POINTS TO REMEMBER:

- Head to the SugarMamma.TV website to find out your sweet spot and to work out what upfront and ongoing action you need to be taking today.
- Your sweet spot doesn't need to be your financial goal, but it is good to know the different options and outcomes available to you if you feel inspired.

- Compounding interest is going to be one of your biggest and best financial friends, so always reinvest your income when and where possible rather than spending it.
- Regular investing is key. This is why doing your budget and looking to add a side hustle can have a big impact.
- Regularly invest whatever you can afford within your budget and look to build and improve it when you can. Even starting with $10 per month is okay, because you can find ways in the meantime to add more to this.
- The important part is to create a habit – just like cleaning your teeth twice a day, you can get to a stage with saving and investing where you don't think about it, you just do it.
- See what your Pareto power can do to help create your sweet spot – the 20% can dramatically change your world.
- The sooner you start carrying out your game plan, the better.
- To build long-term passive income streams, you want to be investing in growth assets. Typically these are domestic shares, international shares and property.
- Cash is for your expenses and the goals you want to reach within the next seven years.
- When you earn more in passive income than what you spend, you have even greater financial freedom and your net wealth continues to grow indefinitely.
- We want our money working for us, the boss.

Chapter Eight

Sharks and Sexy Shares

'I'm working full time on my job and part time on my fortune.'
– Jim Rohn, American entrepreneur

If you were swimming in the ocean and came across a ten-metre whale shark, you'd probably freak out. But if you learnt about this incredible animal, you would discover that they're actually docile creatures with a fondness for tropical waters, feed mainly on plankton, and are happy for humans to swim alongside them. You are definitely off the menu! And so you don't really need to be frightened; in fact, you may even *want* to swim along with them!

Whale sharks and shares can be similar. A lot of people perceive shares as scary and risky, but most of the time this is simply because they don't understand what they really are. **We fear what we don't understand**, and label them as risky, wanting nothing to do with them, pushing them away (or swimming away) without giving them a fair chance.

When I sit down with people and explain what shares are, how they work and how they can help them achieve their financial goals, suddenly shares seem quite amazing and pretty powerful. I have even had someone say, 'Shares are pretty sexy . . .'

When you own shares, you own part of a business. Kind of like a silent partner, you get to be part of the action without actually having to do anything. And assuming your business does well, you get to share in the profits as the value of the business goes up beyond the share price and you receive part of the profits through dividends.

Let me give you an example . . .

Let's say I have a friend who is an incredibly talented bag designer with a commercial mindset. As much as she wants to go out on her own, she isn't in a position where she can afford to start her business yet, but I think her bags would sell well and could make some decent money.

After considering all the risks, I decide to invest in her and this business so that she can start this handbag business. Her plan is to sell a wide range of high-quality bags in a variety of colours and styles catering to a wide market.

I invest $1000 in the business (this money is used to pay for equipment, materials, marketing, staff and so on). I have previously saved this money up, so it's paid for (invested) with cash.

I set a conservative but realistic goal to achieve a minimum of 10% on the return of my capital, which is the $1000 that I invested into the start up of this business. So my goal is to make $100 profit, after the business has covered all its expenses.

The first year the handbag business goes well, with the word spreading that my friend makes great handbags at great prices, and I achieve my goal of 10%.

Because I want the business to keep going and keep growing in value, I take 50% of the profits ($50) as an income for myself, via a dividend, and then keep the other 50% ($50) in the business so that my friend can invest in more marketing and materials, and new stock. And over the next six years I repeat this 50/50 strategy of paying the profits out as 50% income bonus to me (dividend) and 50% to reinvest into the business for more growth and expansion opportunities.

Year	Assets	Profit / Return on equity @ 10%	Dividend ($)	Inflation @2.5% p.a. of $50	Retained for further business investment ($)
1	1000.00	10.00	50.00	50.00	50.00
2	1050.00	10.50	52.50	51.25	52.50
3	1102.50	11.00	55.00	52.53	55.00
4	1157.50	11.60	58.00	53.84	58.00
5	1215.50	12.20	61.00	55.19	61.00
6	1276.50	12.80	64.00	56.57	64.00
7	1340.50	13.40	67.00	57.98	67.00

See how my dividends (which is my passive income) has grown from $50 per year to $67 per year over the seven years? Now assuming that my living expenses move with inflation, even with inflation at 2.5%, my cost of living is only $57.98 p.a. – while my passive income is greater at $67 p.a.

This leaves me extra income of $9.02 – 15.55% above what that same $50 is worth even with inflation over the last seven years. How nice is a 15.55% payrise!

I could spend this extra income or reinvest it elsewhere – but I have the freedom to do what I want with this extra money.

My initial investment is worth 34% more than what I orginally invested and I have received back $407.50 of the initial $1000 that I invested with my friend. All within seven years! How many investments do you know of that can be worth 34% more in seven years but also return over 40% of the initial capital as well?

When you invest in shares in a company, you are essentially becoming an owner of the business. At times, you even have a say in the running of the business through voting rights. And you are entitled to some of the profits as they pay them out, (through dividends) as well as the capital growth of that share price (the value of the asset) growing in value over the long run. Which all contributes to building your number.

The more of the business that you own, the more income you are entitled to, assuming that the business is doing well.

If the business is traded on the share market, these profits can be paid out in dividends directly to you (normally every six months) and the value of the share can be tracked through the stock exchange.

The share market is where most investors buy and sell their stocks – just think of it as the biggest and most important shopping mall you'll ever visit. There are sixteen major shopping malls (stock exchanges) in the world and here are a few that you may have heard of:

- the Australian Securities Exchange (the ASX)
- the New York Stock Exchange
- the NASDAQ Stock Market
- the London Stock Exchange
- the Tokyo Stock Exchange
- the Shanghai Stock Exchange

On the ASX alone, over $4.5 billion worth of shares are traded every day. At the moment, there are over 2200 companies traded on the ASX, and it is the sixteenth biggest shopping mall (stock exchange) in the world.

You use the sharemarket (either your country's local sharemarket or even another country's sharemarket) to buy into (invest in) big businesses – businesses that you see, use, and buy products and services from every day. They are businesses that have operations up and running and have been making a consistent profit and paying dividends for extended periods of time, generally at least seven to ten years.

You can buy shares with as little as $500, and if you set up an online share trading account (most major banks offer this service), the brokerage, which is the cost to buy and sell the stock, can cost as little as $8 to $30 per trade.

It literally takes minutes to buy shares, and it is so easy to do. In fact, I will show you exactly how to buy shares in the following chapter! And if you need to sell your shares (or even just some of your shares) you can receive your money within two working days.

Most brokerage is a dollar amount up until a trade gets larger, which can be anywhere from $10 000. With trades of this size or more, it reverts to a percentage-based fee, which can be from 0.11 to 0.55%. While broker fees have significantly reduced over the last eight years, you still need to keep in mind that brokerage can eat into your initial investment.

Therefore, I recommend that you start with a minimum of $1000 (hence, The $1000 Project). That way, even if brokerage is $20, your buying cost when you invest with $1000 as a percentage is 2% rather than 4% if investing with $500. But of course you can invest in much bigger amounts than $1000 if you like, which reduces your buying cost even further as a percentage.

Our Australian shopping mall for shares, the ASX, is made up of three different indexes, which is like three different groups

CHEAT TIP FROM CC:

My personal share portfolio and The $1000 Project portfolio is with ANZ Share investing. While I would ultimately prefer to be able to access my portfolios with all my other savings accounts as per my advice in Chapter three, after doing my research, I found ANZ worked best for me – I like the available research and educational material, how easy the website is to use, and how excellent its customer service is. Added to these points is knowing there's a high level of security for my trades; I can trade via an app should I need to, and I earn frequent flyer points every time I trade.

I recommend researching different online trading accounts, including your own bank's, so that you're sure it matches your needs, particularly if you can access your investments with your other cash-flow financials for superior efficiency.

of common businesses, used as a statistic measure to help gauge changes in the market.

Again, think of it as all the similar shops within this large shopping mall, grouped together. So all the different shoe shops are grouped together, all the different cosmetic stores grouped together and all the different clothing shops grouped together. By grouping these similar businesses, it's possible to measure how shoes are selling, how cosmetics are selling and how clothes are selling within the one big shopping mall.

Say the shoe index goes up by 1%, it can indicate that those other shoe companies within that index group may also have gone up by 1%. An index is not too dissimilar to a group survey, which is intended to help understand the general consensus about a particular topic, service or product.

These indexes are really significant, as they can help us to make clear comparisons between businesses and judge our investment portfolios with greater accuracy. But it is important to know that these different indexes don't all perform in perfect harmony with each other. The shoe index may be up 2% (so the shoe business is doing well), while the cosmetic index is down 3% – so cosmetics are going through a tough patch.

The three 'groups' or indexes that we have on the ASX are:

- the All Ordinaries Index (aka the 'All Ords')
- the Industrials Index
- the Resources Index.

I will show you in a second what type of businesses belong to each group, but before I do that, have a look at the graph on the following page showing how they each performed over the last thirty-eight years, based on an initial investment of $10 000 in 1979.

The medium-grey line represents the Industrials Index, made up of companies that provide goods and services – transportation companies, food manufacturers, waste management, supermarkets and the like. Examples of these kinds of businesses that you would be familiar with include Woolworths, Wesfarmers, Qantas, Telstra and the Commonwealth Bank. Like I said, these are businesses that have been around a really long time, are well established and are making and selling products and services.

The Resources Index's performance is shown by the dark-grey line, and features companies involved in the mining and exportation of minerals, oils and gases – think BHP, Rio Tinto, Glencore and Fortescue.

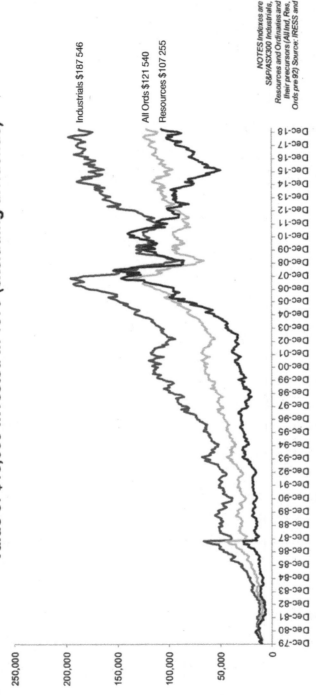

Value of $10,000 Invested in 1979 (excluding dividends)

Industrials $187 546

All Ords $121 540

Resources $107 255

NOTES Indexes are
S&P/ASX300 Industrials,
Resources and Ordinaries and
their precursors (All Ind, Res,
Ords pre 92) Source: IRESS and

The All Ords Index is a measure of the overall performance of the Australian market, shown with the light-grey line. It is comprised of the share prices of the largest 500 companies in the country and can include both industrials and resources.

When you invest in an index, you don't have the pressure of investing in one stock or even just a few stocks, but a group of different stocks, like a managed fund but so much cheaper and so much more cost effective. This is called diversification, which is essentially not putting all your eggs in one basket – it reduces the investment risk of picking some bad investments that may fall in value. So when you use the wider shopping basket of an index to hold your different investments from the shopping mall, the negative returns (which will most definitely happen from time to time) will over the long run be outweighed by the stronger performance and returns of the other investments within the same shopping basket.

Looking at this chart, if you could go back in time with the financial goals of long-term wealth accumulation and efficiency, where would you have preferred to invest? I am pretty confident that you would pick the Industrials Index, which is the medium-grey line, because you would have ended up with the largest amount of money in comparison to the other indexes.

If my parents had invested $10 000 into a parcel of the top fifty **ASX Industrial stocks** for me when I was conceived in 1979, I would have an impressive share portfolio today worth over $187 546, with the dividends paid along the way every year. And the last dividend would have been $8252 in March '19, with the average dividend being $4252 p.a. over the thirty-nine year period. So the average dividend represents a return of 42.5% of my parent's initial $1000 investment and the last dividend represents an 82.5% return on their initial $10 000 investment.

But what is even more impressive is that the portfolio would have yielded dividends every year prior to this. In fact, over the last thirty-eight years over $140 000 would have been paid out. Sure, initially it would have been a small amount each year, but it would have slowly grown over time.

That is, the initial investment that my parents made of $10 000 would have been paid back over fourteen times – yet I would still own the portfolio with the dividends continuing to grow and paying more passive income every year.

Now you know the effect of investing for the long run, using shares, you could include investing in shares to help build your number – and make dividends your source of passive income. Which is exactly what I'm going to discuss in this chapter and the next.

But first, let's have a look at how it can get even better! What if, during that period between 1979 and 2018, the dividends *weren't* paid out but rather reinvested in that portfolio?

DIVIDEND REINVESTMENT

As you know from Chapter seven, reinvesting is where you choose not to spend the dividends as cash but rather to use those profits to buy more stock in the business – therefore increasing your ownership in the business and potentially increasing your passive

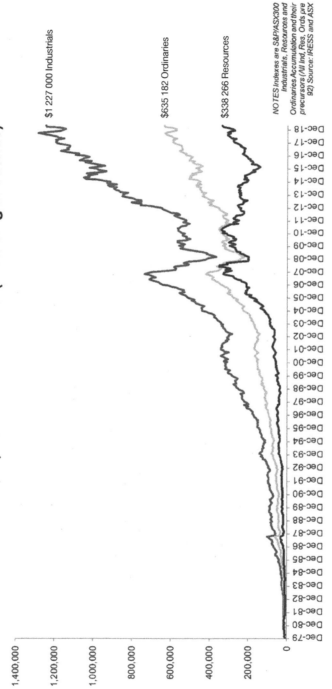

Value of $10,000 Invested in 1979 (including dividends)

$1 227 000 Industrials

$635 182 Ordinaries

$338 266 Resources

NOTES Indexes are S&P/ASX300 Industrials, Resources and Ordinaries Accumulation and their precursors (All Ind, Res, Ords pre 92) Source: IRESS and ASX

income. So let's say my parents chose not to take those dividend payments and spend them, but instead allowed that money to go back into the portfolio to buy more of those stocks in that portfolio.

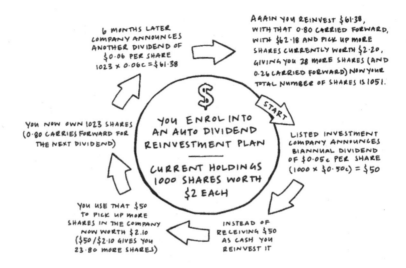

The portfolio would be worth over $1 227 000 and it would be paying a passive income of $49 080 p.a., which is now more than four times the original investment. It's being paid year after year, plus the portfolio is still growing in value over the long run.

Keep in mind that no more new money has been added to this portfolio other than the dividends being reinvested. It was basically a set-and-forget plan. And one that you could definitely do for yourself or your children, now that you know this. But more on that to come! (And by the way, no, my parents did not do this for me when I was conceived.)

This is why dividend reinvestment is one of the easiest and most effective ways to build your weath and your number, through shares without having to work too hard. Plus when you set up an automatic dividend reinvestment plan (which I will show you how to do), you don't have to pay any brokerage, and sometimes you even get a small discount on the share price. At any stage, should you decide that you would like your dividends to be paid to you, rather than being reinvested, you can instruct the dividends to be deposited into your bank account as cash.

If you hold individual stocks rather than the index, and are enrolled in an automatic dividend reinvestment strategy, there are definitely some risks and limitations that you need to be aware of. One major risk is becoming overexposed to a stock – that is, disproportionately over-weighted in comparison to other stocks in your portfolio that aren't enrolled in a dividend reinvestment plan. This is because you're reinvesting and owning more of this stock year after year, so it may be better to consider investing in other companies or industries that could provide you with other capital growth and investment opportunities.

However, if you are enrolled in an automatic dividend reinvestment plan through an index investment, you don't need to worry about this as all reinvested money is invested equally back into the index, helping ensure that it remains diversified and thus reducing your investment risk.

Another risk of dividend reinvestment plans is that you have no say as to the price you pay when you pick up more stock from a dividend reinvestment plan. The price is determined by the market value at the time of the dividend. So it could be cheap and a great time to accumulate more at a discount, or it could be expensive.

But there are some really easy and effective ways to grow your portfolio without these risks, or at least involving reduced risks, which I will be sharing with you shortly in the next chapter.

As an important point of comparison, if my parents had chosen to put that $10 000 into a one-year term deposit in December 1979, the term deposit would still be worth $10 000, and would have paid $220 in interest. Which investment is more efficient, helpful and powerful over the long run to help achieve your number? Cash or shares?

CHEAT TIP FROM CC:

Whenever I'm given the option to enrol in an automatic dividend reinvestment plan, I always take it. I like that it saves me brokerage fees, removes the temptation to spend the dividends and saves me the mental space of remembering to reinvest it. I make sure to keep reviewing my portfolio so that I have a good spread of investments in different companies and industries, and not too much weighting towards one or two individual company stocks that might dominate my portfolio (where the weighting is 15% or more) and increase my investment risk.

As I earn new money to add to the portfolio, I can ensure my portfolio is diversified by buying more stock manually in the companies that don't offer dividend reinvestment, or I can add new stocks to the portfolio for further diversification.

I personally like to hold twenty to thirty different companies. But the automatic reinvestment means one less thing for me to remember or worry about. And as I've said before, this book is a guide for managing your money in the real and busy world. Dividends are passive income, and that means not having to slave over a computer screen to manage it.

Setting up your automatic dividend reinvestment takes less than thirty seconds. When you've purchased your stock, the share registry, which is a company that holds all the details of people who own shares in the companies (either Link Market Services, Computershare or The Boardroom), will send you paperwork confirming your number of shares in the company. Attached to this paperwork is a form that you need to complete and sign – it even comes with a reply paid envelope – but most paperwork you can do online.

You need to register your tax file number, your bank details and, if available, your dividend reinvestment plan instructions. You have three options if the company offers a dividend reinvestment plan.

- **No dividend reinvestment** – dividends will be paid as cash to your bank account.
- **Partial dividend reinvestment** – where you nominate a percentage to be reinvested and a percentage to be paid as cash.
- **Full reinvestment** – *Tick this box!*

However, some companies don't offer dividend reinvestment plans, or they temporarily pause them for various reasons, both internal and external. When or if they do, they will have to pay the dividends to your bank account. So if you want to reinvest your dividends, you'll have to make this happen yourself by manually buying more shares in that company like I mentioned above.

CHEAT TIP FROM CC:

With any stock that doesn't offer dividend reinvestment plans, you will need to have your dividends paid into your bank account. I strongly recommend registering the BSB and account number of your **financial goal account** rather than your everyday account. This will help ensure that you don't miss the dividend being deposited and accidentally spend it. And as this account accumulates, you can get ready to use this money to buy more shares, i.e. more passive income sources.

BUT IT GETS EVEN BETTER...

Most industrial companies pay dividends with franking credits attached. Franking credits, which are also known as imputation credits, are a type of tax credit that allow Australian companies to pass on any tax that they have already paid (at a company level and rate) to the shareholder – you. You can then use this as a credit towards your own tax bill and either reduce your tax bill or potentially even get a refund.

Let me show you an example with my handbag business again – this time compared against another investment income that has no franking credit, such as a term deposit. To make a fair comparison, the income amounts are the same.

If my handbag business floats on the ASX and the company needs to pay out a dividend of $571, they will pay 30% to the Australian Tax Office (based on the company tax rate of 30%), and pay me $400, with a $171 franking credit.

I then declare the total $571 as income, and, if I am taxed at the top marginal tax rate of 47%, I would be up for $269 in tax. However, I can apply my $171 tax credit and only have to pay $98 in tax instead of the full $188 if I have earned that same $4000 from a non-franking credit source such as a term deposit! So my very valuable franking credit really helps me to save tax and boost my net income.

	A fully franked dividend	A term deposit
Income	$400	$400
Plus franking credit	$171	$0
Total taxable income	$571	$400
Less tax @47%	–$269	–$188
Add back franking credit	$171	$0
Net tax payable	–$98	–$188
Gross income	$400	$400
Net tax payable	–$97	–$188
Total income after tax	$302	$212

Now, that was assuming I am on a 47% marginal tax rate. However, say Honey's passive income is purely from her Australian share portfolio which is 100% industrial shares, all fully franked.

She received $63 000 in dividends for the financial year, which have already had $27 000 deducted for company tax (30%). After checking her dividend statements for the financial year, she declares the full combined amount of $90 000 for the financial year and any other income (such as her salary), and is taxed on the total amount at her marginal tax rate, but can now bring forward the $27 000 of franking credits. For simplicity's sake, though Honey isn't working as she is raising a young family, she would have technically overpaid her taxes and she is entitled to a refund of those excess franking credits of $5483.

	A fully franked dividend
Income	$63 000
Plus franking credit	$27 000
Total taxable income	$90 000
Less tax (based on $90,000 income)	–$21 517
Add back franking credit	$27 000
Net Tax Refund	$5483
Gross Income	$63 000
Net tax refund	+$5483
Income Total after refund	$68 483

* Assumptions: 2018–19 tax rates(incorporating the proposed changes supported by both major political parties), income tax based on $90 000 and includes Medicare levy

Not only is Honey earning a passive income, but also her tax dollars are working so efficiently that she's potentially getting an extra $5483 p.a. in a tax refund each year. She could put this towards more travel, more experiences, more charity or more investments – whatever she wants.

CHEAT TIP FROM CC:

Now in Australia, the income within superannuation is taxed at 15% p.a. so if you utilised industrial stocks that pay fully franked dividends, you could potentially cut that 15% tax rate down to 0%, with a refund back into your superannuation account. More on this in Chapter thirteen.

The one caveat is that even though excess franking credits have been refunded since 2001, there's always a chance that the government may change tax rates or decide to no longer issue this refund. Because of this, Honey views her tax refund as a blessing and never banks on receiving it every year or even at that level. That way, she not only remains financially independent but she also would never need to adjust her living expenses or work situation as she doesn't rely on the refund to supplement her living expenses.

MORE BONUSES

Another alternative to a dividend reinvestment is to participate in a Bonus Share Plan. This is where you choose to receive more shares as a bonus, but there is no tax payable on them. It is like getting a Christmas present and birthday present every year from your share portfolio without having to pay tax on receiving them like you would with normal dividends. If you go to sell those bonus shares, you will be taxed on them, but if you are sticking to our long-term 'buy and hold' and live off the dividends strategy, then this is a brilliant advantage of shares. However, not all companies offer bonus shares.

I hope that by now you're starting to realise that shares are not intimidating at all! It's like owning businesses within one large shopping mall, where you buy into a business to earn part of its profits, through collecting dividends every year – all for doing nothing.

Just maybe that person I mentioned overhearing earlier was right: shares, in particular industrial shares, are really quite sexy. Especially now that you can see the power of those dividends to help build your number and help ensure that it grows your number.

In the next chapter I will show you how to quickly and easily build a diversified share portfolio. However, when it comes to pickings stocks, I generally follow these seven rules:

1. I only buy businesses that I understand and would like to own more of and can see their potential to grow and succeed.

2. I choose businesses that have been paying consistent and growing dividends for at least ten years (you can check this online through their website) – no start-ups, thanks!

3. I prefer companies that pay fully franked dividends and that provide goods and services i.e. industrials.

4. I choose companies that help diversify my portfolio without compromising the quality of investment. (I own about twenty-five different stocks in my personal portfolio.) Occasionally companies might cut or reduce their dividends for various reasons – this is another reason why diversity is so important.

5. I choose companies that have positive long-term recommendations from the research houses.

6. I always buy and hold, so I ask myself, if I buy this stock, am I in it for the long run, i.e. indefinitely? Remember, we never want to cut off our passive income supply.

7. **I cheat a lot** – I'll explain this in the next chapter, but about 40% of my portfolio is made up of pre-diversified shares – through listed investment companies (LICs) and exchange traded funds (ETFs) – so keep reading!

8. While I love Australian industrial shares, I do invest, and diversify, outside Australia too. Australian companies pay out a larger portion of earnings as dividends than international shares (usually 65% compared to around 45% for global shares), but this doesn't really matter as both options drive long-term growth.

POINTS TO REMEMBER:

- Owning shares in a company is like being a silent partner in a business.
- Shares are two-dimensional assets – they pay income (dividends) and provide you with long-term capital growth opportunities.
- You buy and hold shares in companies to earn an income via dividends.
- Occasionally a company may need to cut or reduce their dividends. Make sure you have a multiple supply of passive income sources (i.e. diversity) so that your total income is not affected greatly.
- Where possible, enrol in an automatic dividend reinvestment plan so that you don't thoughtlessly spend your dividends.
- For stocks that don't have a dividend reinvestment plan, give them your financial goal account and, as this account accumulates, buy more stock in that company so that it has the same or a similar effect on auto dividend reinvestment.

- Regularly check that you're not becoming overexposed to one company (for me, that means 15% or more of my portfolio devoted to one company).
- If this happens, use new money to add new companies to your portfolio, or build up the holdings you already own in the existing companies. This tactic avoids selling, which can trigger capital gains tax or a capital loss, plus you incur brokerage fees.
- Stocks are long-term investments – perhaps even forever, as they're one of your passive income sources. If you sell the asset, you cut off your passive income.
- Industrial stocks that pay fully franked dividends may be more beneficial over the long run, if excess franking credits continue to be refunded.
- Never assume franking credits refunds as part of your number, as the discussion to remove them may reappear in the future, and we never want to sell ourselves short.
- Consider diversifying overseas. This will help smooth volatility and reduce investment risk.
- If you are picking individual stocks yourself, aim to have twenty to thirty across a range of companies and industries.

CHAPTER NINE

Simple Yet Successful Share Portfolios

'The real key to making money in stocks is not to get scared out of them.' – Peter Lynch, American investor

Our lives can quickly and easily become frantically busy, with family and work; even basic life admin can take up so much of our time we feel we are barely left with a spare second to breathe. I completely understand the feeling, which is why I'm driven to make this book about managing your finances easily but efficiently – as well as in a cost-effective and tax-efficient manner. I want to help you build your number as quickly as possible – the sooner the better!

So whether you decide to use shares as your main source of passive income or merely one of your sources to help build your number, you must understand the importance of diversification, the risks involved and how to handle these challenges.

As you'll remember from Chapter eight, diversification essentially means not putting all your eggs in one basket. By spreading the range and type of companies in your portfolio, so that it covers a wide selection of businesses – at least twenty to thirty different stocks and industries, you'll reduce the risk and impact if and when something goes wrong.

You **never** want to be reliant on a single investment in just one company for all your returns and passive income. I will explain why . . .

Our economy is increasingly dynamic, thanks to the speed with which the media reacts to events, and the ability of the public to access an enormous range of information as well as opinions. Not all companies, industries and asset classes perform in the same way at the same time. Businesses can experience challenges and even collapses. A share price can drop quicker than what it can increase at. And, as previously mentioned, dividends may need to be temporarily reduced to help a company get through a challenging period.

Meanwhile, some companies, such as supermarkets and health-care providers, actually thrive in tough economic conditions. This is because no matter what happens, we still need these services and products to get by. We still need to buy bread and milk, see doctors and buy medication, and use electricity and internet, etc. These 'staples' aren't entirely recession-proof businesses, but having a mix of them among your investments can be prudent, so that your portfolio can weather all conditions.

On the flipside, when the economy is stronger, people and businesses are more open to investing in growth. Whether it be homewares, building or renovations, new cars, even higher quality food and luxury designer goods, these businesses can benefit in economically healthy times.

KNOW YOUR ASSET ALLOCATION RATIO

Investing is actually exciting! Be mindful that you're investing not just financially in your future, but emotionally as well. This is about making your hopes, dreams and goals come true.

When you make your first investment, it may feel a little scary, which is quite normal. But once it's done, you'll most likely laugh at yourself at how easy and straightforward it is, and wonder why you were so nervous.

But one important step that everyone should take before they start investing is know their asset allocation ratio. Your asset allocation is kind of like your dress size – it can change over time (go up or down), but being aware of it helps you grab the right size off the rack.

There are two different asset allocation classes that you already know about.

1. Two-dimensional income and growth assets – which is for your long-term financial goals, such as building your number. This is where you have a long-term approach of ten years if not forever.
   These are:
   • shares – domestic
   • shares – international
   • property
2. One-dimensional income-based assets, which are perfect for your short- to medium-term financial goals, such as saving for holidays, deposits on homes, weddings, new cars, etc. – essentially anything that you need the money for within seven years or less.

   Your correct asset allocation ratio will depend on your goals at the time and will need to be adjusted accordingly.

There are no good, bad, right or wrong asset allocation profiles, they just need to be right for you and your current and long-term goals. Identifying yours helps you work out how much, where and when you should be putting money in savings and how much, where and when you should be putting money in investing. Over time your asset allocation ratio may change as your education and experience grows, and this is perfectly natural.

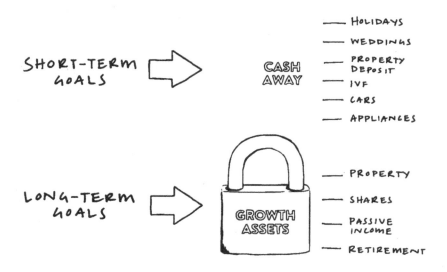

Say that you have a goal to save for a holiday within the next twelve months, but also want to get started on building your number, you could split your regular savings in a variety of different ways. Say you have $1000 available for regular saving and investing.

20% – short-term goals → $200 cash account (e.g. Lifestyle Goal account)

80% – long-term goals – i.e. your number → $800 invested into shares/property

Or you could split this different ways: 30:70 or 40:60 or 50:50 or 60:40 or 70:30 or 80:20. You can adjust or tweak this ratio depending on what you need and want at the time. As long as you know that your cash is only for short- to medium-term expenses and your long-term investment assets are to be used for long-term goals.

TIME FACTOR WITH ASSET ALLOCATION RATIO

Mindful money is not about speculating or trading stocks and assets or adjusting your asset allocation ratio in response to short-term volatility or changes in the share market.

The ratios are not only meant to serve as a guide for you to build your wealth, but also suit and satisfy your immediate needs with safety and peace of mind.

For me personally, the only assets that I hold are my two-dimensional ones which include Australian and international shares and property and then simply cash savings accounts for anything that is short to medium term such as holidays, expenses for the house, cars, etc.

I keep it simple and easy to look after – with no confusion ever.

The fundamental message that I'd like to present through this book is how to build a passive income that lasts indefinitely, giving you the freedom to do what you want, when you want. Holding assets that aren't two-dimensional are only going to hold me back.[2] Looking at the charts on pages 150 and 153, which line would you rather your wealth be riding? I am not prepared to settle for average,

---

2   Remember from Chapter eight the difference between investing $10 000 cash in a term deposit vs investing $10 000 in industrial shares over the period of thirty-nine years. The difference is $10 220 vs $187 546.

so for me, having a larger asset allocation to shares, with all the short- to medium-term ups and downs is well worth the long term and indefinite pay off.

So if you are new to investing, start with a 80:20 ratio of cash to investing and over time, as you see, feel and experience your financial successes building momentum, start to look at slowly shifting towards a different split if and when you can.

This means investing for the long run, buying investments that you want to hold forever, then actually holding those investments forever and never selling them. Selling them would cut off your precious passive income of dividends, forgo great buying opportunities, and jeopardise your financial freedom. Selling your investments would also be likely to trigger capital gains tax or even crystallise a capital gains loss from a short-term pullback, both of which would take a dent out of your net wealth.

I advocate a long-term buy and hold approach, where you never miss out on a dividend and you never crystallise a capital gain or loss, but rather you keep your eye on your long-term goal: your number. This results in a higher weighting towards two-dimensional assets that provide you with growth and income; these will be more volatile over the short term, but they're a more efficient and effective way to build wealth over the long run – which you can afford because you're in it for the long run.

It's particularly important to commit to the long run; some people make the fatal error of selling down their entire portfolio once they hit their number, switching their investment portfolio to cash and term deposits. This is very common with retirees, who leave their working life and then sell down their assets, parking their funds in term deposits and going fishing. Initially the 3.5% term deposit sounds great – no risk, no volatility and a known interest payment made each month by the bank. But when you think about it, life after age sixty-five or even seventy is still a long-term proposition, with life expectancy stats suggesting another fifteen or twenty years ahead of you at least. And medical advancements in curing and preventing diseases continue to push this timeframe out even further.

The effect of inflation over the long run can really kill the yield of that term deposit. Your buying power erodes at a disturbing speed as you eat into your bank balance more and more each year, trying to keep your term deposit income covering your budget, all while knowing there may be many increasingly expensive years ahead of you.

If Amanda did this with her $3 238 485 portfolio at age sixty-five, putting the money in a term deposit earning 3% p.a. and assuming inflation is 2.5% p.a., her entire portfolio would be completely gone within eighteen years . . . yes, the whole $3 238 485 would completely erode away, leaving her broke at eighty-three years old, and possibly out of options and resources to start again from ground zero.

Plus we haven't even taken into consideration the capital gains tax that she would have triggered by selling her passive income stream, so in reality, this amount of money will run out sooner.

This is a huge contrast in comparison to the $6.4 million share portfolio Amanda would have at age eighty-five if she simply held on to and kept spending her growing dividends. What would you do if you were Amanda? I am pretty sure you would hold on to that two-dimensional investment portfolio (see page 198).

As you now know, the key to avoiding this situation is to retain those growth assets in your portfolio so that it can continue to grow and your income can flourish and keep up with inflation.

THE TWO-YEAR SLEEP WELL STRATEGY

If you acknowledge the importance of growth assets for long-term financial freedom and income sources, but would still prefer to have a greater sense of peace of mind, I recommend that once you've built your number, or are well on your way to building your number, you always keep two years' worth of passive income in a separate cash savings or a term deposit account.

You can start building this separate two-year savings account at any time; however, make sure to keep it in a separate account so that you don't spend it or invest it.

Alternatively, if you want to focus 100% of your energies now into building your number, you could choose not to invest that 10% ongoing investment back into the portfolio once you start drawing it, but place that money in a savings account until you have built your two-year supply, before returning back to using that 10% p.a. again for new, additional investing.

However, this lump sum in cash savings, which is always easily accessible, should give you some comfort in the knowledge that should your portfolio suffer a decrease in value, a cut in dividends or an issue with your tenants, you have bought yourself a safety net of two years to either fix the problem or allow time to heal and recover from the situation, which is six months longer than the average time markets take to recover.

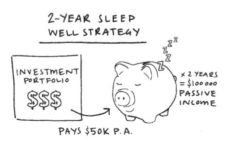

2-YEAR SLEEP WELL STRATEGY

INVESTMENT PORTFOLIO

$$$

x 2 YEARS = $100 000 PASSIVE INCOME

PAYS $50K P.A.

BUILDING YOUR PORTFOLIO

Now that you know your asset allocation ratio, we need to build the assets within your portfolio.

For your Australian shares (or domestic shares) you may want to build a share portfolio of individual stocks that you research, pick and buy. If this is the case, I recommend holding at least twenty to thirty different stocks so that your portfolio works across fluctuating economic climates, and the combined returns give you a healthy average yield in line with or even better than the index.

Researching stocks doesn't have to involve spending hours in front of a computer screen or punching numbers into a calculator as you go cross-eyed over company profit and loss statements and balance sheets. There are plenty of high-quality research houses to which you can subscribe, for access to their reports and opinions, which are usually summarised into a one- or two-page document written in layman's terms. Some examples of research houses include:

- **Intelligent Investor** – value-based research with over twenty years' experience, identifying good buys in the Australian market
- **Morningstar** – available globally, great research tools, allowing comparison of companies and easy-to-read reports and opinions
- **The Motley Fool** – available in most countries and offering a wide range of investment recommendations for different investors with different goals, but focused on long-term investing. I particularly like the Dividend Investor section

Some of these services have free trials and then revert to a monthly or yearly fee, which in some cases may be tax-deductible. As another free option, most online broking facilities include share market research, although it can be limited.

If picking individual stocks isn't for you, great! It means you'll have more time for you. And the good news is that you can build a diversified share portfolio really quickly and easily – actually within minutes, and perhaps even achieve this from one single trade. So you don't need to stress yourself out spending your precious spare time trying to work out which shares you should be buying.

Let's look at the investment products that I personally invest in for The $1000 Project portfolio, my personal portfolio and my superannuation account.

ETFs & LICs

Exchange traded funds (ETFs) and listed investment companies (LICs) are just like managed funds but better. They offer the fastest and easiest way to build a diversified investment portfolio – and you can start with as little as $500. One share in either an ETF or LIC represents ownership of lots of different companies in different industries.

ETFs and LICs are traded (bought and sold) on the stock market and are like pre-packed shopping trolleys. Say you need to do your grocery shopping for the week. Instead of walking down each aisle, slowly searching out and choosing each individual item you need, you can quickly grab one of the pre-packed trolleys at the entrance of the supermarket, which contains all the vegetables, fruit, meats, bread, milk, cleaning products and so on you require for a week. Whether you choose the prepacked shopping trolley or prefer to select your own items, you still end up with pretty much everything you need. But you will have saved a lot of time and stress by picking the prepacked trolley. And while it might be argued that choosing your own individual items allows you to customise the particular brands, flavours and varieties you like, with the prepacked trolley you can still quickly add those additional must-have items to what has already been chosen for you.

If you were to invest $1000 into the Vanguard Australian Large Companies Index ETF (ASX code VLC), your $1000 would be invested in thirty large Australian companies (benchmarked against the index). Through the ETF, you would be holding shares in companies such as Commonwealth Bank, BHP or Woolworths. Your diversification into Australian shares is all done for you by this one ETF.

Or if you were to invest in the LIC Whitefield (ASX code WHF), you would own shares in up to 1600 different Australian industrials companies, similarly diversified across a variety of sectors such as healthcare, real estate, banks, utilities and the like. Again, the diversification and management of your investments in these companies is taken care of for you.

Say, for example, after investing in an ETF or a LIC, you really want to buy additional stock in another company that catches your eye, even if the ETF or LIC already includes it. You are free to buy that stock or any others that you really want to own. But having the baseline of a large proportion of your portfolio invested via ETFs and LICs means that most of your diversification work is done for you, allowing you to cherrypick further stocks as you wish.

You can find ETFs and LICs that invest purely in shares, both Australian and international. Or you might prefer even more

CHEAT TIP FROM CC:

One of the biggest benefits of using an ETF or LIC is that you don't need to worry as much about diversification and being overexposed to a particular company in your portfolio, which was one of the risks I mentioned in Chapter eight. This is taken care of for you by the fund manager or listed investment manager running the fund. They'll have done extensive research into the companies and identified the value in owning them, taking those stressful investment decisions off your shoulders and ensuring that the portfolio is well diversified. And when those dividends are reinvested, or if you decide to buy more shares in the ETF or LIC, your investments remain diversified, with no risk of overexposure to one or two particular stocks. It's important to research the ETF/LIC as some can be concentrated or target one sector only.

So if you want an incredibly efficient and effective way to build a diversified investment portfolio, simply buy shares in an ETF or LIC – or even both if you like! They're very similar in function, but there are a few differences that we'll look at a bit further down. First though, let's see how ETFs and LICs work and what additional options there are should you choose to get more involved in stock selection.

diversified ETFs such as balanced ETFs and high-growth ETFs, which invest in other assets such as property, fixed interest and cash. This gives you even more of a spread and likely reduction in risk.

Their fees are also usually more cost effective, ranging from 0.05% to 0.5% p.a. compared to managed funds, which range between 0.8 to 2.5% p.a. Let's take a moment to discuss managed funds.

Managed funds definitely have their place, and there are many expert fund managers building unique portfolios and achieving great goals. However, I want to show you how to build a diversified investment portfolio that is cost-effective and transparent, minimises crystallising tax and, most importantly, provides you with long-term passive income, via those dividends. I believe this is preferable to suggesting an option that may cost twenty times the ongoing fee; also, when fund managers crystallise losses, you as the investor wears the bill. Worst of all, you could miss out on potential dividends as they jump in and out of stocks trying to make a profit and possibly taking on more risk than necessary.

When you invest in an index-style ETF, or a LIC with a low turnover, it means that they basically buy and hold the market, minimising having to sell any holdings. This means if a company is going up in value, with the share price increasing say 8%, they do not sell that stock. Rather, they keep holding it, which avoids triggering a tax bill for you on the 8% profit. It's more important that you continue to hold those income streams that pay you those dividends and continue to enjoy these long-term capital gains and growing passive income streams without disturbing them by selling them off.

THE DIFFERENCE BETWEEN LICs AND ETFs

LICs and ETFs are very similar, in that both offer a simple way to spread your investments across a wide range of assets. The major difference between the two is that LICs are **closed investments**.

That is to say, there's a limited number of shares available. They cannot issue more shares just because suddenly an LIC is 'in vogue'. You can still buy them quickly and easily on the ASX, but because their supply is capped, their share price may not reflect the true value of the assets in the fund.

To illustrate, if my handbag business was an LIC, I wouldn't be able to simply make more bags. If you want to buy one of my handbags, you have to find someone who is willing to sell theirs to you via the stock market. Fortunately there are always people wanting to trade my handbags, so this isn't a problem for someone wanting to buy another one of my bags.

As a result of this closed investment, an LIC can experience variances in net asset valuation (NTV) and/or as a net tangible asset (NTA). The NTV and NTA is the net value of the underlying investment expressed on a per share basis. This means that sometimes the LIC can be trading at a premium to its value (as in the share price is a little higher than what it should be) or traded at a discount (the share price is a little lower that what it should be – a good buying opportunity). LICs will publish their NTA on their websites on a monthly basis, so you can check the value and then search the share price on the stock market and see for yourself if it's good value or not.

ETFs, on the other hand, are what we call **open-ended**, with an unlimited supply. This means that if the demand does not impact the share price, the manager behind the ETF can issue more units. Using the example again of the handbag business but being a fund, I would simply make more handbags to meet the demand.

Also, the tax structures of the two are quite different. In essence, an ETF is a trust structure and an LIC is a company structure.

In Australia, trusts do not pay capital gains or income tax – these are passed on to the individual investor to declare. A company structure, on the other hand, must pay company tax on any income or capital gains. This means that LICs, having a company structure, can either retain the profits or pay them out to the investors via dividends, while ETFs as trusts only have to pay out the profits to the investor as dividends. So there are advantages and disadvantages to choosing both LICs and ETFs.

CHEAT TIP FROM CC:

Online brokerage costs between $8 and $30 per trade, which means you pay each time you buy or sell. To help minimise these costs, I recommend that you invest a minimum of $1000 for each transaction. If you spend $20 in brokerage, it represents a 4% entry expense on a $500 initial investment but only 2% on $1000.

HOW TO BUILD A DIVERSIFIED SHARE PORTFOLIO WITH LICS OR ETFS

If you go to my YouTube channel, SugarMamma.TV, and search 'How to quickly and easily build a diversified share portfolio' you can watch a tutorial of the instructions below. These are the same steps to follow when you want to buy individual stocks as well.

1. Open an online share-trading account – most banks offer an online share-trading platform, such as Commonwealth Bank's CommSec, St George Bank's Directshares and ANZ's Share Investing, or there are more discount providers such as CMC, IG or Bell Direct.

2. Transfer the money (say $1000) from your financial goal account into this account when you're ready to start investing.

3. In your online trading account, click on 'trading', then click 'buy' and then enter the code of the ETF, LIC, or company you want to buy stocks in – for example, WHF, which I mentioned previously.

4. Work out how many shares or units you want to buy, by dividing the amount that you have to invest minus $20 brokerage (for example, $1000 to invest less $20 brokerage) by the current share price (say $4.60). After accounting for brokerage, you'll be able to buy 213 shares and you may have some small change left over, which is fine – it can sit there until you're ready to buy more shares.

5. Select 'at market'[3] and press 'buy'.

6. Depending on the level of security of your online share-trading account, you should get an email confirming that your order has been sent to the market, followed by another email confirming if it has gone through.

7. A week later you will receive a letter in the mail, welcoming you as a shareholder. Congratulations! Attached to the letter will be a form (mentioned in Chapter eight), and you must either complete the form on paper or online to provide them with your tax file number and bank details . . .

---

3 You can select 'at market' or 'limit price'. 'At market' means you are happy to buy at the best available price, whereas a limit order lets you set a maximum purchase price for your order. For orders of $2000 or less, I will usually go with 'at market' as the savings to potentially get a better price on my order aren't worth my time. But for orders over $2000, I will try to set my 'limit price' a bit lower so I can buy more stocks with my money.

and, of course, your dividend instructions! If a dividend reinvestment plan is available, this is your moment to tick the **full dividend reinvestment** box.

8. Celebrate! You are officially an investor who earns passive income!

9. Continue the process, not only reinvesting, but also contributing to your portfolio when you can, and always adding to your portfolio. Don't forget to update your wealth and passive income worksheets. You're now making progress, so you must document it!

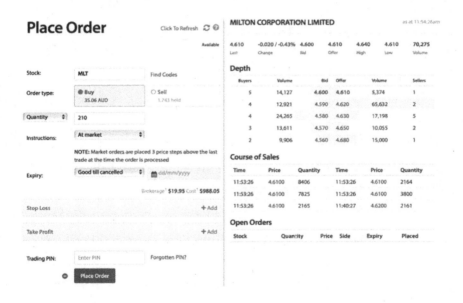

LICs AND ETFs TO RESEARCH

My aim is to give you quality general advice, but there are some specific ETFs and LICs that I believe have fantastic websites full of helpful information about how they build a portfolio and what the goals of their investments are. This background can help you in your investment decisions.

Vanguard has been in operation for more than forty years, and has over twenty-four different ETFs in Australia and more than fifty-nine available overseas. They are a low-cost fund manager, with over $6.8 trillion invested on behalf of other people and institutions. They have ETFs that include allocations that focus on particular assets such as property, Australian shares, US shares, emerging markets, Asia, etc. – each allowing you to diversify within those individual sectors. So if you want simplicity, you could pick the three different ETFs and use this for your two-dimensional investment portfolio, matching your asset allocation ratio. For example:

$10 000 – to invest initially towards your number
$2000 – to remain in savings for holiday money

$10 000 gets split and invested here:

$5000 – Australian Shares Index Fund (ASX code: VAS)
$5000 – Vanguard International Shared Index (ASX code: VGS)

Ongoing regular savings in total = $5000 per quarter, can also be split
$1000 – Holiday savings account – lifestyle goal account
$2000 – Australian Shares Index Fund (ASX code: VAS)
$2000 – Vanguard International Shared Index (ASX code: VGS)

iShares backed by BlackRock offers a wide range of ETFs, similar to Vanguard, and has a fantastic website clearly explaining how they work and how to pick the right ETF for you. It's great for specifying certain countries or industries that you might want to invest in.

BetaShares are another ETF provider, with an extensive list of ETFs that specialise in certain areas. So when you invest in shares, you can include a fund that focuses on something like ethical investments, property, commodities, currency, or even have a geared ETF, which means that within the fund, they have already borrowed money to buy more shares.

FOR AUSTRALIAN SHARE ASSET ALLOCATION THROUGH LICs:

Whitefield is an LIC that has been around for almost eighty years. Its investment strategy is mainly focused on industrial companies in Australia. It's a perfect option for those who want to own a diversified portfolio of Australian industrial shares without any complications. It also offers an automatic dividend reinvestment plan and their fees are around 0.4% p.a.

Milton is an LIC that has been operating for almost seventy years, with extremely competitive ongoing fees and a well-diversified portfolio of investment assets. It prides itself on its cost-effective fees and growing fully franked dividends paid to investors over time and has recently started an automatic dividend reinvestment program for shareholders, so nice and easy! Their fees are around 0.14% p.a.

Argo is another LIC that has been around for over eighty-two years and offers complete transparency. It's ideal for high-growth investors looking for long-term passive income and capital growth opportunities. It offers a share purchase plan on top of a dividend reinvestment plan, where shareholders can purchase up to $15 000 worth of stock in Argo without incurring brokerage, and sometimes at a further discount. Their fee is 0.15% p.a.

MARKET VOLATILITY

One thing that's certain is that your investment portfolio will experience volatility in its value. Over the short to medium term, you'll see it bounce around like a yo-yo, and you might find this quite stressful. But when you're investing for the long run (which you should be if you're building towards achieving your number), the volatility isn't really that scary. Actually, it can be exciting, as it can create more opportunities for you.

The Vanguard Index Chart, which can be found at vanguardin vestments.com.au, shows a chart of market returns over the previous thirty years.

When you look at isolated situations within short periods of time, it seems dramatic – the 1987 crash, the dotcom crash around 2000, even the global financial crisis commencing in 2007. This isn't helped by the clickbaity media, which often follows the maxim 'what bleeds, leads'. The result is that news organisations continue to damage public perception of the share market with dramatic headlines.

However, when you step back, gain some perspective and look at the big picture, the long-term trend is upwards – human endeavour always prevails. If you look at the Vanguard chart, you'll see the overall directions of lines measuring market returns, when read left to right, goes onwards and upwards.

It's worth noting the dividends actually rose during the 1987 and dotcom crashes. So if you didn't sell, not only did you keep receiving dividends, you also got a pay rise. If you stayed the course, your portfolio returned to its previous value and remained on track to keep growing in the long term. Moreover, if you were savvy and tuned into buying shares for income, you could have capitalised on this buying opportunity and bought more shares at a discount,

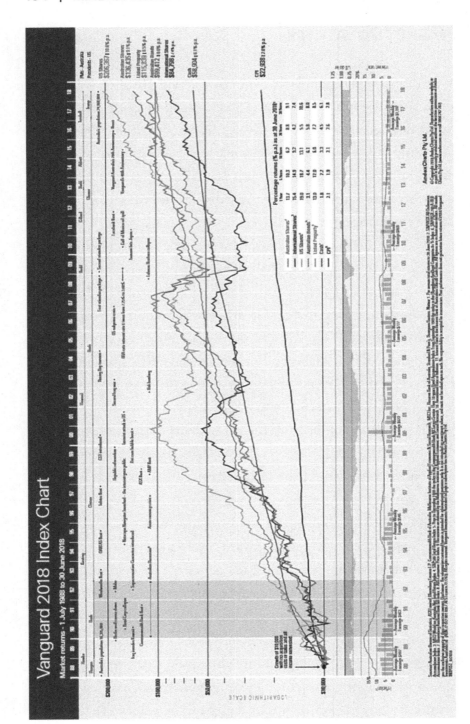

Vanguard 2018 Index Chart

Market returns – 1 July 1988 to 30 June 2018

ultimately realising a bigger dividend due to the temporarily depressed share price.

This shows us that share prices are volatile, dividends are not. In fact, since 1979, Whitefield has increased its dividends each year by 6.5%.

According to the ASX, over the last 141 years Australian shares along with their dividends have generated a positive return on 113 occasions, which is just over 80% of the time. Furthermore, the average return was 16.1% p.a. and during negative years the market fell by 10.6% p.a., making the average return 10.8% p.a. over this same period of time.

You can check out lots of amazing market insights and indexes for free through the ASX website, marketindex.com.au/statistics and plenty of other markets online.

WHAT TO DO:

So what do you do when these so-called crashes happen? There is no doubt that there will be more GFCs, healthcare crises, property bubbles and, sadly, terrorism attacks and wars. However, knowing what to do is what will help make you a great investor and remain on track to achieve your financial goals and continue reaping the rewards.

You have two options and one essential action.

YOUR TWO OPTIONS:

- **Ride the storm.** When you see your diversified portfolio's value drop, keep your emotions in check and turn down the volume of the news. History shows us that the market needs the benefit of time to recover after a pullback or 'correction'. Time heals all wounds! Check the chart again to remind yourself that you're in it for the long run. This can be eighteen months, but to play it safe, I like to allow twenty-four months. There is a reason why the listed fund and investment managers I've described have been in business for over seventy years, and that's because they're good at their jobs. Let them do their job for you, and remember, you only lose your money when you sell. Allow your portfolio to recover and check that your dividends are still coming in; sit on your hands or find a new hobby to distract yourself.

- **Stock up.** These 'horrible', 'scary' financial crises can actually be incredible buying opportunities. It's like having $1000 allocated to buying a new summer wardrobe, only to discover your favourite store has a 30% off sale. You can either buy the summer clothes and walk away with some change for another time, or you can spend it all on more clothes for the winter as well. The choice is yours. Think back to those twenty-eight dips in the stock market over that 141-year period – if you'd used those times to 'shop for discounts', the downturns would evaporate as you'd have turned them into an opportunity for bigger growth and greater income opportunities, **achieving your number a lot sooner**. These volatile times may produce incredible long-term buying opportunities. I love these times!

This is also where that two-year sleep well strategy we covered earlier in this chapter can help, as you have some cash readily accessible to use for these stocktake clearance moments if you choose to.

YOUR ESSENTIAL ACTION:

As explained in Chapter two, every time you invest, buying and building more passive income streams, you must update your workbook. Seeing the progress that you make is intoxicating and motivating. And when your newsfeed or TV is blasting doom and gloom about the future economy and all its problems, seeing your achievements and how much passive income you've already built will help alleviate stress and worry from your finances.

CHEAT TIP FROM CC:

I check my personal portfolio and The $1000 Project Portfolio once a month, if that. The only time I log in is to buy more stocks, ETFs and LICs. If I am not buying, I don't log in as I don't really care what the portfolio is worth, I care about the dividends; I'm buying long-term income sources towards my financial freedom. I don't chase capital growth, I chase passive income. This is why you'll never (well, rarely) see me mention what The $1000 Project Portfolio is worth, but rather how much has been hustled, saved and invested and most importantly **what the updated passive income and progress is as a percentage towards my goal**.

Whether my portfolio is worth $2 000 000 or $1 300 000 I really don't care as long as it is still paying me $100 000 p.a. like it did before it dropped in value, as it hasn't impacted my financial security. While the passive income continues to come in and slowly grow over the long run, I can rest assured my mindful money application is working well.

POINTS TO REMEMBER:

- Work out your asset allocation ratio.
- For long-term growth, having two-dimensional assets, such as domestic and international shares, as well as property will help.

- Short-term goals – cash accounts only – as in high-interest savings accounts or even term deposits. Don't ever gamble with your short-term money.
- No income? No thanks – we aren't interested in trading stocks or speculating on capital growth, we want to invest in healthy businesses that can afford to pay out some of the profits and reinvest for future growth in the business.
- Use ETFs and LICs to build a diversified share portfolio. Don't try to pick individual stocks unless you really want to.
- For individual stocks, subscribe to research houses such as Intelligent Investor – even just for fresh ideas and inspiration.
- Always look for opportunities to expand your passive income sources by buying more shares. However, if you use index ETFs and LICs you don't need to worry about this.
- Remember, in times of high market volatility, some of the best investment opportunities can be found.
- You only lose money when you sell, by cutting off those valuable dividends.
- Continue to review and update your wealth accumulation worksheet, particularly your passive income thus far in relation to your number.
- When worried about the market, turn down the news, look at your dividends and your goals and refer back to the wealth accumulation chart, then get outside and enjoy your life.
- Chase passive income, not capital growth.
- Remember, those overly dramatic news headlines of the day may not mean a negative return for the year. Focus on the long term, the big picture.

CHAPTER TEN

Game Day

'Action is the foundational key to all success.' – Pablo Picasso, artist

So you now understand some really important concepts about investing.

- You understand the power of compounding interest.
- You know the impact and improvement of additional regular investment – even a small amount makes a massive difference.
- You've discovered why being able to stretch yourself a little more earlier in life can really pay off.
- You get the no-brainer of reinvesting your passive income rather than spending it while you work towards your number.
- You understand the real numbers and direction of the market beneath the sensationalist headlines.

I really hope that you're feeling excited, motivated and keen to keep learning. And I highly recommend that as you learn new concepts, you flick back and forth through this book, even if only to refresh your memory! This approach makes perfect sense, and keeps you on the right path of learning.

In this chapter, we'll focus on Honey and Amanda from Chapter two. They're keen to get cracking immediately, and best of all, they now understand the concept of reaching their sweet spot, where they see the financial and emotional payoff from a little extra work, knowing that it is well worth it and will result in their passive income growing indefinitely.

AMANDA'S STORY

You'll remember that Amanda has been through a nasty divorce involving selling and splitting up everything that she had. She is walking away with a settlement of $120 000 cash, and her superannuation is worth $75 000. She realises that she has much less super than she should, which is a result of being out of the work force on maternity leave for several years, before returning to work part time.

She knows that while superannuation is important and counts towards her financial security, it won't be enough on its own. Amanda wants to do something now to build her financial independence, separate from her super, so that she never needs to rely on the government or another person and has funds that she can access at any time.

While she is recovering emotionally from her divorce and focusing on settling her boys into their new home and routine, at a practical level she plans to focus on rebuilding her life in such a way that she is responsible for all her financial decisions. Part of her drive to take care of herself and her boys is to lead by example, as well as to be able to leave them some money as part of her estate.

After doing her budget and figuring out her number, which is $80 000 p.a. in today's dollars, Amanda works out how much she can afford to put towards rebuilding her financial future. She works out that with her new promotion, her side hustle and her realistic budget, she can put aside $5400 per quarter to invest, which works out to be on average $1800 per month including her extra 20% sweet spot effort.

To stay focused on averaging $1800 per month, she creates mini short-term goals, and always puts any extra savings or earnings into her financial goals account, which is nicknamed 'My $80 000 p.a. Passive Income Investment Money' – this makes her feel excited and motivated every day when she logs in to her bank accounts and feels inspired to keep going and add more when she can.

She knows that she can live off her current living expenses budget, so she plans to reinvest all of her dividends back into her portfolio for compounding growth opportunities.

Being clear about her family living expenses, Amanda puts $20 000 from her cash settlement into her high interest–earning Life + $20 000 Emergency Money account to help protect her family from any sudden surprises. She is determined to only use this emergency money for real emergencies, and to top it up again as soon as she can, if she ever dips into it.

Amanda decides to invest the remaining $100 000 in order to begin building her passive income. She identifies herself as a long-term investor at age thirty-eight; she sees her time horizon as twenty-seven years, so that when she reaches age sixty-five, she will be able to stop work and start living off this passive income.

After reading about investment risks, natural and normal market volatility (the value of the shares bouncing around like a yo-yo), and the time needed for the market to recover when inevitable crashes happen, she settles on an internationally diversified ETF for her international exposure and an Australian LIC for her domestic invest-ment exposure. Knowing what she now does, she feels confident this level of diversification is the most efficient portfolio for her to achieve her goals within her long-term timeframe and comfort levels, but she realises she can also learn to embrace the 'wild' volatility of the share-market with excitement rather than trepidation.

Amanda decides that with her high-growth asset allocation, she'll have 60% of her shares in domestic industrial shares via a LIC and 40% in an international ETF: $60 000 goes into an Australian LIC that holds shares in 1600 different companies, and $40 000 goes into an international index ETF which holds shares in over 1500 different companies around the world.

This ensures a well-diversified share portfolio across a range of different companies and countries without having to individually own them and deal with lots of administration and paperwork. Instead, Amanda will get reports from the LIC and the ETF provider.

The listed investment company has a management fee of 0.40% p.a. and the international index ETF has a management fee of 0.18% p.a. This means that all her portfolio investment decisions and portfolio management is being taken on by two different but highly experienced fund managers, costing $240 p.a. for her Australian shares ($60 000 × 0.004 = $240) and $72 p.a. for her international shares ($40 000 × 0.0018 = $72). So the total cost per year to Amanda is $312, which is 0.312% p.a.

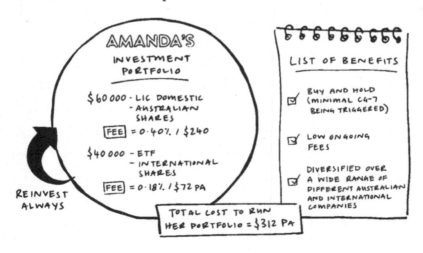

Amanda feels that this cost is well worth it in order to never need worry about which stocks to be buying or reinvesting in; it's all done for her so that she can focus her energy on her boys, her life and her career.

She gets a broker to set up her account and buy her two investments for her; the broker charges 0.55%, or $550, which Amanda pays for out of her own money. Although this is more expensive than an online broker, she feels this is worthwhile for a large initial trade, especially considering this is her first time buying shares. The broker she uses knows these stocks well and is experienced in choosing the best time of day to put this order through the market, and with this expertise can maximise buying as many shares as possible with Amanda's $100 000 total investment spend.

CHEAT TIP FROM CC:

For larger trades of $30 000 or more, I recommend using a professional stockbroker. While it may cost you more, they have greater knowledge and access to in-depth, up-to-date information, tools and research, resulting in you getting greater value for money. For my personal recommended and independent broker, head to SugarMamma.TV.

Going forward, though, Amanda will do her own investing of $5400 per quarter through her online broking account, where her new stocks can be consolidated.

Once the $100 000 is invested, she completes the important paperwork sent to her a week later in the mail by providing her:
- tax file number
- bank details – she lists her financial goal account

- email address, minimising future snail mail
- preference, most importantly, for *full dividend reinvestment.*

She then posts the forms back using the reply paid envelopes provided.

It's important to submit your bank details even though you're reinvesting your dividends; in the event of a fund manager pausing or cancelling a dividend reinvestment plan, there's no wasting time depositing cheques at the bank!

Amanda commences working on her mini short-term goals, putting $1800 per month on average into her financial goal account and buys more shares each quarter worth $5400 (3 × $1800), split 60/40 between the LIC and ETF. Some months she falls slightly short of her mini goals, and some months she manages to come up with extra, but she always averages around $1800 per month or $5400 per quarter. Every time she buys more shares and reinvests the dividends, she tracks her passive income in her worksheets as it slowly grows each year.

All pay rises, bonuses, tax refunds, job promotions, extra money from side hustles and financial windfalls Amanda keeps for herself and her family. She either deposits excess money into her lifestyle account for holiday goals, upgrades or cars, or into her Everyday account for a few little treats here and there.

Any money she gains above her ongoing monthly investment commitments gives her the freedom to choose between spending it guilt-free or putting it towards her lifestyle account. She could even set up a secondary financial goal account for other savings that could go towards a deposit on a home, for instance.

She can rest easy knowing she has planted the right seeds to grow over time to ultimately give her the freedom and independence that she wants.

In the meantime, Amanda enjoys her free time with her kids and her other family members, catching up with her friends and meeting new people, attending courses that will further her career opportunities, and looking after her own emotional, spiritual and physical health as she gets herself back on track to loving life.

The only time she needs to check in with her portfolio is when she adds more shares to grow her passive income, which is when she updates her passive income worksheets – noting her financial position improving and always moving closer to her number.

Date: 01/07/2019
My Number: $80 000

My Financial Snapshot
Assets:
Cash savings $5000
Emergency Cash savings: $20 000
Superannuation: $75 000
Shares $100 000

Liabilities:
Credit card: $0
Loans: $0

My Gross wealth: $200 000
My Net wealth: $200 000

My Passive Income Progress
Current estimated passive income: $5000 (assuming 5% p.a. dividends and excluding super)

Passive Income Progress: 6.25% ($5000/$80 000) –
<u>'I am 12.5% towards achieving my number'</u>

Seeing her progress gives Amanda a powerful sense of how far she has come, allowing her to feel proud and in control. Plus she has done this all on her own! She has peace of mind knowing that her money is well diversified, both locally and internationally, with experts making those important decisions and costing her less than 0.40% p.a. of her portfolio. She keeps her eye on the long-term big picture (her number) and is careful to read the news with a view to potential discounted buying opportunities for her portfolio, rather than market volatility triggering any emotional reaction.

Furthermore, because both the LIC and index ETF that she picked are buy and hold[4], both of them rarely trigger capital gains tax (or losses) for her, minimising any eroding growth effects and allowing her money to work as hard and efficiently as possible for her.

Now let's look at how Amanda's passive income and portfolio grows over time. And to show you how conservative I have been in my assumptions, I have listed the current statistics for comparison.

- Dividends paid are 4% p.a. net of fees (average Australian annual dividend is 4.1% p.a.).
- Dividend growth is 5% p.a. (industrial shares have grown on average 6.5% p.a. since 1979).
- Capital growth is 3.5% p.a. (therefore, combined growth is 7.5% p.a.*) However, since 1900 the ASX has averaged a combined growth including dividends of 13.1% p.a.
- 100% of all dividends are reinvested.

---

4   With minimal turnover among the stocks held.

- Period of investing is twenty-seven years.
- Inflation is 2.5% p.a. (currently 2.1% p.a.).

*According to Fidelity,[5] over the last thirty years up until December 2018, Australian shares have grown 9.1% p.a. (income and growth) and international shares have grown 7.1% p.a. Over the last ten years, growth has been 9.6% for international shares and 9.0% for Australian shares.

At age sixty-five, Amanda is earning 100% cash-flow positive passive income of over $92 000 p.a. in today's dollars in the form of dividend income (which is $12 000 more than she needs as determined by her number), and her portfolio is worth $3 238 000, which is the equivalent of $1 622 000 in today's dollars. Plus, her initial investment of $100 000 is being returned to her at 92% p.a. and growing each year.

Even better, her income is not only keeping up with inflation but rather exceeding it, giving her greater financial security. **Amanda has hit her sweet spot!**

Meanwhile, her gross wealth continues to grow, so at any time she can choose to either give some of her wealth away, sell some of her shares or even improve her lifestyle. She also still has $8000 p.a. available (which was our 10% allocated amount in the budget for new regular, ongoing investment) to reinvest back into her portfolio if she wants to – but she doesn't have to.

Amanda has achieved this outcome without relying on anyone else, or having to consider selling assets, like the family home, or even having to fall back on her $75 000 superannuation account, which

---

5 fidelity.com.au/insights/resources/adviser-resources/sharemarket-chart/a4-handout/

Future Age	Year	Year #	Actual Annual Dividend Paid	Inflation Adjusted Dividend Paid in Today's $	Year-End Actual Portfolio Value	Year-End Inflation Adjusted Portfolio Value in Today's $
38	2019	1	$0.00	$0.00	$126 689.95	$123 854.55
39	2020	2	$0.00	$0.00	$162 574.99	$154 741.21
40	2021	3	$0.00	$0.00	$197 650.94	$183 538.54
41	2022	4	$0.00	$0.00	$235 570.92	$213 415.63
42	2023	5	$0.00	$0.00	$276 604.46	$244 478.04
43	2024	6	$0.00	$0.00	$321 048.91	$276 839.47
44	2025	7	$0.00	$0.00	$369 232.61	$310 622.56
45	2026	8	$0.00	$0.00	$421 518.32	$345 959.71
46	2027	9	$0.00	$0.00	$478 307.17	$382 994.11
47	2028	10	$0.00	$0.00	$540 043.02	$421 880.74
48	2029	11	$0.00	$0.00	$607 217.39	$462 787.56
49	2030	12	$0.00	$0.00	$680 374.98	$505 896.82
50	2031	13	$0.00	$0.00	$760 119.89	$551 406.46
51	2032	14	$0.00	$0.00	$847 122.63	$599 531.72
52	2033	15	$0.00	$0.00	$942 127.98	$650 506.92
53	2034	16	$0.00	$0.00	$1 045 963.90	$704 587.36
54	2035	17	$0.00	$0.00	$1 159 551.54	$762 051.54
55	2036	18	$0.00	$0.00	$1 283 916.56	$823 203.53
56	2037	19	$0.00	$0.00	$1 420 201.98	$888 375.70
57	2038	20	$0.00	$0.00	$1 569 682.57	$957 931.66
58	2039	21	$0.00	$0.00	$1 733 781.34	$1 032 269.64
59	2040	22	$0.00	$0.00	$1 914 088.09	$1 111 826.15
60	2041	23	$0.00	$0.00	$2 112 380.48	$1 197 080.18
61	2042	24	$0.00	$0.00	$2 330 647.97	$1 288 557.82

Future Age	Year	Year #	Actual Annual Dividend Paid	Inflation Adjusted Dividend Paid in Today's $	Year-End Actual Portfolio Value	Year-End Inflation Adjusted Portfolio Value in Today's $
62	2043	25	$0.00	$0.00	$2 571 119.09	$1 386 837.44
63	2044	26	$0.00	$0.00	$2 836 292.31	$1 492 555.49
64	2045	27	$0.00	$0.00	$3 128 971.35	$1 606 413.04
65	2046	28	$184 579.39	$92 451.72	$3 238 485.35	$1 622 085.36
66	2047	29	$193 808.36	$94 706.64	$3 351 832.33	$1 637 910.59
67	2048	30	$203 498.78	$97 016.55	$3 469 146.46	$1 653 890.20
68	2049	31	$213 673.72	$99 382.81	$3 590 566.59	$1 670 025.72
69	2050	32	$224 357.40	$101 806.78	$3 716 236.42	$1 686 318.65
70	2051	33	$235 575.27	$104 289.87	$3 846 304.70	$1 702 770.54
71	2052	34	$247 354.04	$106 833.53	$3 980 925.36	$1 719 382.93
72	2053	35	$259 721.74	$109 439.23	$4 120 257.75	$1 736 157.40
73	2054	36	$272 707.83	$112 108.48	$4 264 466.77	$1 753 095.52
74	2055	37	$286 343.22	$114 842.83	$4 413 723.11	$1 770 198.89
75	2056	38	$300 660.38	$117 643.87	$4 568 203.42	$1 787 469.13
76	2057	39	$315 693.40	$120 513.24	$4 728 090.54	$1 804 907.85
77	2058	40	$331 478.07	$123 452.58	$4 893 573.70	$1 822 516.71
78	2059	41	$348 051.97	$126 463.62	$5 064 848.78	$1 840 297.36
79	2060	42	$365 454.57	$129 548.10	$5 242 118.49	$1 858 251.48
80	2061	43	$383 727.30	$132 707.81	$5 425 592.64	$1 876 380.76
81	2062	44	$402 913.66	$135 944.59	$5 615 488.38	$1 894 686.91
82	2063	45	$423 059.34	$139 260.31	$5 812 030.47	$1 913 171.66
83	2064	46	$444 212.31	$142 656.90	$6 015 451.54	$1 931 836.75
84	2065	47	$466 422.93	$146 136.34	$6 225 992.34	$1 950 683.94
85	2066	48	$489 744.07	$149 700.64	$6 443 902.08	$1 969 715.00

has also been growing and compounding over the last twenty-seven years as another nest egg. Her financial success is completely off the back of her own initiative, hard work, dedication, commitment and, of course, mindful money practices.

Let's just consider her super for a moment. Before Amanda invested her initial $100 000, while she was waiting for her settlement money to come through, she used this time as an opportunity to sort out her super.

She had always assumed that being in an industry super fund, her money was invested in the cheapest account – she'd noticed that the fees were always being promoted as one of the lowest in the market. She'd previously thought that cheap must be better, but had never considered where the money was invested or, even worse, who invested it and *how* it was invested, let alone whether there were fees charged to manage the account on top of the 'cheapest' admin fees.

After making some phone calls to her industry super fund, she discovers that while the administration fees are low, the ongoing management fees are 1% p.a. and that she has no ability to change the fund manager or asset allocation that the industry super company has selected to run the investment. Plus she does not have the option to buy any shares, which includes not being able to access LICs or ETFs, and she finds the list of managed funds is limited and even more expensive.

But worst of all, there is no ability to in-specie transfer from super to pension without triggering an avoidable capital gains tax event, which could deplete her super account balance, just when she is about to retire and shift her money into a pension account.

Amanda does plenty of research online and chooses a new superannuation account that allows her to use her superannuation money to buy a range of index-style ETFs, direct shares, including LICs, has an in-specie transfer service, and a range of personal insurance, including income protection up to age sixty-five.

The fees are competitive and capped after her account balance hits a certain level, and she can easily access her super portfolio, transactions and account details through an app or an easy-to-use, intuitive website.

For her investment selection, Amanda again chooses a blend of LICs and ETFs, and cherrypicks a few stocks in companies where she really liked the businesses. She cuts her ongoing management fees down by more than 50% p.a. as the index ETFs and LICs are much better value for money than the old managed funds she was using! She is happy knowing that just like her share portfolio, limited capital gains tax or losses will be triggered due to the the minimal turnover of stocks within LICs and index ETFs – this is a long-term buy-and-hold strategy.

She checks her superannuation account transactions once a quarter to make sure her employer always pays her correctly and on time. She ensures that the funds are invested promptly as per her instruction and updates her worksheets, as her superannuation also contributes towards her financial security. It takes her merely a few minutes, and she walks away knowing exactly what her super is worth and how she is going from financial strength to strength.

For her life and total and permanent disablement (TPD) cover, she applies for enough cover to pay for a house outright. Should anything happen to her, either through death or becoming disabled, there would be enough money for her boys to have a roof over their heads.

Amanda also applies for an income protection policy within her super, covering up to 75% of her income after a ninety-day waiting period, to age sixty-five. Her Life + $20 000 Emergency account, along with her sick leave and annual leave, is more than enough to safely cover her living expenses for three to four months before running out.

All three policies are owned and paid for via her new super account, but aren't excessive or expensive enough to deplete her super balance.

As soon as her personal insurance application through her super is complete and her policy is in force, Amanda rolls over her old super (closing it off and cancelling any previous personal insurances attached to this account), by giving the old account details to her new super account provider.

Her next step is to take out a separate trauma policy with a reputable personal insurance company that has won numerous awards and has been around a long time – even so, Amanda only settles on this company after reading the policy documents. She takes out a policy with enough cover to pay a lump sum that would allow her time off work for up to two years and an extra $100 000 for medical treatment. She has run the numbers, looked at her situation and what is important to her to cover and, of course, ensured that the premium is within her budget, even with premium rises in the future.

After all this, Amanda can relax knowing that not only is she building her number, but also her superannuation is consolidated for the first time and invested in line with her long-term financial goals. Plus she has the security and comfort of knowing that her family security is protected to the best of her ability in the event of something untoward happening to her.

Look at what Amanda can realistically create for herself! All this is within her reach – and quite possibly within yours if you want.

LEAN IN BABY STEPS

You might long to do this for yourself, but feel you have a stumbling block as you lack $100 000 cash to kickstart your investment or $1800 per month.

That is okay, you can lean in. Start seeing if you can save a small amount per month, and then as each month goes by, slowly challenge yourself to increase it. **Setting those mini short-term goals really helps you achieve so much across a long period of time** because you can see what you can do right now. And doing something is so much better than nothing.

Also, your number may not necessarily be as much as Amanda's; I actually encourage clients to keep their number lower initially as it is so much more obtainable and they tend to be more engaged and committed with making this happen, which is displayed in the results.

As we are making impressive headway, we then look to increase or change the number. Or maybe you have some money in your superannuation account that you can start working on building? I have excluded superannuation or retirement savings of any sort because I wanted to show you how to build passive income that is not restricted or controlled by a government. I want you to be able to start spending your passive income when you want. But if in the meantime your super or your country's respective retirement scheme is all you have, nurture it, build it and grow those passive income streams from it.

Or perhaps your employer will pay part of your required minimum monthly investment through your compulsory 9.5% p.a. super guarantee contributions? For example, if you need to be putting $1000 per month towards your long-term number, maybe your employer is already contributing $300 per month, leaving you to only find $700 per month.

And of course, over time with more knowledge, experience, career development and opportunities, your financial situation will grow and evolve, allowing you to contribute more. So look to do what you can do now, and build up from that. You will be amazed what you can come up with and do for yourself.

But if you are starting even earlier in life, with no or very little money, you can still start from something – so let us now move on to Honey to show you more mindful money in action.

HONEY

You'll remember that Honey is twenty-four years old, working in marketing, full of energy and excitement for life. Her number is $63 000 in today's dollars and she is slightly different from Amanda in that she is starting with a lot less. She doesn't dream of retiring as such, but rather wants to go part time, so that she can stay up to date with industry changes and remain relevant.

When it comes to investing, she is happy to take an educated risk as long as it's safely diversified across two-dimensional assets, which includes borrowing to invest, and she can still afford to service the loan, even with a 3% interest rate rise. She has the benefit of time to see through all the natural highs and lows of market volatility and really wants to maximise the opportunities to build her number and enjoy her passive income.

Also, she decides that she wants to invest purely in Australian shares, through a LIC, so that she can maximise any franking credits, minimising her tax and potentially providing more passive income through refunded tax credits. However, while utilising LICs, she will also stock up on Australian companies that have business operations overseas, so that she can still benefit from international exposure.

She loves her job and learning new things, but would love to build a passive income that allows her to cut back and work part-time by age forty. With this time and freedom, she wants to have the option to either launch her own business or raise a family.

She loves the fact that she is building her own financial independence to the point that even reducing her workload to three days per week will not mean she has to borrow money or rely on someone to support her financially. She also enjoys knowing she has a financial safety net growing under her all the time while she adds to it.

Here is Honey's situation:

Credit cards: $0 balance – with a low $1000 limit, no fees and a good frequent flyer program to help create some holiday savings

Savings for financial goal: $10 000
Life + $5000 Emergency account: $7000
Shares: $5600 given to her by her grandfather

So while Honey's actual number is $63 000, she would like to be earning just under half of this by age forty. This means she needs to be earning $30 000 p.a. as passive income, allowing her to be able to afford to cut back to three days per week, focus on her business goals or raise a family while keeping her foot in the job market and her skills up to date.

Honey previously learnt her lesson with debt after getting a little overexcited with a credit card when she finished school. After learning the hard and painful way by taking almost a year to pay off her credit card debt, Honey has removed almost all temptation and has only one credit card with a $1000 limit and no fees, which she doesn't even keep in her wallet. She much prefers her debit card to pay for things.

Furthermore, she used her debt reduction skills once her debt was paid off to build her Life + $5000 Emergency account – which always floats around $7000 and has completely kept her out of debt. And she's built up savings of $10 000 which is sitting in her financial goal account, ready to invest today and help build her number.

Her grandfather gave her $5600 worth of banking stocks before he passed away seven years ago, and the dividends were always paid into her everyday bank account and spent on stuff, with nothing left to show for it. So Honey contacted the share registry and now has the dividends paid to her financial goal account. This means they don't get accidentally spent, and she can ensure that they're reinvested to help build her portfolio and passive income. Also, at any stage Honey can use any saved up dividends that cannot be automatically reinvested and diversify into other companies, should she wish.

Even though Honey has previously misused debt, she understands the difference between healthy, helpful debt and toxic debt. She's keen to use some form of gearing in her game plan to build towards her number through borrowing to invest, whereby she borrows some money to help buy and build more passive income streams – but only in a wise and conservative way, with lots of research and triple-checking, and with the right safety nets in place.

So Honey takes her $10 000 in investment savings and her $5600 worth of shares, and applies for a special investment loan called a margin loan. A margin loan is a loan made to you to help you invest more. To be able to borrow money, you must offer security for the loan, which is normally through cash or existing investments. Depending on how much security you can offer and how much you can afford to safely borrow, the margin loan provider will lend you up to a certain amount, which is usually a maximum of 70% of the value of the existing shares, while they hold the entire portfolio (cash included) as security.

If the value of your portfolio drops below a certain value, it triggers a margin call, which is essentially where the size of the loan is too big in relation to the total value of the portfolio. In this event, the margin loan provider requires you to do one of three things:

- Transfer some cash towards the margin loan to help pay some of it down so that the loan-to-value ratio (LVR) is back in a safe zone.
- Sell some of the investments within your portfolio to help pay the loan down so that the LRV is back in a safe zone.
- Add additional security, such as transferring other cash or shares of managed funds held elsewhere, to help bring the LVR back to a safe zone.

Borrowing money to invest is considered a risky investment strategy, particularly when not set up and handled correctly. This is because:

- The losses can be magnified if the market experiences a downturn or pullback.
- You may be forced to sell your investments at a bad time, crystallising losses.
- Unexpected margin calls may occur if your loan provider reduces their lending requirements (such as reducing the maximum allowed LVR).
- The loan provider may not be able to get hold of you in time in the event of a margin call.
- The cost of borrowing through a margin loan is more expensive than borrowing through your home equity loan.

The good news is, when used carefully, with lots of planning, thought and preparation, a margin loan can be very powerful in helping you get ahead when you have time and a secure cash flow available, and most of its associated risks can be very easily managed for you.

To recap Honey's situation, she has $10 000 in cash and $5600 already in shares, so her total security is $15 600. She applies for a margin loan of $15 600, with her cash ready to invest of $10 000 plus her existing $5600 bank shares transferred (but not sold) across into the new margin loan account – her margin loan is approved, meaning her LVR is smack bang on 50%.

Knowing she has the interest payment of $85 per month (6.5% × $15 600) being debited out of her account, Honey has already started to quickly save her emergency margin loan amount of $2000.

CHEAT TIPS FROM CC:

I have a margin loan that I use with great care and respect, and I've never experienced a margin call as I follow these strict rules:

1. Never let your LVR exceed 50% +/- 5% *ever*!
2. All the shares, ETFs and LICs should be grouped together in the one account so that you can maximise your security.
3. Make sure your email address, phone number and a second person's contact details are listed in the event of a margin call – so that they can *always* get hold of you.
4. Always have some money within your financial goal account so that if your margin loan ever exceeds 50% +/- 5%, you have enough cash to keep it at 50% or lower.
5. Margin loans are *only* for long-term passive income building strategies.

6. As you start to build your passive income, you can slowly pay off your margin loan. I round my monthly interest repayment up to the nearest $100 so that I'm paying off my margin loan and reducing my LVR.

7. Always ensure that your interest loan expenses are paid out of your monthly cash flow – that is, not capitalising against the loan, which is where they add your monthly repayment to the loan, making the loan bigger each month. This is a big no-no!

8. Always ensure that you can comfortably service the margin loan interest in your budget – this interest expense should be paid every month via a direct debt from your Everyday account.

9. Factor in an interest rate rise of 3 to 3.5% p.a. to ensure that even with interest rate rises, you can still afford to service and slowly pay off the margin loan as you approach your number.

10. Margin loans are for buying the fruit and vegetables of your investment portfolio, not the expensive champagne. I only use my margin loan to buy stocks in large companies, mainly LICs and ETFs.

11. Take twenty seconds once a month to check your loan and make sure the LVR is always in the 50% zone.

With her $10 000 cash and new loan of $15 600, she buys $25 600 worth of a LIC, so that her money is immediately diversified across a wide range of investments across different companies and industries. She still holds her grandfather's shares, honouring his memory, but has reduced her investment risk by holding

stocks beyond the one bank. Her portfolio is worth $31 200, with a
$15 600 margin loan attached.

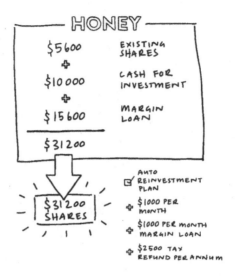

Honey looks up the previous dividends paid by the bank and LIC,
which are clearly displayed on the companies' websites, and works
out approximately what her new passive income is – then updates her
passive income worksheets to see her net wealth.

Like Amanda, Honey completes the paperwork with her bank
details (listing the BSB and account number of her financial goal
account), her tax file number and ticks that very important box,
full dividend reinvestment!

She works on her mini short-term goals. Focusing on saving an
average $1000 per month by finding savings from her budget and
doing some part-time freelancing work, which will all contribute
towards her business plan and skills.

The regular $1000 savings goes into her financial goal account,
and every quarter she transfers that $3000 to her margin loan
account and applies for another increase on her margin loan –
always at a maximum of 50%. So with the $3000 that she transfers

each quarter, she borrows another $3000, giving her an additional combined quarterly amount of $6000 p.q.

Again she adds $6000 more to her LIC. Honey plans to only own Australian shares for her investment portfolio (we'll look at this game plan shortly), as she appreciates the franking credits that come with these shares, and the LIC is invested in over 1600 different stocks – still safely diversified with a long-term buy-and-hold approach.

She continues with this strategy, and every year adds $2500 as an additional lump sum, which is normally how much she gets back from her tax refund as she knows the legal deductions for her profession. (The average Australian gets back $2300 p.a. in tax refunds.)

She essentially adds $26 500 p.a. to her portfolio, of which her margin loan is growing by $12 000 per annum.

Honey continues to always reinvest her dividends, her interest is always managed through her cash flow, and her interest expense always offsets the dividends and franking credits that she receives from her dividends each year.

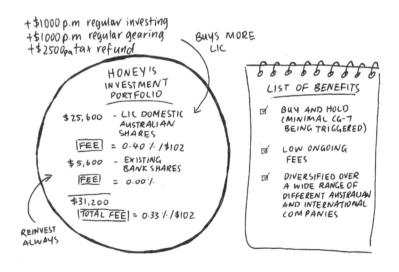

+ $1000 p.m regular investing
+ $1000 p.m regular gearing
+ $2500pa tax refund

BUYS MORE LIC

HONEY'S INVESTMENT PORTFOLIO

$25,600 — LIC DOMESTIC AUSTRALIAN SHARES
[FEE] = 0.40 % / $102

$5,600 — EXISTING BANK SHARES
[FEE] = 0.00 %

$31,200
[TOTAL FEE] = 0.33 % / $102

REINVEST ALWAYS

LIST OF BENEFITS

☑ BUY AND HOLD (MINIMAL CG-T BEING TRIGGERED)

☑ LOW ONGOING FEES

☑ DIVERSIFIED OVER A WIDE RANGE OF DIFFERENT AUSTRALIAN AND INTERNATIONAL COMPANIES

Every time she buys more shares in her LIC, she increases her passive income supply and updates her workbook, tracking her progress towards her number. Because she is regularly increasing her borrowings to invest, Honey keeps a close eye over her loan, which is growing by $12 000 p.a., but always under her LVR of 50%. The two main reasons that this LVR remains safely under 50% is because the dividends are being reinvested, and she is adding $2500 equity each year to the portfolio.

She sticks to her strategy, while spending any pay rises, job promotions, bonuses or side hustle money either on herself and her regular holidays and travel, or putting some extra money away in one of her savings accounts and always accounting for any additional tax as her combined gross income (i.e. her salary + passive income) increases over time. Honey has the luxury of choice, knowing that she has planted the necessary seeds; as long as she sticks to this strategy and allows it to gestate over time, it will work for her.

Let's see what happens over the next few years.

Assuming the same assumptions for Amanda, by the time Honey is forty, her gross passive income is $48 580 p.a., which is just under $32 000 in today's dollars. Her portfolio is worth $998 000, which is worth $656 000 in today's dollars, and she can now switch

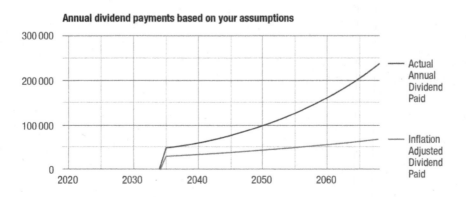

Annual dividend payments based on your assumptions

Future Age	Year	Year #	Actual Annual Dividend Paid	Inflation Adjusted Dividend Paid in Today's $	Year-End Actual Portfolio Value	Year-End Inflation Adjusted Portfolio Value in Today's $
24	2019	1	$0.00	$0.00	$58 957.70	$57 638.19
25	2020	2	$0.00	$0.00	$94 163.61	$89 626.28
26	2021	3	$0.00	$0.00	$128 949.30	$119 742.24
27	2022	4	$0.00	$0.00	$166 515.59	$150 854.91
28	2023	5	$0.00	$0.00	$207 126.04	$183 069.24
29	2024	6	$0.00	$0.00	$251 071.43	$216 498.11
30	2025	7	$0.00	$0.00	$298 672.84	$251 263.08
31	2026	8	$0.00	$0.00	$350 285.03	$287 495.24
32	2027	9	$0.00	$0.00	$406 300.27	$325 336.15
33	2028	10	$0.00	$0.00	$467 152.62	$364 938.88
34	2029	11	$0.00	$0.00	$533 322.77	$406 469.16
35	2030	12	$0.00	$0.00	$605 343.39	$450 106.64
36	2031	13	$0.00	$0.00	$683 805.28	$496 046.28
37	2032	14	$0.00	$0.00	$769 364.16	$544 499.94
38	2033	15	$0.00	$0.00	$862 748.41	$595 698.06
39	2034	16	$0.00	$0.00	$964 767.75	$649 891.61
40	2035	17	$48 580.94	$31 927.16	$998 534.62	$656 232.02
41	2036	18	$51 009.99	$32 705.87	$1 033 483.34	$662 634.28
42	2037	19	$53 560.49	$33 503.57	$1 069 655.25	$669 099.01
43	2038	20	$56 238.52	$34 320.73	$1 107 093.19	$675 626.80
44	2039	21	$59 050.44	$35 157.82	$1 145 841.45	$682 218.28
45	2040	22	$62 002.96	$36 015.33	$1 185 945.90	$688 874.07
46	2041	23	$65 103.11	$36 893.75	$1 227 454.00	$695 594.79
47	2042	24	$68 358.27	$37 793.60	$1 270 414.89	$702 381.08

Future Age	Year	Year #	Actual Annual Dividend Paid	Inflation Adjusted Dividend Paid in Today's $	Year-End Actual Portfolio Value	Year-End Inflation Adjusted Portfolio Value in Today's $
48	2043	25	$71 776.18	$38 715.40	$1 314 879.42	$709 233.58
49	2044	26	$75 364.99	$39 659.67	$1 360 900.20	$716 152.94
50	2045	27	$79 133.24	$40 626.98	$1 408 531.70	$723 139.79
51	2046	28	$83 089.90	$41 617.89	$1 457 830.31	$730 194.82
52	2047	29	$87 244.40	$42 632.96	$1 508 854.37	$737 318.67
53	2048	30	$91 606.62	$43 672.78	$1 561 664.28	$744 512.02
54	2049	31	$96 186.95	$44 737.97	$1 616 322.53	$751 775.55
55	2050	32	$100 996.30	$45 829.14	$1 672 893.81	$759 109.95
56	2051	33	$106 046.11	$46 946.93	$1 731 445.10	$766 515.90
57	2052	34	$111 348.42	$48 091.98	$1 792 045.68	$773 994.10
58	2053	35	$116 915.84	$49 264.95	$1 854 767.27	$781 545.26
59	2054	36	$122 761.63	$50 466.53	$1 919 684.13	$789 170.10
60	2055	37	$128 899.71	$51 697.43	$1 986 873.07	$796 869.32
61	2056	38	$135 344.70	$52 958.34	$2 056 413.63	$804 643.65
62	2057	39	$142 111.93	$54 250.01	$2 128 388.11	$812 493.83
63	2058	40	$149 217.53	$55 573.18	$2 202 881.69	$820 420.60
64	2059	41	$156 678.40	$56 928.62	$2 279 982.55	$828 424.71
65	2060	42	$164 512.32	$58 317.12	$2 359 781.94	$836 506.90
66	2061	43	$172 737.94	$59 739.49	$2 442 374.31	$844 667.94
67	2062	44	$181 374.84	$61 196.55	$2 527 857.41	$852 908.60
68	2063	45	$190 443.58	$62 689.15	$2 616 332.42	$861 229.66
69	2064	46	$199 965.76	$64 218.15	$2 707 904.05	$869 631.90
70	2065	47	$209 964.04	$65 784.45	$2 802 680.69	$878 116.12

off that automatic dividend reinvestment plan and start living off her passive income, which should continue to grow over the long run. Just like always, Honey is on top of her taxes. So even if she is working full time, part time or not at all, she pays the correct taxes by checking her combined gross income against the ATO's income tax calculator and factoring it into her budget throughout the financial year. She uses a different savings account to hold this money separately from her spending and investing money.

Her margin loan, which has increased at $12 000 p.a. for the last sixteen years, is now sitting at $202 000 (16 years × $12 000 p.a.+ initial loan of $10 000).

However, she never needs to increase this again, nor add any further investment to her portfolio, like she has previously been doing every quarter. And the previous $2500 p.a. that she was investing from her tax refund can now go towards paying off the margin loan along with the almost $2000 p.a. surplus she has each year in passive income.

And should Honey ever decide to change her plans, or even not use this passive income, she can either take the passive income of $48 500 to pay off the margin loan in just over five years, or simply reinvest that passive income and slowly pay down the margin loan over her working life.

So her total capital invested, including her initial investment, the regular investment, plus the growing margin loan, is $464 500, and from now on she is getting back $48 000 p.a. indefinitely – and it is still growing.

Let's see what happens if Honey decides at age forty to never add more money to her share portfolio, but to instead reinvest the dividends and slowly pay off the $202 000 margin loan up until she wants to retire at age sixty.

At age sixty, Honey is receiving a passive income of over $170 000 p.a., which is $101 000 in today's dollars, and her portfolio is worth over $3 308 000, or $1 969 000 in today's dollars.

Her total investment outlay is still $464 500 as she stopped contributing to it, and now over the space of twenty-five years, she gets her complete initial investment paid back and still owns the investment assets.

By age forty, she will have planted the most valuable financial seeds of her life if she sticks to her regular investment rules ($14 500 p.a. in additional investment out of her own money, which is $1000 per month plus $2500 p.a.) along with her $12 000 p.a. margin loan. By prioritising her passive income during her twenties and thirties, it will always be there for her in her forties and beyond, rain, hail or shine.

Just like Amanda, Honey wants freedom to access her investments when she wants. She can sell all or part of her portfolio at any stage, if she chooses to. However, considering what this passive income gives her, she sees the importance to her financial goals of keeping this passive income supply.

And beyond these considerations, Honey still has her super. She chose a good value superannuation provider that offers index ETFs, LICs and shares, and she has the ability to select sectors beyond the generic diversified pre-mix, and that very valuable in-specie service for when she retires.

While she has based her investment portfolio purely on Australian shares, due to the franking credit benefits that help offset her income tax, Honey still wants to invest beyond her local borders and spread her investment risk and wealth creation opportunities further. She chooses to make 100% of her superannuation investments through an international index ETF with an ongoing MER (management

Future Age	Year	Year #	Actual Annual Dividend Paid	Inflation Adjusted Dividend Paid in Today's $	Year-End Actual Portfolio Value	Year-End Inflation Adjusted Portfolio Value in Today's $
40	2019	1	$0.00	$0.00	$697 177.85	$681 574.56
41	2020	2	$0.00	$0.00	$760 097.46	$723 471.71
42	2021	3	$0.00	$0.00	$818 882.38	$760 413.70
43	2022	4	$0.00	$0.00	$882 723.81	$799 704.20
44	2023	5	$0.00	$0.00	$952 100.56	$841 518.17
45	2024	6	$0.00	$0.00	$1 027 540.92	$886 045.32
46	2025	7	$0.00	$0.00	$1 109 628.13	$933 491.57
47	2026	8	$0.00	$0.00	$1 199 006.59	$984 080.55
48	2027	9	$0.00	$0.00	$1 296 388.83	$1 038 055.30
49	2028	10	$0.00	$0.00	$1 402 563.22	$1 095 680.15
50	2029	11	$0.00	$0.00	$1 518 402.78	$1 157 242.76
51	2030	12	$0.00	$0.00	$1 644 874.95	$1 223 056.45
52	2031	13	$0.00	$0.00	$1 783 052.64	$1 293 462.72
53	2032	14	$0.00	$0.00	$1 934 126.68	$1 368 834.05
54	2033	15	$0.00	$0.00	$2 099 419.78	$1 449 577.05
55	2034	16	$0.00	$0.00	$2 280 402.32	$1 536 135.86
56	2035	17	$0.00	$0.00	$2 478 710.18	$1 628 996.08
57	2036	18	$0.00	$0.00	$2 696 164.82	$1 728 688.97
58	2037	19	$0.00	$0.00	$2 934 796.01	$1 835 796.25
59	2038	20	$0.00	$0.00	$3 196 867.57	$1 950 955.39
60	2039	21	$170 515.41	$101 522.53	$3 308 757.93	$1 969 989.10
61	2040	22	$179 041.18	$103 998.69	$3 424 564.46	$1 989 208.50
62	2041	23	$187 993.23	$106 535.25	$3 544 424.22	$2 008 615.41
63	2042	24	$197 392.90	$109 133.67	$3 668 479.06	$2 028 211.66
64	2043	25	$207 262.54	$111 795.46	$3 796 875.83	$2 047 999.09

Future Age	Year	Year #	Actual Annual Dividend Paid	Inflation Adjusted Dividend Paid in Today's $	Year-End Actual Portfolio Value	Year-End Inflation Adjusted Portfolio Value in Today's $
65	2044	26	$217625.67	$114522.18	$3929766.49	$2067979.57
66	2045	27	$228506.95	$117315.41	$4067308.31	$2088154.98
67	2046	28	$239932.30	$120176.76	$4209664.10	$2108527.23
68	2047	29	$251928.91	$123107.90	$4357002.35	$2129098.22
69	2048	30	$264525.36	$126110.53	$4509497.43	$2149869.91
70	2049	31	$277751.63	$129186.40	$4667329.84	$2170844.25
71	2050	32	$291639.21	$132337.28	$4830686.38	$2192023.22
72	2051	33	$306221.17	$135565.02	$4999760.41	$2213408.81
73	2052	34	$321532.23	$138871.49	$5174752.02	$2235003.05
74	2053	35	$337608.84	$142258.60	$5355868.34	$2256807.95
75	2054	36	$354489.28	$145728.32	$5543323.73	$2278825.59
76	2055	37	$372213.75	$149282.67	$5737340.07	$2301058.04
77	2056	38	$390824.43	$152923.71	$5938146.97	$2323507.38
78	2057	39	$410365.65	$156653.56	$6145982.11	$2346175.75
79	2058	40	$430883.94	$160474.37	$6361091.49	$2369065.27
80	2059	41	$452428.13	$164388.38	$6583729.69	$2392178.10
81	2060	42	$475049.54	$168397.86	$6814160.23	$2415516.42
82	2061	43	$498802.02	$172505.12	$7052655.83	$2439082.44
83	2062	44	$523742.12	$176712.56	$7299498.79	$2462878.36
84	2063	45	$549929.23	$181022.62	$7554981.25	$2486906.45
85	2064	46	$577425.69	$185437.81	$7819405.59	$2511168.95
86	2065	47	$606296.97	$189960.68	$8093084.79	$2535668.16
87	2066	48	$636611.82	$194593.87	$8376342.75	$2560406.38
88	2067	49	$668442.41	$199340.06	$8669514.75	$2585385.96
89	2068	50	$701864.53	$204202.02	$8972947.77	$2610609.23

expense ratio) of 0.18% p.a. Thus, even while her Australian share portfolio is growing, her superannuation portfolio is exposed to similar opportunities outside of Australia – by experts who know how to invest for long-term wealth creation through these assets.

Including her employer's contribution along the way, super-annuation represents an important part of Honey's overall wealth. It's bubbling away for the long run, invested in a tax-efficient, cost-effective manner, and all correctly aligned to her long-term financial goals and high-growth risk profile.

Honey also takes out the right level of life and TPD cover, ensuring that her growing margin loan is always covered, so there is enough money to pay out her loan and leave the portfolio to her sister and nieces and nephews without any debt should the situation arise. She takes out enough TPD cover (as a separate stand-alone policy to her life policy, still both within super) to pay off the expected total margin loan of $202 000, plus allows enough money to buy a home outright so that she can always remain independent. The reason she decides to cover the expected total loan of $202 000 is to ensure that money is always set aside and invested as per her game plan. It's a way of reinforcing that, no matter what happens, she will stick to her strategy.

Honey takes out her income protection policy, affording to stretch out her waiting period to ninety days and covering herself to age sixty-five. She also takes out a trauma cover policy of $302 000, for the same reasons as the TPD cover: no matter what happens from a medical perspective, Honey will always ensure that she can stick to her investment plan, even if she can't borrow the money; plus she has an additional $100 000 for recovery and rehabilitation expenses. This trauma cover is owned and paid for separately from her super, and sits comfortably within her current budget.

CHEAT TIP FROM CC:

While you can set life & TPD cover as separate stand-alone policies within most super accounts, sometimes the cost of having them combined, with the life cover at the same or higher level of the TPD cover, doesn't actually cost much more. If you ever see yourself taking on large debt (such as a mortgage) or having a family, it may be worth taking it out earlier, while you are fit and healthy. As this helps avoid future risks of loading and exclusions later in life when we have more health risks, concerns or symptoms.

So as you can see, by understanding both Amanda and Honey's numbers, we are able to devise two similar but equally effective set-and-forget (but always monitored) wealth creation strategies that help them create their own financial freedom and, most importantly, provide them with their number through their own efforts and mindful money applications, habits and mindsets.

Both Honey and Amanda have made multiple mini short-term goals to reach their numbers, after working backwards from what their dreams and ambitions are. This helps reassure them they are on the right track, as long as they stick to their game plans and those mini goals are ticked off as they travel along. Life will throw up some surprises, unexpected bills and unforeseen illnesses may crop up, but so too will new jobs and exciting opportunities that will help anchor them to their paths, and, who knows, quite possibly take them well beyond their numbers.

POINTS TO REMEMBER:

- Break it down into mini short-term goals – over the long run, this is so powerful in getting things done.
- Lean in, if you can't save $1000 per month to put towards your number, start with $50 or $70 and slowly start building it up month by month.
- Remember short- to medium-term expenses – separate cash accounts.
- Index ETFs and LICs are a really cost effective and efficient way to build a diversified investment portfolio.
- We never want our asset base to stop paying us our dividend income.
- Chase the dividends, not the capital growth.
- Market pullbacks are often amazing once-in-a-lifetime buying opportunities to pick up discounted passive income streams.
- Always update your workbooks when you buy more passive income streams, marked against the progression towards your big goal.
- Enrol in automatic dividend reinvestment plans where possible.
- Be aware of and understand what is going on in the world and economy, but know when to turn down the noise.
- Always keep an eye on your combined gross income (i.e. your salary + net passive income) as you may need to pay additional tax at the end of each financial year.
- Refer to the ATO's income tax calculator so you know what your total tax is. If necessary, open a second financial goal account with a budget allocation for tax due to ensure you are never caught by surprise at tax time.

CHAPTER ELEVEN

Property

'Some people want it to happen, some people wish it would happen, others make it happen.' – Michael Jordan, American basketball player

Now that you can see the power of two-dimensional assets and collecting them as part of building your number, we can continue on to discuss another type of asset class that fits this requirement: property.

Investment properties are also two-dimensional assets. The value of the property can grow over the long run, and you can receive passive income through rent. Property investment is a tool that can either be used alone or in combination with the other two-dimensional assets previously discussed to help build up towards your number. That is to say, you don't have to do one or the other; you can choose to invest in both shares and property.

Investing in property goes beyond the popular residential property you might be imagining. There are commercial properties, such as shops and offices; industrial, such as factories; and rural, such as land where you rent the space out to farmers (for example agistment and cropping).

For simplicity, I'm going to use the example of residential investment properties to demonstrate how to build up to your number. But I do recommend looking at other forms of property, so that you discover what's right for you, even if it is a mix of different property investment types – don't just follow the residential herd. That said, residential property is easier to secure loans on compared to other property types.

The strategy that I am about to discuss can be tweaked as you see fit but always err on the side of caution – which I will show you how to do.

START WITH SMALL SUCCESSES

Let's go back to Ben, and his aimed-for number of $30 000 p.a. Ben has never purchased property before, but would like to get his foot in the door by owning at least one property in a major city, so that even if it's rented out most of the time he owns it, he always has the option of having a base to come home to one day.

Ben is conservative by nature, and does not want to get in way over his head. He has seen some of his friends borrow large amounts of money with small deposits of 10% or less and interest-only loans that have not worked out quite as planned, leaving them heavily in debt years after purchasing their properties. It creates financial stress for them, and they struggle with interest repayments that take a large percentage of their salary.

In looking to learn from his friends' errors, Ben decides he doesn't want to over-extend himself, even if it means taking longer to save a bigger deposit or buying a property in a lower price bracket, or both. And he certainly doesn't want to bank solely on capital growth to increase his income, so interest-only loans are out of the question. He feels that his mental health is worth more and plans to prioritise his financial health, by first building his number; then those bigger lifestyle goals can be achieved in good time, with less pressure and more enjoyment and balance.

After looking at a few different options and coming back to his number of $30 000 p.a., Ben decides that he wants to work towards an entry point of $400 000 to get his foot in the door of the market. He feels this is a good and achievable starting point, and that he can build and diversify from then on, if he wants to. Plus if he can save a decent deposit, of at least 20%, he will still be able to handle an interest rate rise in his mortgage of 3% p.a. without too much stress and pressure on his cashflow, which he knows for sure as he has run the numbers and checked it against his budget.

He has saved $50 000 since starting his job eight years ago, plus $10 000 in his separate Life + $8000 Emergency Savings account; he's already paid off all his HECS debt and has no credit card debt.

Previously he didn't have any particular goals to work towards, so he was casually drifting along with no real goal to sink his teeth into. The $50 000 slowly accumulated in his account with regular savings, the odd bonus and tax refund here and there, and a few pay rises along the way.

But his breakthrough has come from stopping and thinking about his financial future and what financial freedom means to him, and having that goal of $30 000 p.a. in passive income has bought him to life again with a new rush of motivation, excitement and direction.

Ben starts by reviewing his budget, making a few spending adjustments and increasing his regular monthly savings plan by cutting out some of his living expenses. Taking his lunch to work three days per week, getting up fifteen minutes earlier to have coffee at home before work and skipping two Friday night after-work drinks per month really frees up some cash. He also sells some old sporting equipment that he no longer uses, and picks up some extra handyman jobs to do over the weekend.

And most importantly, he renames his savings account that holds the $50 000 as 'My Investment Property Deposit' – which becomes his financial goal account.

Every time he saves some money, sells something or earns some money from side hustles, he immediately deposits it into his financial goal account.

Ben continuously sets small short-term financial goals for himself, like 'To save $1000 over the next five weeks' and 'To save $300 before the end of the month'. He knows it all adds up when he is in saving mode and when he sees his account growing, it is exciting as his life gets a new rush of purpose and direction.

He puts his tax refund, the after-tax difference of his new pay rise, his bonus, every spare dollar that he can find, into this account so that he isn't tempted to spend it. He knows that if he sees the money in his everyday account, he will find something to blow it on, so he simply removes the temptation.

As he watches his savings grow, and more interest being earned each month, Ben's motivation and focus grow as well, and he uses this time to research and learn more about property.

He studies the property listings online every week, and calls agents to ask questions. He starts to inspect properties rather than just look online, and begins to get a feel for the areas he wants to buy into. He develops a sense of comparison and value as he learns why some properties are better value than others and realise higher sale prices. All of this comes from researching, reviewing and inspecting different properties, in different buildings, in different streets, in different suburbs and different neighbourhoods.

Ben also starts to factor in how his cash flow and outgoings will look if he goes through with this potential investment property purchase.

He runs the following calculations and factors these in to his budget so that he knows he can afford to hold the property:

- **the potential rental income** – a rough estimate given by the agent selling the property, reduced by 5% to 10% to allow for any 'agent exaggeration'.
- **the possibility of being between tenants** – (two weeks per year is the average) and the property being vacant.
- **the total outgoings** for the property, including but not limited to:
  - **strata or body corporate fees** – usually quarterly and advised by the agent.
  - **council rates** – quarterly and advised by the agent.
  - **water** – quarterly and advised by the agent (this one is usually a flat regular amount, so quite reliable).
  - **landlord insurance** – quotes available online; can be monthly or yearly.
  - **property management fees** – quoted by the agent but includes two weeks' rent letting fee and a schedule of other various admin expenses. You can negotiate a better rate, but keep in mind that a good property manager can save you thousands through proactive, responsible management of one of your biggest financial assets.
  - **the mortgage repayment** – given current interest rates, say 5% p.a. for principal and interest repayments (not interest only).
  - **the mortgage repayment with an interest rate increase** – for example, going from 5% p.a. to 8% p.a.; Ben needs to ensure that if this happens, he can still afford to hold the property as well as continue to pay down the principal.

And in the meantime, he never stops saving for his deposit, even if he exceeds his goal deposit. Ben knows that all this growing knowledge and a bigger deposit will not only help him buy well (not needing to borrow as much if his deposit is bigger but his budget remains the same), but also give him confidence that he'll make an educated and informed purchase at good value when he's ready.

CHEAT TIP FROM CC:

There's a rental property calculator on SugarMamma.TV to help make this quick and easy for you. You just enter in all the numbers and it helps work out your net rental income, which you can then compare against other properties that you've been considering. You can match these net numbers against your mortgage repayments to help make sure the numbers stack up and will help you build towards your passive income number.

		Smith street		John Street		Mount Street	
Property price		$ 480,000.00		$ 690,000.00		$ 350,000.00	
Stamp duty		$ 20,000.00		$ 35,000.00		$ 10,000.00	
Other buying costs		$ -		$ -		$ -	
Total		$ 500,000.00		$ 725,000.00		$ 360,000.00	
	Frequency		Per Year		Per Year		Per Year
Estimated rent	Weekly	$ 420.00	$ 21,840.00	$ 720.00	$ 37,440.00	$ 415.00	$ 21,580.00
Gross return			4.37%		5.16%		5.99%
Expenses							
Strata fees (apartment)	Quarterly	$ 690.00	$ 2,760.00	$ 1,050.00	$ 4,200.00	$ 1,000.00	$ 4,000.00
Council rates (house)	Quarterly	$ 300.00	$ 1,200.00	$ 300.00	$ 1,200.00	$ 200.00	$ 800.00
Landlord Insurance	Annually	$ 350.00	$ 350.00	$ 350.00	$ 350.00	$ 350.00	$ 350.00
Building Insurance	Annually	$ -	$ -	$ -		$ -	$ -
Water rates (house)	Quarterly	$ 150.00	$ 600.00	$ 150.00	$ 600.00	$ 400.00	$ 1,600.00
Total			$ 4,910.00		$ 6,350.00		$ 6,750.00
Net income p.a.			$ 16,930.00		$ 31,090.00		$ 14,830.00
Net return			3.39%		4.29%		4.12%

When you find a location that you want to buy in and start looking at specific properties to invest in, it's a good idea to find one or two real estate agents who have been selling (not renting) property in the area for at least five years, and pick their brains.

Preparing to buy a property is worth investing time in. You can make more money when you buy better by allowing greater opportunity for capital growth. Make sure you do all your due diligence first, prior to making any offers. It gives you a chance to be assertive and astute. When you make that offer to the agent, make it unconditional, but make it clear you have a strict deadline for the vendor to come back to you or you will move on to another opportunity. Some questions to ask include:

- **What's the estimated rent and what comparable properties do you have currently rented out?** This stops the exaggerated numbers!

- **Why are the owners selling?** This could identify a weakness that you could capitalise on, such as negotiating a better price. For example if you know the vendor has to sell or has already committed to a new property. On the flip side, it might reveal a problem with the property, which no longer makes it suitable to your investment requirements, such as upcoming strata issues, or noise pollution with new infrastructure, etc.

- **How often are properties up for sale/rent in this building/ street/area?** Be careful of high turnover areas – this could make it slow to rent out your property, perhaps even putting pressure on you to lower your price or potential rent.

- **What do you see as the best selling point of this property?** The agent may show you something that everyone else has missed. Look for unique characteristics that make your property stand out, such as a courtyard or high ceilings.

- **What key aspects do tenants need in a property?** It's really important to know this so that your property will be in demand and always be rented out. Does the property have aircon, and if not, will strata let you install it? If leasing a property in summer, no aircon could mean fewer interested tenants. The same goes for proper heating, especially if renting out during winter. A good property will be great in all seasons. Young families often prefer a property with a bathtub rather than shower for bathing babies and children. Or the elderly may prefer lifts or ground level access or secure parking. Ask the agent what are attractive rental aspects.

- **What is the noise factor and natural light like?** Sometimes open inspections are held at 'convenient' times so potential buyers don't notice traffic or neighbourhood noises, or lack of natural light. You can ask for a special inspection time to thoroughly check everything. Listen for noises, check natural light and take note of the character and movement of the neightbourhood.

- **What changes or improvements would you make to this property to help increase its value?** A good agent will see quick and easy tweaks to a property that would make it more desirable – from a fresh coat of paint to knocking down a wall to make a space more open-plan. Even converting a studio apartment into a one bedroom apartment by building a wall to separate the spaces. You don't need to do what they suggest, but it's good to know and it might be something you can come back to at a later date to add more value to your property.

- **What would you (as in the agent) pay for the property?** This is a question that agents rarely get asked and will most likely put them on the spot, but it will help give you an insight into what the agent really values the property at and if it matches what they are selling it for.

- **What comparable sales are available?** Make sure that these are recent (within the last two to three months) and have similar scope, e.g. same number of bedrooms and bathrooms.
- **What areas do you see value in?** Where would you be investing and what would you be buying? Great insight into whether this property is a good buy in the agent's mind.
- **What areas do you think are overvalued?** What property types would you steer clear of? The answers will change depending on what is going on in the property market and economy. Agents have sometimes inadvertently steered me clear of buying properties when they've answered these questions and they've innocently let their opinions slip, saving me a lot of money and helping me avoid a bad decision.
- **What sort of people would you expect to rent this property?** Young family? Professional couple? What facilities are within close proximity that makes this property more desirable? (public transport, cafes, schools, etc.)
- **If the property is currently being rented, when was the rent last increased?** If it hasn't been increased for more than twelve months, I would be asking why that is and see if there is potential to increase it within the short term.
- **Is the property easily rented out?** What is the vacancy period like for a property such as this? Remember that each week you are without a tenant your net income return rapidly decreases and this can cause issues with deductibility of the interest during this process.
- **How long has the property been on the market for?** If it has been on the market for longer than six weeks, ask why it hasn't sold. There could be many reasons, but if it was initially overpriced, the vendor may have burnt early potential buyers,

opening up an opportunity for you to now acquire the property at a more reasonable price.

- **What is the best offer you have had?** Why was it knocked back? Has the vendor changed their mind and is it more open to offers? What would buy it today? These answers can give you huge insight into what price you could secure the property at.

Over the course of a few years, Ben manages to save an impressive $100 000. He has a 25% deposit on his intended budget of $400 000, so saves over $7000 in mortgage insurance which he would have had to pay if he had only 20%. Mortgage insurance can be around 2% depending on your deposit, how much you want to borrow and what the property is actually worth.

Ben's loan-to-value ratio (LVR) is 75%, which is calculated by dividing the total loan by the value of the property: $300 000/$400 000. The lower the LVR, the less risk you pose to a bank or lender. Ideally you always want your LVR less than 80% to not only avoid having to pay mortgage insurance (which in my mind is an expensive waste of money, as you're paying for the bank's protection), but also as it can mean being rewarded with lower interest rates, higher ongoing discounts and better package deals.

Now he calculates that he needs to save the remaining $15 000 for stamp duty, which is kind of like a government buying fee for getting into the property market, and legal expenses for solicitor fees and conveyancer costs. So in Ben's case, $13 500 stamp duty and $1500 in legals. Motivated by how close he is to buying his first property, he quickly saves up this amount.

After researching and inspecting properties, Ben finds an apartment that matches his criteria, and he can see that it's a good deal. It's in a popular area, with more businesses, cafes, schools and transport options popping up all the time, and there is a shortage of rental properties already. He predicts that the type of person looking to rent in this area will most likely be a young professional person or couple, and this apartment has the amenities to make it more attractive.

Ben negotiates a purchase price of $400 000, exchanges contracts and pays the stamp duty and legals at settlement (when you take possession of the property), after gaining pre-approval on a $300 000 principal and interest loan. He hunts for the lowest-cost basic package on a thirty-year term, so that even though he is going to try and pay this loan off as fast as possible, his actual minimum repayment is very manageable and can always easily be paid.

He has his own savings accounts and investment strategies, so he doesn't need any credit cards or overdrafts or offset facilities attached, as he knows these will jack the interest rate up and create more distractions and temptations to keep him indebted to the bank.

He goes with a no-frills principal and interest package at 5% p.a. because he knows that the lower the interest rate, the quicker this property will be paid off, allowing him to start searching for his next property sooner or diversify and invest elsewhere. And with his mortgage coming down, the property becomes more cash flow-positive sooner, which also helps reduce his risks – he is lowering his LVR by manually creating equity above and beyond any capital growth.

Ben also takes out landlord insurance to protect the property in the event of any issues, such as the tenant not paying rent or not vacating the property, fire and other mishaps, which is also paid for out of his own budget.

Ben then updates his passive income worksheet and financial snapshot worksheet. He documents his **gross passive income** and the percentage of passive income he has created divided by his personal goal number:

Gross passive income

$350 p.w. rent × 52 = $18 200

$18 200/$30 000 × 100 = 60.6% achieved

CHEAT TIP FROM CC:

I have used an average interest rate of 5% p.a. (principal and interest) for conservative measures. At the moment, though, you could possibly secure an interest rate of more like 3.59% p.a. through new digital loan providers such as Athena. A lower interest rate means that your loan could be paid down even faster, as less money is going towards the interest expense. However, always do your research into the best rate and package for your needs, and make sure it's designed to be paid off as it works towards building your number.

While this is the gross passive income and doesn't take the repayments and ongoing holding costs including property management fees into consideration, Ben has officially built 60% of his gross passive income source and has a game plan already in place to make sure this is 100% cash-flow positive as soon as possible and ensuring that the cash-flow positive income can easily pay for all the property's outgoings.

As the six-week settlement period passes, Ben gets ahead of the game and hires a property manager to start advertising the property for rent, which he previously negotiated as part of the purchase price so that he has a tenant ready to move in shortly after he reaches settlement to start covering as much of the mortgage repayment as possible.

Ben also uses the time to build up a lump sum of six weeks' worth of his mortgage repayments, to get a head start on reducing the loan and building passive income. This is really easy for Ben, as he has such an ingrained habit of saving from building his deposit; he rounds the amount up to the nearest $100 and makes an upfront lump-sum repayment of $2500 the moment the property and loan settles.

This simple but proactive strategy has already saved Ben over $8000 in interest and knocked six months off his home loan, assuming that he keeps his repayments unchanged at 5% p.a. over the thirty-year life of the loan.

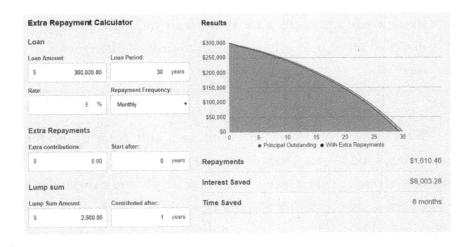

Ben's property manager secures a tenant at $350 per week. Ben calculates that $1520 per month will be coming in from rental income, while his principal and interest mortgage repayments will be $1610 p.m. at 5% p.a. His first investment property will cost him $90 p.m., excluding the outgoings.

CHEAT TIP FROM CC:

If the property you purchase is vacant, you can sometimes negotiate a deal where a new tenant can be found and the vendor gets to keep the rent up until the property settles. This will minimise any shortfall in cash flow for you from the moment the property settles. Alternatively, you might be able to secure a property with a quality tenant already in place. If this is the case, find out when their last rental increase was and if they are interested in extending their lease. This will help create greater cash-flow security for you.

When an investment has been bought with a loan, even a small loan, we call this a **geared investment**. When the loan on an investment costs more in interest than the income (in this case the rent) that we receive, it's called **cash-flow negative**. When the income we receive is the same as the interest we pay on the loan it is called **cash-flow neutral**, and when the investment income that we receive is greater than the interest repayment, we call this **cash-flow positive**.

When it comes to building your number, we need our income to be cash-flow positive. Otherwise we can't spend it, as it has to go towards the loans and defeats the purpose of building passive income in the first place.

The way to beat this is to pay down the principal and interest loan by making extra repayments out of your own cash flow, along

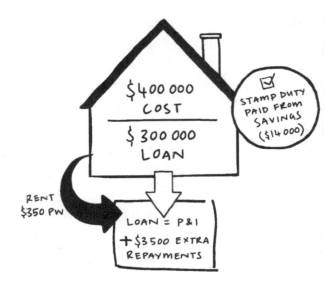

with the income that you receive from the investment. That way, the investment asset (that is, your investment property) can have the opportunity to grow in value over time with capital growth, and any extra contributions you can make towards reducing the loan, along with the rent which should also be slowly increasing over time, will mean that the gap between the value of the asset and the loan gets bigger and bigger. And over time, your property's rent will not just cover the interest but also pay down the principal for you.

Because Ben is keen to reach his number as quickly as possible so that he can jet off overseas, he capitalises on the savings habit he developed when building his mortgage. He not only pays the shortfall in rent of $90 per month as well as all the outgoings for the property from his own budget, but on top of this he makes extra repayments of $3500 per month towards reducing the loan of $297 500.

If Ben sticks to this, and the interest rate averages around 5% over time, his loan will be completely paid off in just over 5.5 years and save him almost $230 000 in interest!

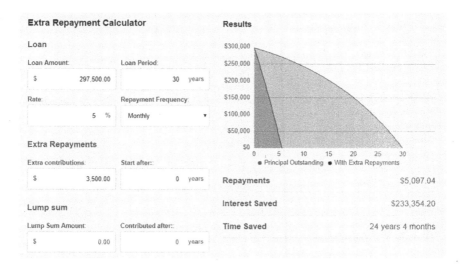

If Ben wants to speed this up even more, he can put more towards the loan along the way, such as pay rises, bonuses, extra cash from his side hustle, and use his mini, short-term goal strategy to help along the way. He may even have a few rental increases – assuming his property manager puts his tenant's rent up in line with inflation at 2.5% p.a. over the 5.5 years, and it's in line with the going market rates within the states guidelines, the rent should then be just over $400 per week, which is $20 592 p.a. – all contributing towards his number of $30 000 p.a. For conservative measures I have kept rental increase at 2.5% but it could be as much as 5% or higher.

Every time the rent goes up, Ben updates his worksheets to monitor the progress he is making towards his number.

Year zero – date xx/xx/xx $350 p.w. = $18 240 = 60.6%

Year one – date xx/xx/xx $359 p.w. = $18 720 = 62.4%

Year two – date xx/xx/xx $368 p.w. = $19 188 = 64%

Year three – date xx/xx/xx $377 p.w. = $19 658 = 65.5%

Year four – date xx/xx/xx $386 p.w. = $20 127 = 67%

Year five – date xx/xx/xx $396 p.w. = $20 649 = 68.8% – **Mortgage paid off**

Obviously, Ben has to pay income tax on his rental income each year; however, the interest on the loan is tax deductible, along with all those outgoings such as insurance, strata fees and council rates (which he pays for out of his budget). Plus he can claim a little bit of depreciation along the way. He covers all shortfalls out of his own pocket, with rental increases eventually covering these outgoings and still providing Ben with his passive income.

He also updates his superannuation passive income in his work-sheets, which is growing thanks to his employer contributions each year. However, as he wants to access his passive income as soon as possible for his overseas adventures, he is focusing his energy on his investment portfolio, which is liquid and can be drawn on with no government restrictions.

CHEAT TIP FROM CC:

Most attentive property managers will increase your tenant's rent by 5% to 10% p.a. after giving sixty days' notice once the lease is due for renewal. You are only allowed one rental increase per twelve months. However, for conservative meas-ures I have kept the assumption of an increase at 2.5% p.a. If your tenant's rent is increased, it means more passive income, taking you closer to your number.

So within 5.5 years, Ben has achieved 68.8% of his gross passive income goal – but he needs to keep going.

OPTION 1

Ben can use the cash-flow positive income from rental payments to help buy a second property worth, say, $400 000 again. He can borrow the full $400 000 from the bank, but also use his first investment property as security to help keep the LVR safe at 50%. (That is, $400 000 new loan / $800 000 new and existing property – which could actually be worth more after 5.5 years, but to be safe and conservative let's say it hasn't grown in value.)

By using his first investment property as security, it means that should he default on the loan repayments, the bank can legally go after his first property if they aren't fully reimbursed from a sale of the second property. As Ben has a game plan in place, this isn't a serious concern for him; nonetheless, he understands the risks of this and he has already checked that he can still service these loans with a 3% interest rate rise.

Now, assuming he doesn't save up another deposit, he could use the rental income from his first property to help pay down the loan on the second property.

Also, the rent from the second property is going towards the interest and will then help reduce the loan, while Ben can continue to use his surplus cash flow of $3500 p.m. (after factoring in the outgoings on both properties). He essentially has up to three sources of cash flow to put towards the loan, extinguishing it faster.

Assuming a $400 000 mortgage, an average interest rate of 5% p.a., extra repayments of $20 649 from property one and Ben contributing $3500 p.m. in extra repayments, this loan could be paid down in just over five years.

In less than eleven years, Ben has built a passive income sourced from two investment properties, both owned outright, together paying him over $40 000 p.a. He has achieved his passive income goal of $3000 p.a., which with inflation is now $39 363 at 2.5% p.a. – Ben monitored this inflation to keep on track with his goal.

Also, remember from Chapter two that within this required passive income is $3000 p.a. that we allocated for new investment? Going forward, Ben's long-term wealth and passive income should continue to grow if he sticks to buying new passive income sources, further diversifying his spare money and watches the ongoing costs of holding these properties.

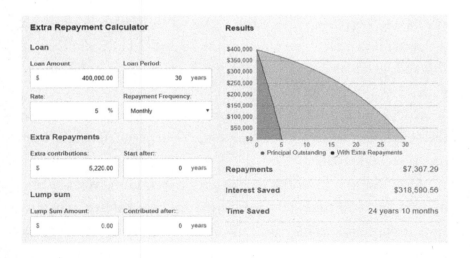

Extra Monthly Repayment Breakdown for Option 1:

Surplus Cash = $3500 p.m. +

Surplus passive rental income = $20 649/12 = $1720

Total surplus for extra repayment = $5220

OPTION 2

If Ben is enjoying the feeling of having his foot firmly established in the residential property market, he could look to diversify elsewhere. He could use the equity within property one and borrow a more conservative amount of $200 000 to invest into a portfolio of ETFs and LICs.

Assuming the dividend return is 5% p.a. after franking credits and tax, this would yield another passive income supply of $10 000 p.a., which gives him a new total passive income of over $30 649 p.a. – plus those franking credits may grow over time, giving him more potential tax breaks in the future.

He has a mortgage investment loan of $200 000. By using his surplus cash flow of $3500 p.m. plus his rental income of $20 649 p.a. and the new dividends income of $10 000 p.a. he could have this loan paid off in less than four years and save another $163 000 in interest along the way (as the dividends are paid every six months, for conservative measures we've assumed a 1-year delay in making these extra monthly contributions, so in fact the interest and time savings may be even more).

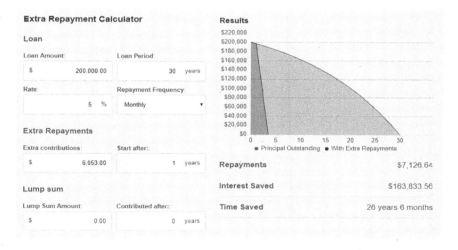

Extra Repayment Calculator			Results	
Loan				
Loan Amount:		Loan Period:		
$	200,000.00	30 years		
Rate:		Repayment Frequency:		
	5 %	Monthly ▼		
Extra Repayments				
Extra contributions:		Start after::	Repayments	$7,126.64
$	6,053.00	1 years		
Lump sum			Interest Saved	$163,833.56
Lump Sum Amount:		Contributed after::	Time Saved	26 years 6 months
$	0.00	0 years		

Extra Monthly Repayment Breakdown for Option 2:
Surplus cash = $3500 p.m. +
Surplus passive rental income = $20 649/12 = $1720
Surplus dividends = $10 000/12 = $833
Total surplus for extra replayment = $6053

As a slight alternative to help balance and diversify Ben's portfolio further so that the spread between property and equities (via the ETFs and LICs) is a little more even, Ben could opt for the dividends from the ETFs and LICs to be automatically reinvested back into the share portfolio for further capital growth and income opportunities. This means he takes a little bit longer (only four months) to pay off the $200 000 loan.

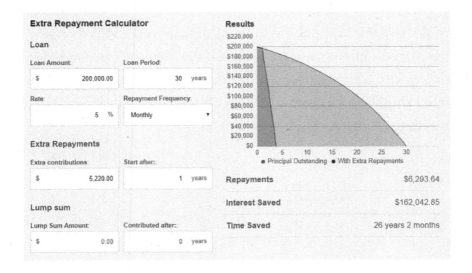

Extra Monthly Repayment Breakdown for Option 2:
Surplus cash = $3500 p.m. +
Surplus passive rental income = $20 649/12 = $1720
Total surplus for extra repayment = $5220

All in all, Ben can realistically achieve his number. And by prioritising his passive income goals before expensive lifestyle goals, such as buying a family home, he is choosing to establish a firm foundation of financial security and independence in his life.

Furthermore, he's now freer financially to go back to building up his superannuation accounts, as this will provide him with some helpful tax savings along the way and enable him to build his wealth at an even more efficient speed.

So as you can see, Ben's number is actually really achievable *and* really flexible. He isn't locked into anything as long as the mortgage repayments are decreasing, and if he decides to delay his travel, he can use what he has built thus far to create more financial freedom in his life.

He has choice, he has freedom and he is back in control of how he wants to live his life, all because of the way he now looks at money with more mindfulness as a range of solutions and opportunities.

CHEAT TIP FROM CC:

Although I own properties as part of my investment portfolio and strategy, I actually much prefer my share portfolio of ETFs and LICs. You can start investing and building a passive income sooner than it takes to save a deposit on a property, plus the dividends tend to increase at a faster rate than rental income does.

Furthermore, the ongoing holding costs of property can really eat into your passive income, reducing your net return. And there may be times when you are in between tenants, leaving your property empty; you may also have special strata levies and costs associated with natural wear and tear on the property, such as needing new paint and carpet, which can make a dent in your net passive income. And finally, you can't really 'reinvest' in an investment property like you can with shares.

However, the benefit of investment properties is that the bank allows you to leverage more when you have the security of property. So instead of using the equity in my properties to buy more property, I can use the equity to buy more shares. This lets me diversify into other two-dimensional asset classes, spreading my passive income sources. I will cover this in Chapter thirteen!

POINTS TO REMEMBER:

- If you want property to be your source of passive income, diversify and look beyond residential property. Different property types pay different income yields. They aren't all the same.
- Research research research! You make most of your money when you buy. Never rush out and buy the first thing that you see. Take your time, this is one of the biggest purchases that you will ever make.
- Factor in the impact of a 3% interest rate rise so that you know you'll still be able to afford the repayments.
- Always make your loans principal and interest – remember, we want to eventually own our passive income sources outright so that they are 100% cashflow-positive passive income.

- Check all outgoings for the property, such as council rates, strata or body corporate fees, landlord insurance and water.
- Check to see how long you could afford to keep the property empty if you have difficulty finding tenants. Consider adding this to your emergency money amount.
- Your loan should be no-frills, basic principal and interest, and at the lowest rate possible. You don't need credit cards or offset accounts with the associated higher interest rates and fees.
- Make extra repayments and lump sum repayments towards the loan as often as you can. The goal is to pay this property off as quickly as possible so that it can start paying you passive income.
- Use our property calculator to see how the cost of holding property impacts your net passive income and compare different properties.
- The more repayments that you can make, the quicker your property will be cash-flow positive and paying itself off via rental income, freeing you up to move on to the next property or other investment opportunity.
- Regularly update your passive income worksheet and track your progress against your number.
- Never let your LVR exceed 80%.
- Mortgage insurance is a waste of money, and you're paying for the bank's protection rather than your own protection. It's better to save more or lower your budget.

CHAPTER TWELVE

Your Money, Your Priorities

'Pay off your toxic debt first. The increased freedom and happiness that you gain once you come out the other side will be one of the most valuable lessons you will ever learn and will give you a new sense of respect and gratitude for what you build going forward.' – Me

If you're starting to feel excited about investing in your financial future and building towards your number, I am so pleased and proud. But before we can get started, we need to ensure that we are building on a solid, concrete foundation and not quicksand. I am talking about debt – the bad kind.

There are two types of debt: healthy debt and toxic debt. When used conservatively and for the right reasons, debt can help build your financial freedom. Then there is debt which is used for the wrong reasons – often for our egos, for instant gratification or to keep up with the Joneses.

But this chapter is not about judging you or berating you for your previous financial decisions, it is about helping you draw a line in the sand and get your debt vanishing quickly and for good, so that you're in greater control and can use your energy and focus for building wealth, which is easier and so much more fun.

I'll start with the most toxic type of debt first, as this is the debt that you need to prioritise. You must then move down the list until you are debt free.

CREDIT CARD DEBTS AND PERSONAL LOANS

This type of debt is a huge financial handicap to building wealth. It can damage your credit rating and limit how much you can borrow, and at what interest rate. This also includes any potential margin loan or investment property loan that you may want to take out one day to help build your financial wealth. And, most obviously, why would you want to waste thousands of dollars in interest when that money could be going towards building your number? For example, that $10 000 in credit card debt at 22% p.a. interest is costing you $2200 p.a. That money could be going towards your number!

Moreover, there are a lot of toxic emotions that come with this type of debt, such as shame, remorse, embarrassment and guilt. So if you're in credit card debt, I'm going to help you get out of it as fast as possible and stay out of debt. You may even end up regarding the credit card debt as a blessing in disguise, as the new habits that you will develop will be incredibly useful in helping you build your number once that horrible debt is paid off and avoid ever repeating history.

Most financial experts, including Google, will tell you that the fastest way to get out of credit card debt is to consolidate it into a personal loan and pay it off through a repayment plan. In theory this works – but in reality it doesn't. I have seen this backfire so many times.

What tends to happen is that people apply for a loan that's something like 0% interest for the first twelve months. Once approved, they roll the debt over, breathe a sign of relief that they have twelve months to pay it off, and go about their business as normal, with the 'I have twelve months to figure that one out' attitude.

Suddenly a year has gone by, and they've made only some – if any at all – inroads into their credit card debt. And now that honeymoon rate is over, and the real rate kicks in, along with panic and anxiety. On top of this, their spending and lifestyle habits have never changed, so they're often in double the debt by now and feeling like they're drowning in their own anxiety. This happens all the time, and the banks know it, which is why they love to advertise (and can afford to) provide these low or zero-interest loans.

This is why I'm hesitant to recommend the quick-fix debt-consolidation strategy of a personal loan. Instead, follow my **Hit-List Strategy**, which has helped thousands of people get out of debt, and let's get you out of debt for good – learning those valuable lessons I spoke about in the first chapter.

To be totally upfront and transparent, I should say that this method may cost you more in interest. From a purely financial basis, paying the debt with the higher interest rate first is technically the fastest and cheapest in theory. But in reality, this isn't always the case. What does work is facing the cold hard truth, taking responsibility of your financial situation, including the pain. This will help prevent you from repeating your bad habits in the future.

So grab your workbook and a pen. We have a hit list to write.

Step 1: Write down, from the smallest debt to the biggest, where you owe money and exactly how much. We're going to 'hit' the smallest debt first as it will be the quickest to get rid of. Importantly, this will give you a sense of progress, which will fuel your motivation to move on to the next and progress down the list until you're completely debt-free. You must review and update your hit list every time you make an extra repayment or finally pay one of the debts off.

Your list may look like this:

Mum – $500
HSBC – $1300
Mastercard – $2300
Virgin – $5800
Amex – $12 500

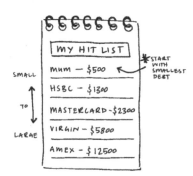

Step 2: Cut up the cards. You are on a credit cleanse and will only spend cash or use your debit card. No ifs, ands or buts; we need to get you out of this debt before it gets any worse.

Step 3: Set up minimum monthly repayment plans for each debt and factor them into your budget, with the money to come out of your Everyday account. Your minimum repayments should cover your interest expense as an absolute minimum, so check with your credit provider when setting this up. This way, at the very least your debt is quarantined and won't escalate further out of control as long as you use cash or your debit card and maintain the minimum payment.

Step 4: Review your budget every day along with your hit list. You're now living on cash, so you need to know how much money you have in your Everyday account and Life + $X Emergency account and check what bills you have coming in against your budget. In particular, look out for those irregular or one-off expenses, cross referenced against your calendar, such as upcoming birthday presents or car rego. You need to prepare in advance for them and not use credit.

Step 5: When the going gets tough, the tough get going. You need to go through your budget and look at what you can reduce or cut out, both temporarily and permanently. For example, if you decide to cancel a monthly membership which was costing $50, start pro-actively putting that $50 per month towards the first debt on your list. Keep doing this with every expense that you can cut back on, and once the first person or institution on the list is paid back in full you immediately move on to the next.

Step 6: Hustle – in order to get this debt paid off faster, you need to look beyond your current financial position and find ways to earn extra money. (Go back and re-read Chapter five!) Every time you make some extra money, immediately transfer that to the debt at the top of your list. No excuses.

Step 7: When you're finally debt free, take a deep breath, pat yourself on the back, cancel the card(s) and never have a credit card again. The danger, temptation and self-destruction just isn't worth it. We want to build wealth, not be constantly chasing our tails – life is too short for that.

Your final step is to use all your new money-making and saving skills to build up your Life + $X Emergency account. I never want you reaching for a card again to get you out of trouble, because that is what your Emergency account is for.

CHEAT TIP FROM CC:

Seriously ask yourself if you really need a credit card. Many people think they need a credit card to have a credit score. However, utility and mobile phone accounts are also a form of credit. Some people think they need a credit card in case of an emergency – but now that you have cash savings, this is no longer applicable to you. Plus you can pay for any online shopping with a debit card anyway. So there really isn't a need for a credit card at all. Unless it works for you and pays itself.

For example, if your credit card costs $300 in annual fees, but it gives you travel insurance which saves you more than $300 p.a. and is linked to your frequent flyer program which saves you even more money, it may be worth it. The benefit should exceed the cost tenfold!

If you really feel the need to have a credit card, ideally make it one only, and particularly one with no fees or competitive fees with a benefit program that suits you. And ideally have it with the same bank as your everyday accounts so that you can view its balance anytime you log on to your internet banking. And keep it out of your wallet, stored away somewhere safe, like with your passport. I even know one person who keeps their credit card in a block of ice in their freezer!

STUDENT HELP DEBT

If you have a HECS/Help debt or a student loan, we need to clear it. Even though this debt may be 'interest-free', it's still indexed, which means that it grows each year, so really it isn't quite interest free.

It's the same as credit card debt: it impacts your ability to borrow, and to get the best interest rate. Furthermore, there's a flow-on effect. The government lent you money to pay for your education so that you could improve your future opportunities and add value to the country and wider world. When you pay back that debt, it means others can benefit from the same helping hand.

And even if you're still a student, start tackling that debt now, rather than waiting until you've graduated. Paying off a $30 000 student loan is a lot easier, cheaper and faster than paying off a $40 000 student loan. I've seen plenty of students who have used these saving and earning techniques to have their entire education debt paid off before graduating.

To find out exactly how much debt you owe, log in to your myGov account or contact the Australian Taxation Office. Keep in mind that compulsory repayments are based on your total income tax level.

CHEAT TIP FROM CC:

I have never met anyone who regretted paying off their student debt. It gives them the same relief and pride that comes with paying off toxic credit card debt. While I understand it might be the last piece of advice that you want to hear from me, it is **good and honest advice**. There's a lot of advice and opinions out there that say to never worry about paying it off because it's the cheapest loan you'll ever get. While that is partly true, having student debt does still impact your future borrowing capacity and sense of responsibility and honour that you're taking on in being more mindful with money. And of course, working on your number.

If you're still hesitant, at the very least make additional repayments as you work in unison with your other financial goals. Working on both at the same time means you can honour your student debt and enjoy the sense of it lightening, while still being excited and motivated to accomplish your other financial goals. Slow option, but a win-win.

LET'S PLAY 'BEAT THE BANK'!

Even though you view your home as an asset, it's more of a lifestyle asset than a financial asset. While it's likely to increase in value, so does everyone else's. So even if you sell it for a much higher price than what you paid for it, you still need to buy somewhere else to live of equal or similar value (unless you are moving in with someone, downsizing or in the business of flipping properties).

Your home doesn't provide you with an income, so other than saving you some money with no more mortgage repayments once the mortgage is paid off, it doesn't offer any financial benefit. And your mortgage is still a form of non-deductible debt, meaning that the cost of the interest is not tax deductible. So you need to be trying to pay it off a lot faster than the bank would like. You can definitely start building your number while having a mortgage (and I'm about to show you how), but it's more efficient to at least reduce your home loan's term.

Ideally you want to get your home loan paid off within twenty years or less, not thirty like the bank prefers to lock you into so that you can borrow more and they make bigger profits (**why I prefer to own the bank rather than owe the bank**). And the first few years are the most effective for saving yourself a huge amount of interest on the loan. So before you jump in to building towards your number, first game-plan your mortgage reduction.

Begin with setting down your mortgage numbers:

- What is your interest rate?
- What is your term (that is, the length of the mortgage – typically twenty-five or thirty years)?
- How far you are into the term?

Once we know these numbers, we can actively work to cut the term down and save you valuable time and interest.

Start by looking to increase your mortgage repayments. Go through your budget and see what savings you can make, and put this money towards your repayments by increasing your automatic repayment amount, either through adjusting your automatic mortgage repayments online (this takes minutes to do) or asking your bank to do this for you over the phone. But it must be set up automatically so that it actually happens, leaving you one less thing to have to remember.

Say for example, you cut out pay TV and limit takeaway dinners to only twice per month. You work out that these measures will save you $100 per month, so you log in to your internet banking and **increase your automatic repayments by $100 p.m.** It is usually approved overnight and you can watch your loan term reduce once this is approved. You can follow the same process for the new money-hustling tricks you've learnt, too – that additional income should also go towards your mortgage.

A small increase of just $300 per month on a thirty-year loan of $400 000 with an average interest rate of 6.5% p.a., commencing three years into the term, can reduce the loan term by over six years and save you more than $116000 in interest! And remember, that's an after-tax saving! Can you imagine having no mortgage repayment six years earlier than you anticipated when you took out the loan? Better still, you can use those six years to focus on building your number sooner.

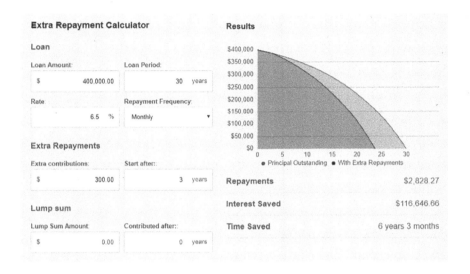

The next step is to make lump-sum repayments whenever you can. This is perfect for when you manage to hustle some extra cash from random jobs, tax returns, bonuses, selling unwanted items and the like.

But every time you make an extra lump-sum repayment or increase your mortgage repayment, **check the term left on your mortgage**. Not only will this feed your motivation to pay off your mortgage faster, but you'll develop greater respect for the impact and benefit of your savings and extra earnings in helping you achieve your goals sooner.

Also, always make sure that even with the extra repayments and lump-sum repayments, your term remains 'as is'. Don't let the bank restart your loan to match your original term. Remember you want to beat the bank!

My rule of thumb is that as soon as you've reduced your mortgage to be paid off 30% or more sooner than the bank had planned, keep your mortgage repayments 'as is', and start working on your number. Though 30% is my rule, you may prefer to wait until your loan term has reduced by half or even more – go with what you feel most financially comfortable with. But keep in mind, don't miss out on losing too much more time to allow compounding interest work its magic for you. This is why I find a 30% reduction in your loan term a healthy balance in leapfrogging your debt reduction period (saving you a large amount of time and interest), while allowing you the freedom to get cracking on building your number.

If your mortgage is due to be paid off in twenty years and you can get the term down to fourteen years or less, that six years of extra time that you've bought yourself can not only be put towards building your number right now, but can also allow you to take advantage of two of the important financial friends you met in Chapter seven: time and compounding interest.

It means that you can get on with building your passive income supply sooner by starting to invest, knowing that your mortgage is now reducing at a faster speed and saving you valuable time and interest. You can feel good knowing that you'll not only eventually own your home outright so much earlier than the average person, but also that you've used the time efficiently to build your financial freedom without the pressure of having to necessarily rely on the option of downsizing your home to free up money.

CHEAT TIPS FROM CC:

You can check the loan term on your mortgage at any time through your internet banking. It takes seconds to find out, and seeing the impact of your small efforts is incredibly motivating.

I do this every time I make an extra repayment on my home loan, however small it might be. Each time you do this, you know you're paying less in interest and having a greater impact on paying down the principal.

Here are another ten hacks for paying off your mortgage faster – you can use all of these, or just pick the ones you like and will work for you. And if you have an honest go at tackling your mortgage, you will be blown away by how much time, energy and money you can save.

1. **Refinance** – keep an eye on what interest rates are around, and consider whether going for a lower option will be worthwhile once any upfront or loan establishment fees are taken into account. Only refinance if the new provider agrees to make your new term the same as where you're up to now, or less. Or if there's a better rate but the new leader has to set the new term at 30% to demonstrate serviceability, once the new loan is set up, go and readjust your automatic repayments back to your original repayments, or even higher, with the new interest savings in place. Set your mortgage repayments the same as what you were previously paying, or even higher if possible. Otherwise

you'll be likely to spend that money elsewhere and take even longer to pay off your home.

2. **Pay your mortgage more often** – most loans default to monthly repayments, because you'll pay less off your home loan, allowing the bank to charge you more interest. Because interest is calculated daily, if you can pay your mortgage repayments weekly or fortnightly, the less your balance will be and the less interest you will pay. So these more frequent repayments will have a greater impact in reducing your principal. Just make sure you factor this change into your cashflow and budget.

3. **Call your bank** – tell them you want a lower interest rate, and reduced or waived fees if applicable to your loan. See what you can negotiate with your existing bank before looking elsewhere, to save on fees associated with changing banks. I've heard of many impressive interest-rate and fee savings that have been granted over the phone by the banks just to keep their customers as their customers. Again, put any savings you create towards the home loan.

4. **Say goodbye to the Rolls-Royce mortgage** – often the loans that come with all the bells and whistles, such as credit cards, offset facilities, overdrafts and special 'private banking' hotline services attract more expensive interest rates, no matter how well they try to package them up. The simplest no-frills loans are the most effective, as they're easy to understand, involve less temptation as they don't come with ridiculous products and services, and almost always have a lower interest rate and often still have free redraw facilities.

5. **Give your mortgage a pay rise** – every time you get a raise, increase your automatic repayment (just watch the term reduce!) by the new after-tax difference. You won't miss the money as you never got to experience it in the first place. And if you get regular pay rises, even if only in line with inflation, this practice can really make a big difference over the long run.

6. **Consider digital lenders** – with new non-bank digital lenders appearing, such as Athena, there are often better mortgage options available if you look beyond the banks, as these providers don't have the same expenses as a bank, so they can pass far better and lower interest rates on to you. Plus they genuinely want you to pay off your home loan as fast as possible. And if there is a special new interest rate promotion, everyone gets it, not just new people signing up, which is a common trick used by the banks with their 'honeymoon' rates only for new customers, and they even have loyalty bonuses.

7. **Pay your mortgage the moment you get paid** – by prioritising your mortgage repayment, you can feel the pressure lift, knowing that you've honoured your biggest expense first. This is less of a money-saving tactic than a psychological one.

8. **Do The $1000 Project** – so many people around the world have used The $1000 Project to not only save the deposit for their home loan but also to help pay it off. This can be a great way to get your home loan term down by 30% or more, so that you can move on to investing in building your number sooner. And you can use The

$1000 Project to set mini goals for tackling your mortgage at any time.

9. **Round up** – if you've exhausted all other options, try simply rounding up your mortgage repayment to the nearest $10, $100 or $1000. Say your mortgage repayment is $1875 per month – change the automatic direct debit to either $1880, $1900 or even $2000 p.m. That way, you're spreading the increase over the month, and you'll likely find that you don't notice the $5, $30 or $130 per month less as it's come out of your bank account before you've had the opportunity or temptation to spend it.

10. **Move out** – if you're really serious about not only getting in control of your finances but also making up for lost time or creating more time for yourself, you could consider moving out of your home for a period of time, renting it out and renting somewhere else which is more cost-effective, or renting with another person or even, if possible, moving back in with your parents. That way someone else is paying some or all of your mortgage for you, allowing you to add extra repayments from the savings created from downsizing. Your interest rate may go up marginally (on average investment loans are 0.5% p.a. more) when your property goes from being deemed as a principal place of residence to technically an investment property now, so you must factor this potential increase in interest, and you must declare the rental income that you receive in your taxable income. But on the other hand, you may be able to claim some interest off your income tax along with some depreciation. Plus if you don't buy another principal place

YOUR MONEY, YOUR PRIORITIES | 261

of residence during that period, you may be allowed to keep your tax-free status on the capital growth of the property for up to six years.

To have a play around with different options and see how extra repayments and lump-sum repayments can save you tens of thousands of dollars in interest plus a huge amount of time, head to SugarMamma.TV and see what you can do to your mortgage!

DEBT-FREE OR MORTGAGE REDUCING RAPIDLY?

If you're in the very fortunate position of not having a mortgage or your mortgage is now on track to be paid off quickly, there are two different strategies that you can use to build your number.

STRATEGY 1: SLOW AND STEADY

The first strategy is to build up savings in your financial goal account and then start investing in line with your asset allocation ratio. Invest on a regular basis as much as your budget can afford. This is a simple regular investment strategy to follow without taking on too much risk or costing you a lot of time or energy.

Every time you buy a new investment that produces an income and capital growth, update your gross passive income worksheet and net wealth worksheet, always tracking your progress against your number.

While this investing strategy may be slower, it's the more conservative approach. Here's an example of building up a passive income of $40 000 p.a. in today's dollars (which will be worth

$84 000 p.a. in thirty years' time) by slowly but regularly investing over a thirty-year period.

We start with $10 000 as an initial investment, and invest $1500 per month, with a buy-and-hold strategy of either a growth or high-growth index ETF or a blend of sector-specific ETFs and LICs (because we have the benefit of time, allowing more diversified risk without the stress of having to research and choose which companies to buy). By the end of the thirty-year period, the portfolio is worth just over $2 100 000, assuming an average net growth rate of 7.5% p.a. with all income reinvested and a buy-and-hold approach, so no eroding capital gain tax or missed dividends are ever an issue.[6]

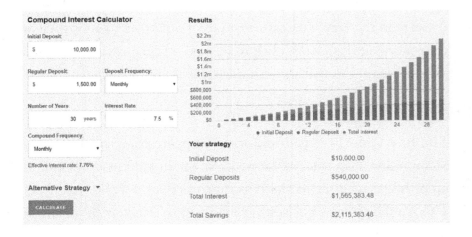

At the end of the thirty-year period, assuming a passive income of 4% p.a., we would have a growing income of $84 000 p.a. ($2 115 000 × 4%).

---

6   Tax will need to be paid on the passive income and should be monitored and accounted for in the cashflow and budgeting. However, if you have included those valuable industrial shares that come with franked dividends, this will help minimise any additional income tax bills.

And if you think this wouldn't be enough, don't forget we still have the superannuation accounts to top up this passive income for even more freedom, which we will be covering in the next chapter.

To get an idea of what you can do, jump on the regular investment calculator on my SugarMamma.TV website and check out the power of regular investing and how it all pays off.

Strategy 2: Financially Fast

If you have a comfortable cash flow, with the mortgage either paid off in full or now heading towards being paid off 30% sooner, and you have a generous amount of equity in your home, you could look at investing a larger lump sum up front – essentially going hard and fast.

It's important not to overextend yourself here, but if you have more than 50% equity in your home – for example, a $400 000 home with a mortgage of $200 000 or less – the bank may lend you money through a separate investment loan, which you can then draw down and invest.

This is called debt recycling, and it means you continue paying your mortgage as you're currently doing, while you open a new investment loan secured against the house. The investment loan is on an interest-only basis and typically has a slightly higher interest rate, (usually 0.5%) but it's still not as high as a margin loan.

You then use the money to make a larger lump-sum investment, and service the new investment loan while also maintaining your mortgage.

The lump sum can be invested as you wish, in either shares or property or even a combination of the both for further diversification. But you must ensure that, firstly, you don't borrow too much. You need to ensure that even with a 3% interest rate rise, you can afford to service the new investment loan and you can afford to continue reducing your existing home loan without too much stress or changes to your lifestyle. (Refer back to my strict margin loan rules on pages 208–9!)

If not, either look to reduce the amount of the investment loan or hold off on this strategy until you have a more relaxed budget or have made further inroads with your mortgage. Borrowing to invest involves a lot more risk, so don't rush in until you are 100% ready.

The effect and results of both strategies – sexy slow and financially fast – are quite similar.

Let's go back to Kim and Paul Howard from Chapter two and their number of $55 000 in today's dollars, which they work out will be the equivalent of approximately $71 000 p.a. in ten years' time using the SugarMamma inflation calculator.

They have a mortgage which is safely and efficiently reducing, with fifteen years left on it. They shift their $20 000 emergency money from the separate savings account where it was earning 3% p.a. and fully taxable (giving them approximately $400 p.a. in interest after tax each year), to their home loan as a lump-sum repayment, but ensuring that the redraw facility is switched on, so they can still access it at any time.

Doing this means they are paying interest on their home loan based at $480 000 rather than $500 000 and potentially saves them up to $21 000 in interest (remembering that this is after tax savings) and almost five months off their home loan. Obviously also assuming that if they ever use some of the emergency money, they always replace it shortly after.

They check their budget and after making a few adjustments, they agree to take out a separate interest-only investment loan of $300 000 secured against their home. They know that even with a 3% interest rate rise, impacting both their mortgage and their new investment loan, they could still afford to service both loans without putting the family under financial pressure. They also agree to each contribute $1000 per month as their mini goals towards the new investment portfolio, with Kim receiving a well-overdue pay rise recently and Paul getting a new job with a better salary. They also agree to sell their old shares, worth a combined value of $17 000 (assuming any capital gains tax is accounted for out of their cashflow in selling their old shares to pay off their home loan), and put the proceeds towards the new portfolio where they can be properly invested, diversified and actually work for them now.

They invest the total funds of $317 000 into a blend of LICs and international ETFs, and set all the dividends to be reinvested. They immediately update their gross passive income workbook, as well as their superannuation passive income workbook and their net wealth workbook, and can see the headway they're already making. They only need to update this once every six months, when dividends are reinvested; they can see how much those dividends have grown and how much they're progressing towards their number. They also keep a close eye on any additional income tax payable as their passive income grows. Kim and David are proactive and have an additional tax savings account so that any tax can be quickly paid. But they also have valuable franked dividends helping keep that income tax manageable.

They also never take their eyes off their super, even though they aren't adding anything to it quite yet. They're focusing on building a passive income stream that they can access as a priority, but they know they'll come back to topping up their super shortly. They still follow the steps recommended in the next chapter, so at least in the meantime they know their super is finally invested properly, in a cost effective account and cost effective investment portfolio for their long-term financial goals.

Kim and Paul sit on the investment loan for five years, not adding any new money to the portfolio other than their $1000 per month each, with all other extra money being used to help pay off even more of their home loan; they can see it reducing faster than ever, helped along with a couple of tax refunds, bonuses, pay rises and promotions along the way.

After five years they increase their investment loan by $300 000 and invest this money with their existing investment portfolio, and continue to leave everything to reinvest. Assuming a net average return of 7.5% p.a., ten years in, they should have a $1 600 000 investment portfolio and a passive income of just over $66 000, with an investment loan of only $600 000 in comparison.

By then their mortgage, which had fifteen years to go when they began investing in shares, has actually been paid off within ten years by picking up some great saving and earning tips and applying the various hacks mentioned earlier. With only the $600 000 investment loan left to worry about, they start paying this off with the money and cash flow habits they were previously using to pay off their home loan. They switch off the dividend reinvestment plan (if they want to) and use this money to also help pay off the $600 000 investment loan. In the meantime, they are still watching their passive income grow.

Now they can take their foot off the accelerator, knowing that they've done all the hard work and can let time and compounding interest do the rest for them. They can think about taking those family holidays and cutting down their working hours.

Another option for Kim and Paul, if they wanted to travel earlier, would be to pack up and rent out their family home, use the rental money and head overseas with the children for a sabbatical. The rent money could cover their living expenses and the $66 000 p.a. dividends could actually now be paid towards servicing and reducing the $600 000 investment loan while they have the adventure of their lives.

All in all, Kim and Paul have used their lifestyle asset of a family home strategically to diversify their wealth and build an investment portfolio that pays them a passive income stream, all contributing towards their financial health. And just like Ben, they still have their superannuation accounts that they can also look at including as part of their wealth accumulation strategy now that their home is paid off (yay!). While their super isn't necessarily accessible until they meet preservation age (age sixty for them) they can still utilise this asset-holding environment for further investment opportunities, particularly in view of the tax savings now and prioritising the financial goals that match their values.

Most of all, they have the comfort and security of knowing they have a growing asset apart from the family home – and it's also paying them a great passive income along the way.

POINTS TO REMEMBER:

- If you're in debt, as in toxic debt, make a decision that from this point on you will work as hard as you can to pay that debt off completely and never get into debt again.
- Once your debt is paid off, build your emergency savings so that you never need to rely on a credit card or personal loan again.
- Use your debt-reduction strategies and cash-flow routines to build savings and then start investing the moment you get out of debt.
- Check the details of your loans, the interest rate that you're paying, the term of the loan and how much longer you have left

to pay it off, then try to cut that time down as much as possible. Make it a fun game. Beat the bank!

- Know your mortgage numbers – interest rate, remaining term and regular repayments – if you don't know this, how do you know if you are being ripped off or not?
- No extra repayment or lump sum is too small. Every dollar counts, saving you valuable time and interest.
- Watch out for the bank trying to restart your mortgage to the original (usually thirty-year) term.
- If you refinance, your loan term must be the same, or your repayments must be the same or more.
- If looking to refinance, consider the new digital loan providers that offer the same rates to existing and new customers . . . no more loyalty tax!
- Check for any new application fees as well as any exit fees on your current loan before making any final decisions.
- When your mortgage looks as if it's reducing at a significant speed (30% sooner is my minimum rule of thumb), look to start building your number so that you can make the most of time and let compounding interest work its magic.
- Check any additional tax that may be payable on your passive income, especially as it grows, and make sure you account for it in your budget. Working with a good accountant and even having a bit extra set aside in a separate 'income tax saving account' will help you stay on top of your tax responsibilities.
- Always check any triggers of capital gains tax (or even crystallising losses) before making any financial decisions.
- Remember those franking credits from Australian industrial shares can help keep any income tax a little more manageable.

CHAPTER THIRTEEN

Secret Success & Protection Power

'*You will never win if you never begin.*' – Helen Rowland, American journalist

Even if you aren't ready to invest – not because you don't want to, but perhaps because you're paying off debt in preparation to invest or because you're focusing on a shorter-term goal such as saving for a deposit – you can still keep working on building **your number**.

This involves sorting out your superannuation or your country's equivalent retirement savings plan. So you need to follow this chapter and its instructions and checklist as a matter of importance. Whether you're starting to invest, paying down debt or saving for a deposit, get your retirement plans sorted now so that it's done and out of the way.

Once your super is ticking along correctly, you won't really need to worry about it again other than watching it grow and adding to it when you can, so any time invested now will be well worth it. It will save you a huge amount of time and energy and even money further down the track. So don't delay.

Note that the advice I'll be giving in this chapter pertains to Australian structures and laws around superannuation – almost every developed country requires its citizens to save for retirement in some compulsory form, but there will be differences around taxation, access and other details. However, even if you reside in a country outside of Australia, you may find a lot of the general advice we'll be discussing helpful for you.

FIRSTLY, WHAT IS SUPER?

Most people will automatically reply that superannuation is your retirement 'savings'. But really it can be seen as your investment portfolio, which is capped at a maximum tax rate of 15% p.a. and wisely locked away by the government for your long-term benefit so that after retirement you can financially support yourself to the best of your ability. The government has removed temptation from the equation, in that you cannot access your super until a certain age or special condition; it's all too evident that many of us could blow it and then be reliant on measly government pensions, living below the poverty line, for the rest of our lives, which is not an outcome you, I or the government want.

And you may not realise this, but your superannuation is already invested. Yes, you actually already own shares; it's just that you hold them through the investment fund with your super and possibly don't see much of what's happening with them. They might be held in the default balanced fund, a high-growth fund, or one of the other types you now know about from reading Chapter nine.

When I ask people where their super is invested, they often answer 'Host Plus' or 'AMP' or 'Rest'. That's not where the money is invested, it's identifying the superannuation account provider. Think of the superannuation account provider as a handbag, or perhaps a grocery basket. Asking where it's invested is like asking what is *inside* the basket. That is, the investment isn't the basket itself; it's what's within the basket that is most interesting.

SUPERANNUATION

We need to know where your superannuation money is invested because we need to make sure that:

- it is invested in line with your long-term financial goals
- it's cost effective and competitively priced without jeopardising quality
- the investments aren't triggering capital gains tax all the time
- it's diversified – helping reduce your investment risk.

These four key factors will dramatically impact the opportunities at which your superannuation portfolio can grow – and remember:

the more money you have in superannuation, the more comfortable your retirement will be. This is because superannuation is one of your biggest sources of passive income, significantly contributing towards your number, with the added bonus of the government forcing your employer to contribute to it, on your behalf. Therefore, it needs to be part of your overall strategy. We should be grateful for having such a stringent policy in our country.

First of all, having the right superannuation account is paramount. It needs to:

- be cost-effective, with low fees
- be consolidated into the one main account with active regular contributions
- have a good range of quality investment options, including shares, ETFs and LICs – where you can customise your asset allocation if you want to, for example 30% or 60% Australian.
- be able to attach personal insurance – we'll see more about this later in the chapter
- offer in-specie transfer service – I will explain this shortly but this is seriously important!

COST-EFFECTIVE

Superannuation accounts are not free; they have fees and charges and you need to know what they are, how they are calculated and how much they add up to as they're deducted from your account balance.

Generally speaking, a super account with low fees will help build your super faster if it invests in the same assets. And despite certain commercials aired on TV by industry superannuation providers, which rubbish retail superannuation accounts, the retail super-annuation account market has actually become increasingly competitive, with more focus on fee reduction without jeopardising quality.

I'll share with you some superannuation accounts that I like; first, though, have a look at the different types of fees that super accounts charge, which can be dollar-based or percentage-based.

- **Administration fees** cover the cost of operating the super account – such as organising the taxes and investing, creating statements, taking your phone calls, providing online access to your account and so on.

- **Investment fees** are charged for managing your investment, which can vary for different investment options such as default funds, shares, index ETFs and other managed funds within the account.

- **Indirect costs** are paid by your super fund to external providers that affect the value of your investment – typically investment managers.

- **Advice fees** are only charged if you employ the services of an adviser.

- **Switching fees** are charged for changing your investment option within the fund. This isn't a big issue, as once you've set this up correctly it should be set up for life and you won't need to pay it again.

- **Buy/sell spread fees** may be paid every time you make a transaction, including making a contribution, switching and withdrawing. The fee covers some or all of the cost of transactions entered by the fund.

- **Insurance premiums** are the cost of any insurance that you have in force and own through your super.

- **Activity-based fees** are only charged if your super fund provides you with a particular service, such as a family law split fee, where they charge you a fee to split your super in the event of a separation and family law court order.

As you can see, there are lots of different types of fees. Although it might appear complicated, something to be aware of is that a 1% difference in fees could result in a 20% difference in your account balance over thirty years. So while a lot of these fees are not avoidable, you need to know the impact on your investment portfolio within super.

My general rule of thumb is that your super fees should not exceed 0.80% p.a. excluding the cost of financial advice. This limits the deterioration of your account balance while still allowing you to access a quality account with a reputable provider and having an intelligent investment selection available to choose from.

INVESTMENT OPTIONS

My pet hate is coming across a superannuation provider who claims to be the cheapest; this is quite possibly true, but it's inevitably at a great expense to quality. These accounts just have the generic five pre-mixed conservative, balanced, growth and high growth options, and that's it. What happens if you want an index fund or ETF? What happens if you don't agree with the fund manager who runs these pre-mixed portfolios? What if you want your superannuation money invested entirely in Australian shares? Or in a fixed interest investment?

My second pet hate is coming across a superannuation provider whose fees are cheap, but the fees they charge on the underlying investments are actually quite expensive. Or even worse, expensive and poor-quality investments. Or portfolios that are run by fund managers that jump in and out of investments, regularly triggering capital gains taxes, which may end up costing you more money in the long run.

This is where quality is sometimes worth paying for. Let me explain the requirements I have for my superannuation account when it comes to investment options:

- **Direct equities**, so that if there's a particular company that I want to invest in, I can; this includes LICs.
- **Index ETF style** (buy and hold the general market so as to remain diversified but avoid triggering frequent capital gains tax) as the ongoing fees are a fraction of the cost of the pre-mixed portfolio but still have index-style ETF pre-mixed portfolios as well as sector-specific index ETFs such as Australian shares, emerging markets, Asia or even ethical investments.

That way I can create my portfolio in a cost-effective way that doesn't churn the portfolio and trigger a capital gains tax from jumping in and out of stocks. I can decide if I want a different asset allocation to the risk profile guides, such as 50% Australian shares and 50% international shares. The main thing is that I have control.

FRANKING CREDITS

In Chapter eight, we talked about franking credits. This is where your dividends have already had up to 30% tax paid on them, and you get a credit for that. As income tax within superannuation is

15%, this means if you invest in fully franked Australian shares (i.e. industrial stocks or LICs), your superannuation may get a handsome refund because you have overpaid the tax on this by 15%. This can really boost your passive income and is even more valuable in retirement when the tax rate drops to 0% p.a. and the full 30% tax may be refunded back to you.

However, as previously mentioned, this may be up for debate again in the future, so never rely on it completely, but view it as a helpful bonus while it remains.

INSURANCE

There are four important types of insurance that everyone should have, and three of these can be owned and paid for via your superannuation account. As well as being convenient, this is often the most cost-effective way of achieving this cover, as your superannuation provider may have access to group discounts. But you need to be careful – the premiums for these insurances come directly out of your super, so it does impact your super account balance. Don't go and take out large amounts of expensive cover thinking 'It's fine, my super pays for it', because *you* actually pay for it, with your balance reducing as it funds these policies. So insure what you need and can afford; nothing more, nothing less.

Also, insurance in your super is not transferrable. So if you were to close your account and roll the funds over, this cover will automatically be cancelled and you could be left uninsured and exposed. I always recommend finding the right super first, then applying for cover. Once it's accepted and you have in writing from the superannuation or insurance company that it is now in force, you can then roll across old superannuation account balances.

Let's look at the three types of insurance that can be owned and paid for in super.

INCOME PROTECTION

One of the most important insurances to have, income protection pays you up to 75% of your salary if you are unable to work due to medical conditions, whether sickness or injury.

Income protection can be paid for via super, and I recommend that you always be covered up to age sixty-five as a minimum. That way, if you ever need to claim and are unable to return to work, the policy will continue to pay you until this age. At sixty-five your superannuation money becomes accessible, which you can then live on. Some income protection policies offer the option to include covering your superannuation contributions while you're on claim. If this is available, tick yes on that application form! And some income protection policies allow you to cover yourself up to age seventy, which may be wise.

Your superannuation balance can really suffer when there are no new monies going in; especially if you are on claim for an extended period of time. When that precious retirement date comes up, your superannuation could be worth barely anything at a time when you need it the most. So take out the super benefit if it is available.

The other key component of income protection is the waiting period, which you can choose. You need to work out how long you can afford to go without an income before running into financial stress. Most people can only last a maximum of three weeks before they start using credit cards and borrowing money to survive. But the shorter your waiting period, the more expensive your premium is.

I recommend making sure you get that Life + $X Emergency account built up as soon as possible, and see how much sick leave you have saved up as well. If you have been with your employer a long time and rarely take a sick day, you may find that you have a month or more worth of sick leave accumulated (along with some annual leave and even long service leave). So you may be able to stretch your waiting period from thirty days to sixty days or even ninety days. This can reduce your premiums by up to 25% p.a.

Again, call your superannuation provider and get some quotes with different waiting periods, **but always insure yourself up to age sixty-five as a minimum**. Ask yourself how you would cope without your income and how long you could survive? And then pick the one that you see as offering best value for money and the best level of protection for you.

LIFE COVER

This pays out a lump sum (the amount you are insured for) to your nominated beneficiary if you were to die. It's designed to help leave your loved ones without any unnecessary financial stress as a result of you not being there to financially support them any longer.

How much to insure yourself for is a very personal question and one that you should think about and get professional advice on. But as a very rough guide, if you have liabilities and loved ones such as a partner and children, you owe it to them to protect their financial wellbeing by covering yourself with enough insurance to wipe out all debts, such as credit cards, car loans and even mortgages. That way, the remaining partner is left with no major financial liabilities and can focus on the children. If your partner makes less money than you through employment and wouldn't be able to afford to take care of the family living expenses, even with the loans paid out, consider an additional lump sum that can be drawn down and used over time, or invested to provide a passive income that can cover or at least partly cover the ongoing family living expenses.

For example, if Paul Howard was to pass away, Kim knows that even with their mortgage and investment loan paid off she wouldn't be able to cover the school fees and basic family running costs, let alone holidays; all this costs approximately $60 000 per annum.

So Paul should consider an amount that would cover not just paying out their mortgage but also include a lump sum of say $600 000, which could be used by Kim to help pay for the living expenses for up to ten years, by which time their youngest child would be out of school. Or if they wanted, they could increase this additional lump-sum cover to something like $1 200 000, where it could be invested in a passive income stream, at say 5%, giving Kim an ongoing income stream of $60 000 p.a. which along with her own employment income could cover the family living expenses.

There's no right or wrong level of cover, but I recommend getting a range of different quotes and searching out value for money. Ask your partner what they want covered and, of course, always check what you can afford.

TPD COVER

Total and permanent disablement cover pays you a lump sum if you are seriously injured to the point that it's highly unlikely you will ever be able to return to work or be able to live without help from a carer. It is designed to help keep you financially independent.

Again, there is no right or wrong level of cover, but regardless of whether you have a large liability or not, I recommend having enough cover to not only pay out any debts but also to provide you with enough money to pay for a home in cash. This might sound extreme and excessive, but if you're young and you seriously injure yourself and can never work again, you'll struggle to find a bank that will lend you the money, especially if you have no pension or passive income to service and pay off a loan. And if buying a home is one of your dreams, I recommend locking it in so that even in this worst-case scenario that dream can still become a reality.

Using Ben as an example, he would be wise to not only choose enough TPD cover to pay out his investment property loan and any other investment loan, but to also allow him enough money to buy outright a home for himself. That way, if something serious happened to him, he would remain financially independent, and he would have the stability and security of owning a home that he owned in full (after paying for it with the insurance money). And since the home was owned outright, with minimal drain on his cash flow other than the outgoing expenses of holding his home, Ben would have an immediate cash-flow-positive income source from his other property or investments which are still rented out or paying him a dividend income to help cover his cost of living and help budget the 25% shortfall from the income protection policy.

CHEAT TIP FROM CC:

I have covered my mortgage and most of my investment loans with my life and TPD insurance. This policy is owned and paid for via my super so that I can focus my cash flow on paying off my mortgage. But I sleep well at night knowing that if anything should happen to me, Rocco, Tom and baby number two would be in a home that is owned outright, they'd have enough passive income to pay for full-time care through a housekeeper and there'd still be enough money to cover school fees. Tom has his own career, so he'd be able to take care of the bulk of the family living expenses with this major stress out of the way. I've never reduced this cover, and the peace of mind it gives me is well worth it.

TRAUMA COVER

Trauma cover cannot actually be owned and paid for in super. But it's equally important, and I would say the most important personal insurance second to income protection. This is because it pays out a lump sum tax free if you suffer a major medical trauma such as cancer, heart attack or stroke, etc. The money can be used at your own discretion, but the cover is designed to help pay for any medical expenses and adjustments to your home or lifestyle, reduce any financial debts and stresses, and even ensure that you can continue to achieve your financial goals and dreams.

Also, with some major medical traumas, you may not necessarily be away from work. A lot of people suffering from cancer or recovering from a stroke or heart attack can still work, and may even prefer to. Yet they still may have expensive medical bills or big lifestyle changes or recovery/rehabilitation costs.

There is no right or wrong level of cover – it's about what is right for you and what you can afford. Especially as the cost of this premium needs to come out of your cash flow and be factored into your budget.

As a starting point, if you don't know what you want to cover or how much is right for you, I suggest covering three times your annual salary if you don't have a mortgage or any debts. Look at the premium in your budget and adjust it up or down as you need. This means in the event of a seriously medically traumatic event, three years' worth of salary tax-free can be put towards building your number or one of your major financial goals.

If you have a mortgage, I would suggest cover to pay this out in in full if you can. If the quote comes back as affordable, look at what other opportunities you can protect. If it's expensive, adjust it down until it's manageable.

When it comes to personal insurance, it's better to have something in place than nothing at all. And the moment something goes wrong – you don't feel well, or an ambulance is called – it's too late to apply for cover. So prioritise taking out these four insurance policies, with the level of cover that you can afford that protects your financial wellbeing to the best of your ability. And over time, increase them if and when you need to. If you never claim, that's a good thing, so insurance is never a waste of money. And as your debts come down and your passive income grows, you can look to reduce that cover to help save more money in the premiums.

CHEAT TIP FROM CC:

I have trauma cover, and I've insured approximately 60% of my mortgage. This level means that the premiums are sustainable within my budget; if anything were to happen to me from a medical trauma perspective, knocking 60% off my home loan would be a huge help, as the remaining 40% could be knocked off quickly afterwards with my income protection policy that would kick in after my ninety-day waiting period.

IN-SPECIE TRANSFERS WITHOUT TRIGGERING
CAPITAL GAINS – YOUR BIG AWARENESS

This is a big one that a lot of financial experts miss, to my surprise, but you must be aware of it and its impact on your superannuation investment portfolio.

An in-specie transfer means to transfer the ownership of an asset from one person to another in its current form, without a change in the actual beneficial owner, e.g. one's super accumulation account to their own super pension account, avoiding the need to physically sell it down as cash before transferring. Because no physical sell-down has occurred, no capital gains tax has been triggered, your assets have remained in the market (not missing out on any potential passive income) and not incurring any selling and buying expenses such as brokerage.

When it comes to super, let's say you've spent forty years or so of your working life contributing to it and ensuring that your funds are invested for the best long-term capital growth and income opportunities through low to minimal turnover index ETFs and LICs. This long-term buy-and-hold approach works well. Cleverly and legally limiting capital gains tax along the way and only paying the 15% income tax on the passive income within your super, which you may have gotten down even further with franking credits!

So up until this point, you have never actually paid any capital gains tax on any of your own disposals because you have always diligently bought and held and rarely or never sold.

As you approach your retirement, you want to commence an account-based pension, which is where your superannuation money gets shifted to a new style of account and starts paying you money on a regular basis so that you can live off it while enjoying the fruits of your hard work. This means triggering a sell-down in order to carry out this shift from your super account to your pension account. And this sell-down means triggering the capital gains created over the last forty years or so. If you've done a good job with your super and contributions along the way, this tax bill for over forty years' worth of growth could be fairly substantial. While capital gains tax within super is only 10% for assets held for longer than twelve months, if you have say $1 000 000 worth of capital gains being triggered (which isn't unfathomable over a forty-year period), you're going to have to pay $100 000 in tax and that is assuming the 10% capital gains tax after the twelve-month discount.

Ouch.

However, some superannuation accounts offer an in-specie service where the transfer also doesn't trigger a capital gain, and where they are able to undertake this shift of your superannuation assets from your normal superannuation account to your new pension account without any sell-down. This means you don't have to trigger any gains, you don't have to pay any brokerage, you don't have to risk missing out on any dividends, and you certainly don't have to pay $100 000 in capital gains tax to the government.

And as you know with life expectancy, retirement can be a journey of twenty or thirty years, so you still need to have your assets invested for the long run, including those two-dimensional growth assets that have helped ensure you a great retirement.

Once the funds are in the allocated pension account, it becomes tax-free from a capital gains and income perspective, and there are maximum limits as to how much you can have in your pension account (currently $1.6 million per person). But if you need to sell down some of your portfolio, say for instance to create that two-year income strategy with cash, you can now safely do it in the pension account where no capital gains tax will apply.

This little bit of knowledge could save you tens of thousands of dollars in tax, if not hundreds of thousands of dollars.

Okay – here are my four favourite superannuation account providers that match my requirement list. That is to say, they all offer competitive fees, some of which are capped at certain account balances; they also offer both pre-mix diversified ETFs, index ETFs and sector-based ETFs, direct equities – including the very important LICs – quality insurance providers and in-specie transfers. I recommend looking at each of their websites and deciding which one suits you the best. But it's important to keep in mind that the superannuation account market has become incredibly competitive. Product providers have been really lifting their game, continuously increasing the quality of their products and service offerings while also reducing fees, so it's even more important now to research the market yourself rather than simply picking from the list below, as there may be a better option out there for you.

- Asgard Infinity Super – I am in this one
- BT Open Super
- Q Super
- CBus – only the self-managed option

TIME TO SHINE

Once you have worked out where you want to invest your superannuation money, you must follow these steps.

1. **Open account online** – completing all necessary details.
2. **Select your investment options** – try to stick with index ETFs and LICs.

3. **Apply for insurance** – all three types.

4. **Give your employer your new account details**.

5. **Wait for your insurance to be accepted** – it must be in writing that your new cover is in force.

6. **Transfer forms** – from your other superannuation accounts to your new superannuation company – you can do this as soon as your new insurance is in force.

7. **Check for those old funds** – make sure they've been rolled across and your employer is contributing correctly. Update those workbooks with your consolidated super account balance and estimated passive income.

CONTRIBUTE

Now that most of the groundwork for your super account is done, and it's correctly set up for your long-term success, you can take a moment to enjoy feeling organised about this major asset.

Your super is now neatly consolidated into the one account, your insurances are at the right levels for you and within your budget, and the money already in there – along with all new contributions – are invested for long-term growth and income opportunities. Perfect! Now on to the next step.

We need to include this asset as part of your overall strategy in building your number.

Even though you cannot access your super until you reach preservation age, which varies depending on when you were born but is generally between age fifty-five and sixty, it's still a hugely important asset and one that is really effective for building wealth.

So many people look to avoid paying tax, pushing the envelope and sometimes not doing the right thing. However, one of the biggest tax savings is right under all of our noses – many people just don't realise it.

Any income earned within super is taxed at a maximum tax rate of 15%. Considering the average tax rate that most people sit on is around 37%, using super to build your wealth may potentially reduce your tax bill by 22% p.a.!

Obviously the downside of this is that once you put money in, you can't get it out again. However, this can be a real blessing in disguise, as it forces you to let time and compounding interest do its thing and work for you.

I'm not recommending that you stash all your money in your super, but if you can, start contributing a little extra each year. It will generate amazing interest, as the super environment allows you to build your wealth far more efficiently even with the tax savings alone.

There are two simple paths to consider when it comes to contributing extra to super. The first is paying money out of your savings account that you have already paid tax on. The second is a pre-tax option, through salary sacrificing, where you forgo some of your pay, before being charged tax on it, and have it placed in your super account instead, on top of the standard 9.5% p.a. that your employer pays. This can be a great way to save on income tax, but ask your payroll to go through a few different scenarios with you and check against your budget to ensure you can afford it.

If you're self-employed, the same two options exist for you, with a twist to the second pre-tax option: your business can claim a tax deduction for your contribution that goes into super with the pre-tax money.

The maximum that you can contribute to super each financial year is $100 000 p.a., or up to $300 000 with no further contributions for three years if eligible for the post-tax contribution. As for the pre-tax contributions, regardless of whether you're an employee or self-employed, the maximum allowed per financial year is $25 000, including amounts your employer pays.

Pre-tax contributions are taxed at 15% upon entry. It's kind of like an admission fee into a trendy nightclub – annoying, I know, but once you're in there, it's pretty cool. As you get to dance all night to your favourite tunes and watch your super investment portfolio grow, you'll feel quite empowered.

Coming back to your number – if you're looking to build your number in such a way that you can have access to those funds before you can access your super, you'll need to focus your energy on your gross passive income as a priority, and then come back to your super. It wouldn't be great if you spent fifteen years beefing up your super with a small fortune and growing impressive passive income only to be able to watch it through a glass window but not be able to touch it for another ten years while you're stuck with your financial freedom delayed. (#torture!)

I am definitely not saying 'forget about your super' if you're young, far from it. But we need to have a balanced approach with an initially greater weight towards building your access-ible passive income even while we also build your superannuation passive income. That way, you can either have a great big pay rise in passive income when your superannuation becomes accessible, or if your accessible passive income is starting to erode (as part of your strategy), you can shift your required passive income source to super, which in the meantime has also been bubbling away for your eventual use.

First of all, ask yourself how much passive income you want from your super. This may be on top of the passive income that you're working on building, or it may be part of your big picture.

If you're starting out later in life, with no other real financial asset behind you, it may even be worth making your number be completely focused on your superannuation passive income. You will be able to access it within the next ten to fifteen years, and the tax savings alone mean it's actually a far more efficient structure to build your wealth in than starting from scratch with an investment portfolio and personal tax rates on the passive income that you build.

For example, let's say you're fifty right now. Your number is $80 000 p.a. in today's dollars, and you want to start drawing on this in fifteen years' time when you reach sixty-five. We need to firstly factor in inflation, which at 2.5% p.a. is $116 000 (using the SugarMamma.TV inflation calculator). This means that between now and fifteen years in the future you have to build a passive income, working from what you already have in super, so that by the time you reach sixty-five it will be paying you a passive income of $116 000 p.a.

To work out how much you need in super to achieve this, head to SugarMamma.TV and use the Super Sweet Spot Calculator (like the Sweet Spot Calculator, but for superannuation). This will give you a few different numbers to work with and a few different outcomes to pick from. You can have your funds last fifteen years, twenty years, thirty years, or even growing indefinitely.

You can then use the SugarMamma Super Savings Calculator to see what you can do to help bulk up your super sooner. Again come back to Chapters five and six to see what tricks you can do to build up the passive income within your super, through making additional contributions via salary sacrificing and setting up a regular investment with your after-tax money. The quicker you get onto this the easier it will be, because you have more time to have compounding interest working for you.

POINTS TO REMEMBER:

- Make sure your super is good value for money without jeopardising quality.
- Ideally go with index ETFs and LICs for a cost-effective, diversified investment portfolio within super that is also tax effective. Remember, they don't trigger as much capital gains tax along the way, which erodes your money.
- Consider your long-term financial goals when it comes to selecting your investments portfolio for super.
- **Make sure your super has an in-specie service.**
- Take out the right levels of personal insurance through your super that are within your budget – and remember the premiums impact your account balance.
- Make sure your income protection policy covers you to age sixty-five at a minimum.
- Take out trauma cover separately; even if you can only afford $100 000 worth of cover, it's better than nothing at all.
- Check every three months that your employer is paying your 9.5% Superannuation Guarantee contributions and on time. If not, alert them immediately. This literally only takes a few minutes to log into your superannuation account. Some providers even have apps to allow quick access.
- Update your workbook every six months so that you can see your progress towards your number.

Chapter Fourteen

What About the Kids?

'The only wealth in this world is children, more than all the money, power on earth.' – Mario Puzo, American author

As I hope you've now begun to realise from reading this book, financial security is one of the essential pillars to our overall wellbeing. Teaching kids good habits from a young age will give them lifelong skills that will serve them well in their adulthood and most likely be passed on to your grandchildren and great-grandchildren.

Helping your children get ahead financially is as important as teaching them good manners, and good manners like being mindful with money go a really long way and can take you to exciting places. (Who doesn't like a polite person?)

It definitely takes time and patience, but if you can do it the right way, **the gift you give them will change their future more than any lump sum of money will.**

I firmly believe spending time with children is far more important than spending money on children. Leading by example, by powerfully imprinting, even if that means showing them your own changing, improving and strengthening ways as your own financial knowledge and money mindfulness flourish, is the first place to start.

If you think about how financial stress impacts your life or others' lives, ask yourself: would you want your child to feel the same anxiety, stress and pressure about money that you do? This is your opportunity to get in early and help have this important area of their life sorted, so that they can move on and focus on other important aspects such as the value they can add to this world, as honest upstanding citizens.

In my job, two of the most common questions I'm asked are: 'How do we give the kids the best financial head start with the cost of housing already so unattainable?' and 'How can we prepare for the possibility of private education?' Let's look at some simple strategies you can put in place to help you achieve these goals.

But before we begin, it's also important to remember that while we want to give our kids everything, this is sometimes to their detriment. Without even realising it, we can rob them of the feeling of pride, accomplishment, respect and realisation of their own hard work. These are some of the vital building blocks that every child needs to help develop their self-worth, confidence and self-motivation.

When we teach children about money (among all the other important life skills), we teach the importance of mindfulness, perseverance, the value of a dollar, the power of a game plan. This helps them identify great opportunities, make good decisions and know how to handle challenging situations with wisdom.

The first and most influential source from which children learn about money is you – your habits, financial attitudes and financial values. Watching you, listening to you, overhearing you. So you need to imprint upon your kids healthy, humble and positive attitudes and actions, and always try to come from a gentle place of education and empowerment.

Money should never be an off-topic subject. By no means do we want to put pressure on your children to be 'financial geniuses' or dump our own financial stresses or worries on them, but being open and communicating simply the family goals and game plan goes a really long way, beyond building numbers.

Subjects that are great for children to be included in are:

- saving up for family holidays
- the importance of sticking to budgets
- setting money aside for a rainy day (emergency money)
- investing and compound interest (for older children)
- the importance of charity

But always explain to children **why these financial responsibilities are important**. For example, if you're planning a family holiday, include your kids in the planning process. If you explain that you're saving up for the holiday and describe all the fun activities that you'll be able to do together, involving your children in this process will help them feel included. It will also give them a deeper understanding and respect for why you might need to say no to a few other expenses during the saving period. By demonstrating your own discipline with money and how you work towards your goals, your children will learn a lot just from observing you and your habits.

To help guide you through the various stages of talking to your children about money, I have included different methods and strategies of how to approach it, and for a range of ages as well. However, you know your children best, so use your own judgement and intuition as to what they're ready for and when, and which ideas resonate with you the most. Look for their signals. Just make sure their financial knowledge keeps growing and evolving as you work down the list, gently and steadily building their skills.

WHEN AND WHERE TO START

It's never too early to teach children about money. I started with Rocco when he was about three. I would give him chores to do that were safe and within his skill set – little things like packing his toys away, helping prepare dinner, taking the plates to the sink. These were unpaid chores, as this is just part of being a family, working as a team and understanding responsibilities.

But when he started to show interest in things in shops, with 'Can I have . . . Can we buy . . . I want . . .' followed by the relentless 'But why *not*?', I gently gave him the idea that he could do some extra things around the house and start earning pocket money, which he could save up in order to buy himself what he wanted.

By coming from a place of empowerment and showing Rocco how he could earn and pay for these items himself, I offered him a chance to rise to the opportunity, and he was thrilled by it. He started to earn $1 per week for feeding the dogs. Since then, his job opportunities have expanded to vacuuming (to my delight) and more recently mopping the floor! As well as a few other unpaid and paid jobs along the way.

Being young, the idea of the cashless society was a little too advanced for him, so I got him a money tin and gave him the coins, so that he could place them in his tin himself and get excited as it filled up and weighed more. When we were in the shops, we would make a note of the price of the things he wanted, and come home to check the tin to see how much more he needed. He quickly started to understand patience, as well as disappointment when he was short, but he also looked for opportunities and solutions to help speed up the process.

For children under six, I recommend using coins and notes and piggybanks as a great starting place. Let them regularly open it up, see it and count it with them. Remind them how much more is needed, then encourage them to keep saving. **Empowerment is key.**

For the more mathematically advanced and inquisitive, you may want to let them sit on your lap while paying the family bills online, letting them see how the numbers in your balance drop, or maybe even show them the special family savings accounts and how the balance goes up as you transfer money into it. Don't worry if they don't get it straight away – they will in their own good time.

When they ask for something that's out of the normal spending habits, suggest that they save up their pocket money. That way they have a choice, and will think twice to see if waiting and saving for that item is really worth it. You are slowly and gently planting seeds of value and hard work, even though at times it may not feel like it.

For kids under six, the key is to keep it simple, light and, most of all, fun in the home.

CHEAT TIP FROM CC:

Occasionally Rocco 'goes on strike' and refuses to do his chores. I don't push it at this age. I let it go but remind him that it's his choice and the consequence is no pocket money, which will delay buying the next toy. Sometimes he's fine with that, and sometimes he quickly changes his mind and gets on with it. But the point is that he's realising he has a choice.

CASHLESS SIX-YEAR-OLDS

For young children, coins and notes are great. But as children approach six, it's time to raise the bar and educate them about using money in a cashless society.

While some parents really value giving their kids physical cash and taking them to the bank to have it weighed and deposited, which is brilliant, we need to prepare kids for the way of the future as well.

Their first official job will most likely be cashless; their first debit card will be used to make cashless purchases. So will their first credit card, their first online purchase and even their first investment. Plus most of us actually already operate in a cashless society, so we are making our jobs harder if we're showing and telling our kids about physical money while we ourselves are rarely seen paying with cash. It creates confusion, which can lead to disengagement. Remember, we are always leading by example and imprinting.

For children over the age of six, I recommend stepping up with confidence into the cashless world. You might start with using pocket money apps, such as Spriggy.

Spriggy not only comes with a debit card, you can add your child's chores, as well as other earning opportunities for extra cash along with the amount they can be paid. Then you can mark it off once the chore has been done and pay them (just like their first pay cheque). You can even control the money and lock the card at any time (perfect for when Rocco goes on strike again!). And the card is preloaded, so there's no risk of debt being created.

Within the app, children can set their own savings goals. It's easy to use and the fact that it comes with a card means children can see the similarity to you and how you use your cards in a cash-less society. It costs $2.50 per month per child, which isn't exactly cheap, but considering how much it educates and creates engagement around money in a busy modern-day world, in my opinion it's well worth the investment.

Otherwise, if you feel this is too elementary, set up your child with an everyday savings account and linked debit card. This is perfect for your teenagers. Do your research as to the best value for money, with either no fees or the cheapest fees and best interest rate possible. (I recommend using independent comparison websites to do your research and see what promotions are going at the time). You need to be able to create additional linked online savings accounts at no extra fees, as we'll use these in a similar way to your banking ritual, with the following three accounts for when your child is ready. Get them to check their accounts regularly and share with you how they are going.

- **Everyday account** – for your child's regular transacting. Their pocket money and weekend job income is deposited here, and they can use this same account for spending money on video games, movie tickets, gifts and so on.

- **Goal account** – for one simple goal at a time. Once you've helped them figure out the goal and how to make it happen with extra chores, it needs to be **nicknamed in relation to the goal** to remind them to stay focused. Encourage them to add some money every time they get paid.

- **Investing account** – the start of their investment portfolio, and also a great account for holding any birthday money, or financial gifts from family and friends until you and your child are ready to invest. No money is to come out of this account until it's ready to be invested. Again it should be nicknamed, but with a reminder that the money shouldn't be spent – a suitable nickname could be 'Future investment money – do not touch'. As this account builds up, you'll need to be careful that it really doesn't get spent. So use your own discretion here with how much access your child has to this money or how much you let this account build up before you start investing it. And you may want to invest that money sooner rather than later, or shift it to an account with no access such as a term deposit or a completely separate account if you are worried that it may be spent before it gets invested.

POCKET MONEY AND BUDGETS

Every family is different, with different situations, personalities and dynamics. And all should be respected, without judgement. But if you're going to give pocket money to your children, you need to establish with them what it's for and what it needs to cover. Will this pocket money be for lunch money, family Christmas and birthday presents, or weekend activities? Be really clear with your kids and then sit down and write out a budget with them.

Even better, put the budget on their phone, perhaps in a budgeting app, so that they can easily access it and remember how it works. And don't assume that they're sticking to it – remember, they're completely new to budgeting. So check in with them to see how they're going with it and what they might need help with, and remind them of what expenses they might have coming up that they need to prepare for.

OPTIONS FOR OPPORTUNITY

No two kids are the same. Which is why I don't have hard and fast rules for kids when it comes to money. You have to take your child's lead and jump on those moments of interest and curiosity from your child, to build their knowledge further. **But always ensure you come from a place of empowerment.** There will be times where they are interested and excited, then there will be times when they just can't be bothered.

Don't push – remember that watching you manage money is equally valuable for them, and that you're still planting seeds, even if they're on strike. However, to help inspire and motivate your children to engage or re-engage with their personal finances, I recommend presenting them with opportunities to earn extra money if they want to. Show them what extra chores and tasks can be done (win-win if they actually help you!) and how much they'll earn.

The inner entrepreneur may be unleashed, and you'll find your child negotiating rates or even 'employing' their siblings. If this happens, monitor it to keep it fair, but embrace it. Let them learn their first and most important business skills of sales and negotiation. If they want to sell homemade biscuits and cakes or have a lemonade stand in your street, encourage it. Don't be embarrassed (even if those biscuits are charcoal); everyone loves seeing a child with some get-up-and-go in this world. It's inspiring to all age groups.

SET GOALS AND COMMUNICATE FAITH

I will come to investment goals shortly, but work with your children when the time is right to set some simple goals. Start with something basic, and make sure it's only one goal at a time. It might be a new toy, it might be some new arts and crafts supplies, it might be some new sporting equipment, a concert ticket or a school camping experience. Guide them towards something connected to their personal interest, whether looking online with them or taking them to the store to look at different options. Show them what they could potentially achieve for themselves.

Make sure it's achievable, but communicate that you have faith in them. It sounds obvious, I know, but when I told my parents that I wanted to buy a home at age nineteen, when I could barely get through university, they never laughed or told me that was unrealistic. They told me to give it a good go, be patient and work hard. They helped me work out how much I needed to save, encouraged me when I felt deflated, and kept me realistic and humble as I approached my goal successfully. It was my parents' belief in me that helped me stay focused, and even though it took me six years, eventually I did it and it felt amazing.

And that experience helped give me the confidence to take on other opportunities and challenges in my life. So, encourage and help your kids define their goals; brainstorm ideas with them to help achieve those goals, such as getting a weekend job or doing more chores around the house; help them set up their savings account and use it as an opportunity to teach them more.

Once you've figured out the goal, make sure you set up a separate savings account linked to their everyday account, and brainstorm together the range of different things that your child could do to help build up enough money to achieve that goal. Just like your own goal accounts, this account should be nicknamed in relation to your child's goal; you can easily change that nickname when a new goal is created.

For younger children, work with that money tin until they're ready to understand a bank account. Regularly pull the tin out, check what is inside and how much more is needed; when there's enough, regardless of their age, make a special fuss of picking up that item, buying that toy or booking that event. Watch them feel proud of what they've managed to do, and tell them how proud you are of them.

INVESTING IN EXPERIENCES

Most kids love lots of stuff to play with, even if it's for thirty seconds. As a result, our homes are drowning in clutter, while our local charities can barely keep up with the daily drop-offs from our Marie Kondo–inspired 'spring cleans'. And sadly our environment is feeling the biggest and most damaging impact of all.

There have been many studies to show that more toys does not mean more happiness for children. In fact, it's quite the contrary; in some children, the more toys, the greater their anxiety and depression. Which is one of the reasons why I recommend parents ease up on the pressure they put on themselves to help children financially, but invest more time in their children.

As your child gets older and shows you the right signs, start encouraging them to consider spending their pocket money on experiences rather than more 'stuff'. When we have experiences, we are more present, we get a better return on our investments, and we create memories – memories that can last a lifetime. If you can share these experiences with your children or as a family unit, you're raising the value of the investment and helping create the opportunity to build a deeper, rock-solid bond.

Here are some great ideas for experiences for different age

groups that kids can save up for in place of adding to the clutter in your home:

- pony rides and petting zoos at your local markets
- movie tickets – see what's coming soon to your local cinema, and watch trailers online to help them get excited
- shows – carnivals, easter shows, circuses, entertainment/theme parks, art exhibitions, plays or concerts
- memberships, such as for the zoo, museum or sports clubs
- classes where they can learn new skills such as painting, pottery or cooking
- lessons – do they want to get better at their chosen sports or games techniques? Maybe they can save up for a special lesson
- holiday activities – maybe your child could save up for a water-skiing experience for your upcoming summer holiday

Again, make it slow and keep it simple, but work with their genuine interest.

RESEARCH QUALITY OVER QUANTITY

While we're on the topic of clutter and excess stuff swamping our homes, there's also the issue of our children's belongings having a short life due to poor manufacturing standards. When your child experiences a toy breaking or falling apart, it can be the perfect opportunity to explain the importance of investing in quality workmanship.

Whenever your child is planning to spend their money, be it on toys, clothes, gadgets or sporting equipment, get them to look at a wide range and compare the quality of items, as well as consider buying it from the second-hand economy, such as Gumtree, eBay, Craig's List, etc.

Rather than encouraging impulse purchases, explain to them that they should want their purchase to last as long as possible, and that although sometimes this may mean paying a bit more, it's worth it. In these situations you can show your children how to research a good buy and good value for money, where to find the best price and what's best for them and their needs, as well as explaining the environmental responsibility of buying second-hand.

We want our children to not only manage their hard-earned money, but also spend it wisely and actually enjoy their purchases, with respect for our environment. This is all part of money mindfulness.

DEPOSITS FOR FIRST HOMES

With the high entry price of properties these days around the world, so many parents are worrying about how their children will ever be able to afford to own their own home. As a result, some parents are giving their children deposits or even buying properties for them.

While this is incredibly generous, I recommend a moment of caution here. If you are going to do this, firstly make sure you can actually afford it without jeopardising your own financial security. Secondly, suggest your child contributes towards this cost in some way, such as matching you dollar for dollar, or something similar. **They must put in some hard work and sacrifice towards this.**

Ensure that they have good cash-flow habits firmly in place beforehand so that they can manage the ongoing cost of holding that property (mortgage repayments, strata, insurances, maintainence, etc.) without too much stress before they take on the big commitment of a property. And that they gain that valuable sense of pride and satisfaction that comes from working on a goal for an extended period of time.

CHARITY

I will be talking about charity in a lot more detail in Chapter fifteen. But for now I'll just say that we need to teach our children how to give back – not just financially, but through their time, effort and awareness.

Of your children's money, they should always have one charity that they have picked themselves and contribute to either when they can afford to or regularly. You must give them guidance as to how much they can afford to give without themselves suffering financially and you will need to do the due diligence so that you know that the charity that they pick is legitimate.

Explain to your children that charity is not about throwing money at a problem, but is about understanding it, spreading awareness about it and giving time to it, all unconditionally. It's a valuable life lesson for children to do some form of physical charity work so they really get this message, whether it be cleaning up the rubbish from the local parks, selling raffle tickets, helping give food to the homeless, or walking dogs for the elderly or unwell. They should be actively involved with a charity that sparks a passion to be a part of the solution.

TEENAGERS

I completely understand the pressure that kids and teenagers put on themselves to do well, not just at school or sport but socially too.

And while I'm not recommending that kids put money-making above their education or school responsibilities, having some kind of part-time job can be really valuable in teaching them the value of hard work and how to juggle multiple commitments.

Casual work such as babysitting, washing cars or dog-walking can be done around school hours and on weekends and school holidays. (I used to take my homework when I babysat and would study once the kids went to bed.) They can start small – an hour or two here and there – and then build it up when they can. The point is that having something to show up for, the experiencing of commitment and feeling pride in a first job, is fantastic for preparing teens for the real world ahead of them.

STATEMENT LITERACY

If this is the only step that you can do successfully with your teenager, I will be happy. Starting the day after their thirteenth birthday, show your teen how to read financial statements.

I personally feel that some financial institutions make it challenging to read your statements, particularly statements of the toxic debt variety. That way they can more easily keep you in debt and paying interest to them for a lot longer. So many people look at their credit card statement crossed-eyed, not really understanding how much they owe, how much more it was than last month, how much more interest they're paying and how much longer it will take to be paid off. As a result, the debt sits there and escalates. Let's not let our children be victims of this.

If you can teach your teen how to read their bank statements, their transactions and even their superannuation statements, they are more likely to be engaged with their finances. They get that their savings are building and they're earning more interest; they get that their expenses got a little out of hand last month and they need to scale it back now; they get that the bank is charging them expensive interest, wasting their money. They get that their investment portfolio is paying more passive income and that they now own a bigger portfolio. They get that their superannuation money is valuable to their long-term financial security and needs to be checked regularly and invested properly, reflecting their long-term financial goals.

COMPOUNDING INTEREST

From reading Chapter seven, you not only understand the difference between savings and investing, but the power of compounding interest, particularly when you add in two-dimensional assets, with time.

It's equally important that children also understand this, even if they don't grasp it straight away. You can show your children that adding even a little bit along the way makes a huge difference to their long-term financial security.

The best way to do this is visually. And to make this as easy as possible, we have created a special kid-friendly Compounding Interest Calculator, which lets you play with the variables such as length of time, how much they contribute upfront and ongoing, how much you might even contribute to help get them started or as a reward along the way, and then together you can compare all the different potential opportunities.

For example, your fifteen-year-old who already has $1500 in their savings account and wants to go overseas for a month when they finish school can see that if they start now, and add $200 per month ($50 per week) to their savings account (as it's a short-term timeframe), they'll have just under $10 000 saved up, of which $627 is interest earned by their money working for them.

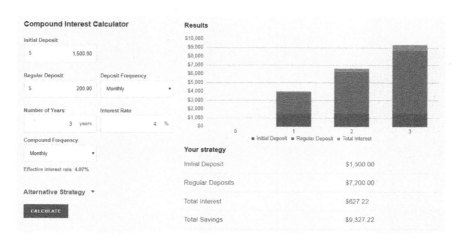

Or take your ten-year-old who dreams of buying their own car when they turn eighteen. Starting with an initial $1000 and adding $220 per month from chores and even a weekend job over eight years, and invested into a longer-term ETF, can potentially give them the cash upfront to pay for that car. This time the interest earnings are over $7832 because the length of time has been stretched out and the type of vehicle is not a savings account but an investment portfolio.

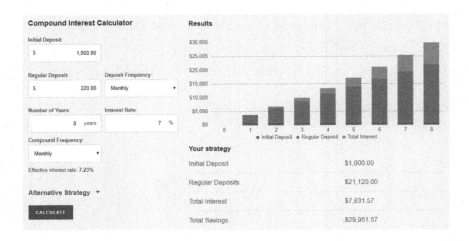

Or even for your newborn child – see what a kickstart of say $3000 initially, with a $300 per month regular investment, can do. When they reach twenty-one, they already have a seriously impressive six-figure investment portfolio[7] that can help set them up financially by using it or continuing to grow it themselves. Just go back to Chapter eight and re-read the numbers of an investment of $10 000 made in 1979 invested into an index of industrial shares. Even a small investment into something like that (such as the Whitefield industrial LIC) over the long run could have a high impact.

But the exciting part is, you and your children can start exploring possibilities and getting enthusiastic about what is realistically within their reach. You can decide together, but also alter and tweak the strategy and goal as time goes by and new ideas, opportunities and inspiration come your way.

---

7   You need to monitor income tax payable.

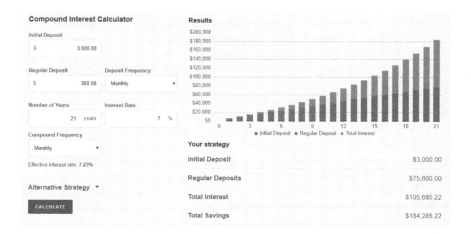

INVESTING FOR KIDS

Starting an investment portfolio for your children is a brilliant idea. It's a great way to get them on the path to financial freedom so much sooner, as they get to benefit from time and allow compounding interest to work its magic.

This is where you can help prepare for their education costs – by building up a portfolio that can either be sold in its entirety down the track to cover the cost of education, or even better, held so that the passive income paid each year can pay for as many education costs as possible, leaving the portfolio to accumulate over time.

But you must prioritise your own financial wellbeing first and foremost, because most of the financial wisdom and guidance will actually be installed and imprinted in your children from your own actions and self-respect. So once you feel that your finances are under control, with your debts or mortgage dropping at an efficient speed, your superannuation accounts sorted along with the right insurances in place, and even your own growing investment portfolio with passive income, then look to add something for the kids. But not before. You can't pour from an empty cup.

Again, you need to use your intuition as to how involved you want them in this exercise, and how much you want to give them, and if and when they will contribute to this investment themselves.

I highly recommend that as children get older, they start contributing at least something to their portfolio. It should be factored into their budget, increasing as their income or pocket money does. Initially it may only be small amounts that they can afford, such as $20 per month, but as they get older, they can work on slowly increasing it (leaning in). Put it in the financial goal account to accumulate over time, and when there is enough to add more, add it straight away. This could be a timely opportunity to include some new financial goals for your child, such as saving $1000 by the end of the year.

There are five ways to invest for your child. I'll start with the structures first, as you need to get this right before you actually start investing.

INVEST DIRECTLY IN YOUR CHILD'S NAME

This is where the child owns the investment and has direct control over it, in the same way you would own any other financial asset. Assuming that the initial money to pay for the investment came from what the Australian Taxation Office deems 'unearned income', which is normally financial gifts, an issue arises when the income from that investment exceeds $416 per financial year – anything above that will be taxed at 66% and then drop to 45% on any further earnings.

Income	Tax rates for 2017–18 income year
$0 – $416	Nil
$417 – $1307	Nil plus 66% of the excess over $416
Over $1307	45% of the total amount of income

But if your child actually earned the money (from a job) and paid for the initial investment through those earnings, they are taxed as an adult – meaning they can earn up to $18 200 per annum and pay no tax. If their income exceeds this, the next tax rate is 19% p.a. and slowly moves higher; there are still low-income offsets that they may be entitled to that help reduce this tax.

You would not have control over the investment – in fact, your child could sell down and spend that entire portfolio at any time.

INVEST AS TRUSTEE FOR YOUR CHILD – RECOMMENDED OPTION

This is the option I've chosen for Rocco. I invest in my own name: 'As Trustee for Rocco', I quote Rocco's tax file number, and declare and pay tax on his dividends until he turns eighteen, as he 'benefits from the income', even though it is reinvested for compounding growth opportunities. Once he turns eighteen, the portfolio can be transferred from this structure into his own name without triggering capital gains tax, as there is a change in legal owner but no change in beneficial owner (this is similar to the in-specie service). I'll do the same for any future children and grandchildren, and I'll add to it when it suits my finances. I make the investment decisions on his behalf.

With this structure, when they turn eighteen they're the legal owner of the shares, with you losing all control. A Change of Ownership form must be completed, and no capital gains tax should be charged as there hasn't been a change in the beneficiary.

It's extremely important that any dividends paid are not used by any adults for their own benefit, as it raises questions around who the beneficiary is. For this reason, aside from the obvious compounding interest benefits, you should enrol in an automatic dividend reinvestment plan so that you never need to worry about this, which is quick and easy to manage.

INVEST IN YOUR NAME FOR YOUR CHILD

One popular and flexible option is to invest in your own name, as the parent. The income will be taxed at your marginal tax rate; if there's the option of putting the investment in the name of the parent with the lowest tax rate, this can help keep the tax bill down and ensure that you still have complete control of the investment as the parent.

The only disadvantage is that capital gains tax will apply if or when you transfer the asset to your child. However, depending on legislation and tax rates at the time, if you live in Australia you may qualify for a 50% capital gains tax discount if the asset is held for more than twelve months. You also have the control to decide if or when you want to transfer the portfolio over to your child; by contrast, when it's invested for your child with yourself as trustee, you are obliged to transfer it to them.

INVEST VIA AN INSURANCE BOND

This is my least favourite option, but one I must share with you. Insurance bonds are among the simplest and most tax-effective investments available. You essentially make an initial investment, and set and forget. After you've held the insurance bond for ten years, you can sell all or part of the bond without paying any tax. If you need to sell it before the ten-year period is up, you can, but tax will apply to the profits; however, you may be entitled to some of the 30% tax rebates previously paid from the bond. Otherwise you can keep holding it indefinitely beyond ten years.

The reasons I don't particularly like this type of investment is firstly due to the management fees, which are typically between 1.5% and 1.8% p.a. (by comparison, an index ETF or LIC fee can be between 0.05% p.a. and 0.4% p.a.), and secondly because there are strict rules around how much you can make in ongoing contributions to the fund. The rule is called the 125% rule, which means you cannot add more than 125% of your previous year's contribution. For example, in the first year you invest $1000, so for the following year the maximum allowed contribution is $1250, etc.

This may not work for you or your child if you want to add more to the portfolio. If new contributions do exceed 125%, the start date of the ten-year period will reset from the date the excess contribution was made. Also, most insurance bonds have a minimum investment amount of $2500, which can take a while to get together. With shares, ETFs or LICs, you can start with as little as $500 (that said, I always recommend $1000 due to brokerage costs being dollar-based).

START A SUPERANNUATION ACCOUNT

Your child will like this option the least, but you may love it the most. While it does come with serious long-term restrictions, it may be suitable for children or situations where you're worried about money not being spent wisely; superannuation offers a way to preserve funds and gives them opportunity to grow without falling prey to sticky fingers.

The first challenge is that your child needs to be over eighteen to open a superannuation account, or for you to open one for them, unless there is an employment contract in place. However, if you work for yourself and can employ your kid as your admin assistant, or if they have a part-time job, you may have a way around this. Technically they need to be working over thirty hours per week and earning at least $450 per month, but some superannuation funds will still accept your payments regardless of this.

The second challenge is that under current legislation, your child won't be able to access this money until age sixty, and it's highly possible that between now and then this age may be pushed out even further. However, perhaps the greatest benefit of this option is that the maximum tax rate on the income earnings within the fund are 15% p.a.

This means it's a seriously great way to build your child's wealth over the long run so that you can help them have a comfortable retirement. It's also comforting to know that under current legislation, money within super is protected from bankruptcy.

Limits apply as to how much you can put into super each financial year, so you can only load these accounts up to a certain level (as explained in Chapter twelve). But you definitely could place a lump sum amount into your child's new superannuation account to get them started, and then encourage them to add money to this along with their financial goal account or regular investing, even if it's through their pocket money.

The long-term wealth accumulation benefits from the compounding interest are astronomical. You and your child could very easily see the benefit of a humble regular contribution, which could actually make them a millionaire before they know it.

To help explain this, I've added a child's superannuation calculator to the SugarMamma.TV website. Jump on and play with the different options. Check out the impact of a sixteen-year-old starting their super with $1000, earning an average salary of $50 000 p.a. throughout their lifetime (conservatively assuming no pay rises, promotions, bonus, etc.), salary sacrificing $200 per month and adding $200 per month from their after-tax savings (never increasing). Based on an average net return of 7.5% p.a. their superannuation should be worth more than $1 409 000 by age sixty-five.

Results

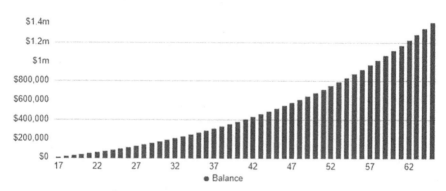

The Projection at retirement is: **$1,409,006.12**

You can refer to the same list of cost-effective, high-quality superannuation accounts that I recommended for you in Chapter twelve. It will make it easier for you to show your child how to read the statements, as they will be displayed in the same way as your own.

$500 FOR FREE – IN AUSTRALIA

And one final special touch is to get your children to make the most of the government's co-contribution scheme if they qualify for it. There are certain rules, such as requiring at least 10% of their income to be earnt from wages and for their income to be under certain levels before it starts tapering off. Always check the ATO website for these limits and thresholds. But by encouraging them to put $1000 of their own money into their account, you can show them they are getting up to $500 'free' money back. Show them the impact of this with the child superannuation calculator over the long run, and instil in them how much more security it adds. The great thing about these options is that you can simply pick the one that works best for you and your child, or even better, pick a few different options. All with great financial benefits.

INVESTMENT OPTIONS FOR CHILDREN

You can essentially invest in anything you like for a child, within reason. However, my three key bits of advice are to ensure that the money is diversified, cost-effective, and that it's easy to add more money if and when you want.

Again, I won't recommend managed funds here as the fees are too high and eat into your returns; moreover, if the fund manager is active, the portfolio may erode due to capital gains tax being triggered, with you or your child footing the bill. This scenario would definitely not encourage a child to want to invest more.

So here are my top three suggestions to get your kids into investing in a way that is cost-effective and tax-minimising, and that is immediately diversified, helping reduce investment risk. And what's also great is that you can make an initial investment and just leave it there (such as a lump sum when they're born) or contribute money along the way if and when you wish. Super flexible!

DIVERSIFIED INDEX ETF

As explained in Chapter nine, you can purchase shares in an index-style exchange-traded fund that comes with its own instantly diversified asset allocation. You can make sure that the portfolio matches your timeframe, your risk profile and your goals.

For example, you might consider the Vanguard Diversified Growth Index ETF or Vanguard Diversified Balanced Index ETF, where the management fee is 0.27% p.a. and your child's money is invested across a wide range of both growth and income assets, including domestic shares, international shares, property, cash and fixed interest. The two different ETFs have suggested timeframes of five to seven years.

SPECIALIST INDEX ETF

If you like this idea of an ETF, but don't want such a wide mix of assets, you can invest in a specialist ETF that focuses purely on a particular asset allocation such as Australian shares, international shares or property.

For example, there's the Vanguard Australian Shares Index Fund, the Vanguard Australian Large Companies Index Fund or the Vanguard International Shares Index Fund. Again, these are cost-effective options with ongoing fees of 0.14% to 0.20%, and allow a portfolio to be well diversified within that particular asset allocation.

And being an index-style ETF (buying and holding the general market), the portfolio is not being churned over; minimal capital gains tax is triggered, avoiding the eroding effect on the portfolio, which in turns helps give it the best opportunity to compound over time.

LISTED INVESTMENT COMPANIES

As mentioned in Chapter nine, you can buy shares in an LIC, which are similar to an ETF in that they are cost-effective, professionally managed and diversified. They usually focus on equities rather than other asset allocations such as cash and fixed interest.

As mentioned in Chapter nine, the suggested ETFs and LICs may also work well for your child's investment if you understand and are comfortable with the risks, and have a long-term investment timeframe.

My final tip would be to pick one that offers an automatic dividend reinvestment option; you can find out if this is available through the fund manager's website. That way, the LIC is much easier to manage going forward and is very much set and forget; you never need to worry about accidentally spending the dividends.

If this isn't available, list the BSB and account number of the financial goal account on the forms sent to you by the share registry, so that the dividends can accumulate safely and be manually invested with new contributions when the time is right.

Whitefield currently offers an automatic dividend reinvestment plan, if you like the idea of a diversified Australian industrial portfolio; and remember, a dividend reinvestment plan can be cancelled at any time.

RETHINK 'SAVING FOR THE KIDS' EDUCATION'

Often our natural initial financial instinct when it comes to planning and preparing for the cost of children's education is to save up for it. For example, when they are born, we start putting money into a separate savings account on a regular basis, with the idea or hope that when they commence paid education, there is enough money available to cover the cost.

And when the child finishes paid education, there is $0 left over. Seems like it has done its job. But what if there is something better and more efficient?

While this regular savings is plausible, now that you understand the power of passive income, compounding interest, the benefit of time and regular investing, you can actually rethink preparing for the cost of your children's education through building your number and actually having a substantial portfolio left over when they graduate, rather than $0.

This could be a new separate number and investment portfolio to match, purely dedicated to your child or children's expenses. For example, imagine building an investment portfolio rather than a savings account, which provides an annual growing passive income that pays or helps pay for your child's annual education costs?

Sure, it may not cover 100% of your child's education, but it may cover enough for you to fit the difference in your budget at that future time. Even better, once your child finishes their paid education, (whether it be private, catholic, college, TAFE or university), you still have the investment portfolio left, still paying passive income and free for you to do what you wish with it. You could use the ongoing passive income for yourself and put it towards building your own number, or if you wanted, even transfer the portfolio to your grown-up child when appropriate for them to continue managing and building.

You can use or incorporate Honey's strategy, Amanda's strategy, the Howards' strategy or Ben's strategy to build a passive income source to help cover the cost of education. The point is to use two-dimensional assets to help you more efficiently use your money and achieve your goals, taking the stress off your shoulders.

And if you live in Australia and already pay for day care, a nanny, babysitter or other paid childcare service, once your child graduates to kindergarten (assuming it's a public kindergarten), reallocate those childcare expenses towards this idea.

Again, have a play with the growing passive income calculators, savings calculators and investment calculators and see what is possible to help you, for your children's mindful benefit.

POINTS TO REMEMBER:

- Start with coins and notes for children under six.
- Let them have paid and unpaid chores.
- Always look to grow their knowledge and understanding of money management when you see that they are ready.
- Always come from a place of education and empowerment.
- Be patient; at times they'll be interested and times they won't – work with their rhythm.
- Remember your own habits, attitudes, language and mindset rubs off on children – they are always absorbing and learning by watching us. Lead by example.
- Encourage your kids to have a part-time job or side hustle, even if it is just for school holidays.
- Rethink 'saving' for your child's education – and build a passive income that helps pay for the cost of education.
- If setting up a portfolio with the intention of eventually paying for education costs, consider using the passive income rather than selling it down in full. That way, the portfolio can continue to grow, and so can the income. This will obviously be subject to your own budget and situation at the time.

- Consider diversified index ETFs and even LICs for a child's long-term investments, invested by yourself as 'trustee for'.
- Knowing your timeframe is important – for short-term timeframes you could consider some of the conservative, moderate or balanced diversified index ETFs, or even stick with cash.
- For long-term investing – that is, ten years plus – you could use a growth or high-growth index ETF, or a specialist ETF such as Australian index shares or international index ETF.
- Ideally pick one that offers an automatic dividend reinvestment plan to make life easier for you to manage. Otherwise, list the financial goal account number and BSB on the share registry forms and make sure you do not accidentally spend your child's dividends on yourself if invested as trustee for your child.
- As your children get older, encourage them to allocate their own money from their budget to their investment portfolio.

CHAPTER FIFTEEN

Sharing is Caring

'Think of giving not as a duty, but as a privilege.' – John D. Rockefeller, American oil magnate and philanthropist

When I was a child, my father would tell me, 'A problem shared is a problem halved.' He was right: when you share something that is bothering you or causing worry, not only do you feel relief in identifying it and communicating it, but also you start to move on to a place of solutions. Solutions coming from two people instead of one double the chances of overcoming the problem.

In our home, Rocco and I have a saying – 'sharing is caring'. It's a great way to illustrate to Rocco the benefits and sense of connection that comes from sharing something you have so that you can enjoy something together.

When you share, not only does it feel good to the receiver, reassuring them that they matter and their problems are valid, there is also something energising to the giver in knowing how much they are helping that person work through something that is tough for them. You then grow on the inside, which is the best growth of all.

I hope that these two sayings can encourage you to help halve problems by sharing and caring.

As you progress towards your number, share, care and give help back.

There are lots of ways that you can share and care, through donating money to causes and people, by giving your time or even simply helping create awareness. But as you grow financially, getting stronger with each action that you take and each day that passes, try to find at least one problem that you can help halve.

Find the problem that you want to help fix, and include it in your financial ritual and financial goals; be passionate about it and wanting to help make a difference.

Whether it be a large charity organisation, or someone who is down on their luck, or a younger person who needs a mentor, invest some of your growing time, freedom and energy in something that means something to you, where you can give back and where you can make a difference.

The problem you pick to try to help solve may change and evolve. It may go from helping a mother who needs a few free hours babysitting to cooking a meal for someone who is unwell. Or reading a book to disadvantaged children or helping keep the elderly company. Maybe even helping use your social media channels to inform people of the problem or communicate how they can help as well. Or doing a charity run to help raise money. Make yourself part of the solution that halves the problem. It all matters and it all helps.

As I said at the beginning of this book, this is a book about authentic wealth, wealth where you feel genuinely happy, healthy and free on all levels, not just financially, and you can be more present and have more time for things that matter to you and to the people you love.

There is no point building a huge amount of financial wealth if you can't share, especially if it is being shared in a positive, empowering way to reduce stress, conflict and trauma.

Here are my steps to help maximise your sharing and caring impact.

1. Find a problem that you want to fix – something that you are passionate about fixing. It could come from something that impacted you or someone you loved in your past, it could be something that worries you now, it could even be something that you are concerned about in the future.

   Consider:
   • the environment
   • healthcare
   • religions
   • animals
   • international welfare
   • education
   • arts and culture

2. Ask how you can help – charity or helping people isn't always about giving money necessarily. Quite often your time and the benefit and value that you can add is worth more than money to them. This could include helping spread awareness, helping keep someone company or maybe helping them find particular items such as spare clothes or food. But ask them what you can do to help them, and then carefully listen to their answer so you know exactly how to serve them best and have the biggest impact possible.

3. Commit and communicate – work out how long you can help for and make sure that you communicate along the way.

Let the mother who needs an extra set of hands know that you can help at this time, on these days, for this many months, for this many hours. Let the person know that you are cooking a meal for them and dropping it over to them on whatever day or night. Let the child know when you will be back to read another book to them. Let the charity know that you are doing a shout-out to help them find toys, bras, clothing, food, etc. When you communicate your wishes, not only does it empower you, but it also helps reassure the person or charity that you are helping halve the problem.

4. Unconditional giving – share and care with no expectations. If you get a thank you or praise, that is a blessing, not a requirement. This is about helping others out and learning more about how deeply the impact of your sharing and caring can really be. Don't expect anything in return.

5. Leave your legacy – if you give to charity regularly or even sporadically but always wished you could give more, but your resources are limited as you focus on building your own number, you would be pleased to know that you could continue or even 'catch up on' your generosity after you have left this planet. This could be done by gifting part of your investment portfolio to your chosen charity, which could be achieved in several ways:

   • Directly by way of **gifting** in your will an asset, such as your shares or property or even a lump sum of money to your chosen charity. This is very simple and provides not only immediate funding to the charity but allows them an asset which could help them indefinitely if the charity chose to hold onto it. However, the downside of this is that once they officially own the investment that you have left them, they are free to decide how they are managed or even sold.

- Create a **testamentary trust will** and name your charity of choice as one of the beneficiaries. You would leave instructions to your trustee (i.e. the person you pick to be in charge of your estate and make major decisions) as to how you want the charity to receive the distributions of the trust, such as the amount and frequency. A testamentary trust will is a type of will that establishes a trust or trusts upon your death.
- Gift your assets to an existing **discretionary family trust** and add your chosen charity as a beneficiary. The charity can receive donations through your discretionary family trust.

If you decide to distribute or gift your asset to a discretionary family trust (or create a testamentary trust will), and intend that the charity only receives income generated by the assets, then the charity would be unable to directly deal with and therefore dispose of the assets. This allows you (or the trustee) some level of control in relation to your assets and the distribution of any of that passive income generated from your assets.

I highly recommended that you see a lawyer[8] who specialises in estate planning laws as this can be quite complicated and you

---

8   A very special thank you to Jenny Needham from Needham Ainsworth who not only helped set up my will but also gave me brilliant advice that was easy to understand, giving me peace of mind that my wishes will be followed through correctly, supporting charities that help make a difference.

need professional advice to help you work out which options are best for you, so that the right type of will is established and most importantly you have documented your wishes clearly so that your family and friends understand and respect your wishes, and best of all you feel proud knowing what impact you are leaving behind.

If you don't have a will already, I recommend having one prepared as soon as you have started on the path to financial independence. It should be reviewed and updated every couple of years, particularly when your situation changes, such as when you have bought a major asset like a property, or when there has been a change in your life stage such as having a child, marriage or divorce. Also consider non-estate assets such as your super or insurance policies, which are usually separate to your estate. You can nominate your estate with these accounts and policies, but get legal advice upfront.

There are will kits available online. However, as this is a specialised area of law, it is recommended that you contact a lawyer or ensure that the will kit you are using is drafted by a lawyer. Your will could be invalidated if it is not properly drafted. This could mean that the wealth you have worked hard to build would not be distributed as you wished, and certain loved ones would not receive the gifts which you intended them to have.

Remember that giving back is part of our responsibility. We come into this world with no physical items and we leave with no physical items but we have the ability to leave a legacy behind of inspiration, presence and love, and of course the valuable example of our financial education in investing and long-term passive income. So consider making even a small percentage of your number part of your legacy.

POINTS TO REMEMBER:

- A problem shared is a problem halved – help lift the burdens of others by sharing and caring as you progress towards your number. From my personal experience, here is a place to start thinking about how you want to give back and enjoy being part of making a difference.

- Find a problem to which you can be part of the solution, whether on a personal level with someone you know or a societal level with issues such as the environment, animal welfare, medicine or education.

- Make sure to ask the person or organisation how you can usefully help, and pay attention to their answer.

- Communicate your commitment so that the person or charity feels supported and reassured, and you reinforce your intentions to yourself as well.

- Give your money or time unconditionally, without the expectation of being thanked.

- Set up your legacy so you can continue to help others after you're gone.

- Consult a lawyer specialising in estate planning to make sure your will is well established and that the beneficiaries receive what you intend, and in a way that legally and proactively minimises tax.

- Public and ancilliary funds can also help set this up, but be careful of the ongoing fees that are charged.

CHAPTER SIXTEEN

Stories of Inspiration

So far you've been reading all my tips and advice, and you've only had my word that it works. Here I want to take a moment to share with you some stories from my readers and YouTube followers so you can see for yourself how my techniques have been applied in the real world, with real people.

DEB

I first found Canna on YouTube while looking at fashion advice videos. I soon found my way to your financial advice videos. I am now a proud owner of your book and participator in my own $1000 Project. I have always been able to save, and live with no debt other than my mortgage; but I didn't have much of an idea what to do with my savings other than just let it sit in the bank . . . until now! You have debunked many share market myths and made investing in shares much less scary than I was led to believe it was. I am young and have a young family, and while my mortgage is my first priority, I have also made efforts to use my $1000 Project funds to begin building a share portfolio and take advantage of compounding interest while time is on my side. I can now see the potential improvements the right investments could make to my life twenty, thirty or forty years from now. Thank you for your real and relevant information.

EM

In 2017, at age twenty-one, I made the big leap to London from Melbourne. While I loved the independence and freedom of finding my feet in a new city and being able to travel around Europe much more easily, I was quickly hit by the financial reality of my newfound lifestyle. Rent, transport and food were so much more expensive than I was used to, and it took a long time to stop converting items back into AUD to judge their value. Then, in July 2017, I received an email from the Australian Taxation Office notifying me I was eligible for mandatory student loan repayments.

I suddenly had to figure out how on earth I was going to pay back my $24 602 Australian student HELP loan while living and working in another country and currency. I had no idea how to transfer money internationally without being ripped off, nor how to work out my worldwide income. Worst of all, the prospect of doing both a UK and Australian tax return every year until I paid back my HELP loan made me dizzy. I felt completely lost and pretty unprepared, anxious, stressed and beaten down as I thought I'd been so ready for this big life change. Around this time, a friend mentioned your YouTube channel. I found The $1000 Project and was hooked. I realised I was going to need to toughen up my budget if I wanted to get rid of the financial stress in my life and start feeling in control of my salary.

I started by putting my $601 tax return towards the loan. I sold old clothes and books. I saved *hard* and took inspiration from all the ideas and resources on your blog and others, and just kept chipping away at the balance to build up parcels of £1000, which I'd then transfer into dollars and send straight to my student loan. Sometimes, I'd hold out for a week or two before transferring the parcel in order to get the best exchange rate possible but for the most part I felt motivated to see the balance decrease with every month and every parcel. It has taken thirteen months, but as I write this, I only have $1263 left to go. A long, long way from the $24 602 I graduated with.

Thank you, Canna. I genuinely never thought this would be possible.

RANIA

Until recent years, my relationship with money had been a negative one. This stems from my childhood – I would listen to what adults around me complained and argued about. Especially my parents. I did not think money came easily or effortlessly. I learned how to save but always ended up binge spending before I reached my savings goal. Then I would feel extremely guilty and embarrassed. What made matters worse is that my father always put me down and criticised my efforts to save money, but didn't give me any guidance or help to get better.

When I was seventeen my father's business boomed and suddenly, we had a huge influx of money. I was given not only a new car but also three gold credit cards! For the first time in my life I felt free and abundant, but this slowly turned into overspending and expensive shopping sprees. My parents joked that I was like Dickie Greenleaf from *The Talented Mr. Ripley*, and that my only talent was spending my allowance. Deep inside I felt insecure that I couldn't earn my own money.

It didn't help that everyone around me also was very skeptical about investing and whenever I tried to learn anything about it I didn't understand it at all and felt completely out of my depth. I didn't trust myself at all. I continued to depend on my father, never saving my own wages from my various jobs. After a few years of living this way, one of my credit cards was hacked. My father lost £250 000! He then cut me off financially and cancelled all my credit cards. He paid my rent off for the rest of that year and said that from now on I was on my own. This was a low point in my life, but it also became the key to my liberation. For the next seven years I struggled to cope with the loss of a living standard I was used to. But then I decided to educate myself about money. I discovered minimalism, how to live within my means and eventually came across SugarMamma.TV. The $1000 Project helped me gain confidence and skills in my relationship to money. I now have a property I call my own, as well as savings, and I am feeling positive about my financial future. Most of all, I know I can depend on myself and don't need anyone's help! Thank you, Canna, for writing a book about finance for young people and millennials, you are helping a great deal start life the right way. Lots of love to you, my son will definitely grow up reading your books.

COURTNEY

I'm forty-one years old and am only this year getting me and my family organised financially. My husband and I both earn reasonable salaries but we never paid any attention to our finances. I also had a spending problem, shopping far, far too much. We earned more than enough but I spent almost all of it. I was living with constant stress, which I tried to relieve by spending more, even spending whatever savings we accumulated. I feel sick remembering it.

The lowest point came when we realised we didn't have enough money to make our mortgage payment that month. I had to pray our salaries would hit our account before the mortgage payment was debited. This was the day I decided things had to change.

Not long after this, I was watching a Chloe Morello video on YouTube where she was doing Canna's make-up, and discovered SugarMamma.TV. It inspired me to make some changes to my financial health. I set up a budget, started a side hustle selling my unwanted items and clothes and used those earnings to participate in The $1000 Project challenge to start investing. I got a new job with a higher salary, then set up salary sacrifice so I could increase my super contributions. I've even been able to invest for my daughter so that she has a nest egg to use as a house deposit.

SugarMamma.TV has given me ongoing motivation when it comes to my finances. Most importantly, it has helped me understand what made me spend so much – stress and boredom. This insight has allowed me to substitute spending with a different coping mechanism – saving money! Plus my eBay side hustle. Thanks to your inspiring videos, I've been able to achieve all of the above.

REBECCA

I was brought up in a family where there was no money and where my father was on welfare payments for many years. While it was incredibly hard at the time, it turned out to be a gift because it made me determined to build a secure future for myself. Although I had very limited knowledge on personal finance and wealth management, my eagerness to learn landed me a position at AMP Financial Services. This role taught me the importance of basic financial knowledge. It was also the catalyst for creating a saving to invest account and going really hard at putting money away every pay cheque. I was really proud that in four years I'd built up a deposit of $100k to buy my first investment property.

But just when I was about to take the plunge and purchase, I found out I was pregnant to a man I had been dating for four months. He left me when I was seven weeks pregnant and my financial situation changed dramatically overnight. My $100k of 'savings to invest' started eroding rapidly on expenses to prepare for the baby. I had to move out of my shared flat into a one-bedroom unit, which meant buying lots of furniture. I had to purchase all of the baby goods myself, plus buy a car so I could support myself while on maternity leave. Desperate not to become a victim of my circumstances and be perceived as a 'poor single mother', I studied for my diploma of financial planning on weekends throughout my pregnancy to build on my knowledge and increase my self-reliance.

I'm now blessed with a darling five-month-old boy who lights up my world. But without child support from my baby's father and limited Centrelink support (I'm a New Zealand citizen), I had to return to work part time when my child was only nine weeks old. Throughout all this, your videos have kept me inspired to work hard and continually re-evaluate areas where I can save money. When I return to full-time work in a few months' time, I plan to put away as much as I can into my savings to an investment account and build up a share portfolio. It's going to be much more challenging to build an investment portfolio on a single income with a dependent and new major expenses such as daycare fees, but I know your vlogs will keep me motivated and on track!

Thank you for being such an inspiration and making a difference in my life, and I'm sure the lives of many others. I can't wait to devour your book as soon as it arrives in my letterbox!

ELLEN

I discovered Canna's SugarMamma channel in 2015 through Chloe Morello's beauty channel. I instantly loved what she was saying about the importance of learning about and taking control of your finances. I learned so much about being smart with money and the steps to secure your financial freedom. I've always had an interest in finance, and my mum has always been quite frugal, but I always thought that I only needed to start saving and investing when I was an 'adult'.

But when Canna started to talk about the power of investing at a young age and the magic of compound interest, I decided to take my financial future into my own young hands. I took part in Frugal February and The $1000 Project, and I modified it to suit my age and needs, making it The $100 Project! I was amazed at how easy it is to save when you are concentrating! 'Energy flows where attention goes!' Eight months later, I was eighteen with $10 000 in the bank. After that, I funded a holiday to Japan with my best friend, where we created some amazing memories. Seven months after that trip, I have $20 000 saved! I have learned so many tips and tricks about not only saving money, but also making extra money by selling things online, taking up extra tutoring, babysitting, pet sitting and market research jobs, and I still implement all of these in my everyday life.

My life is so much simpler now that I only buy things I need or value, and I don't have any unnecessary clutter with guilt attached from how much money I spent on something. I have learned that life isn't about restricting yourself to have the most money in the world, but making smarter choices with your money to get the most value out of your purchases, and setting yourself up for your financial future at the same time. I learned that spending is *not* your enemy, but mindless spending can be. Spending on things that make you happy and improve the quality of your life and relationships is so important to a well-balanced lifestyle.

I am setting aside my $20 000 and will continue to add to that for a house deposit, and I'm also saving for another overseas holiday, contributing to my superannuation account above my employer's contribution and taking advantage of the Australian government's co-contribution scheme, and saving for the start of my investment portfolio of ETFs and listed investment companies to start building up my passive income. I'm so excited about my future because I know I have the financial habits to remain in control of my finances.

POOJA

My husband and I both moved to the US from different countries. When we got married, my husband had no debt (except monthly car lease payments) and I had student loan and car loan debt.

Despite earning well and having no children or other dependents, I was disappointed at how little I had to show for it outside of an overflowing wardrobe. Money seemed to come into my account and disappear soon afterwards. Despite bonuses and pay increases, I wasn't seeing corresponding increases in my wealth and assets. When it came time to do taxes, I was always shocked to see how large my income was for that year and yet the balance in my bank accounts was so small. My lifestyle would always come before my income. I would often treat myself to luxurious things and vacations with the rationale that 'I work hard, I deserve this' or 'I earn so much, I can afford this' or 'I can pay for this with next month's pay cheque'. I am ashamed to admit that I was living pay cheque to pay cheque. A high monthly pay cheque just made my monthly transgressions bigger.

When we were dreaming of buying our first home, my husband made workbooks to show me how we could afford to put 20% down payment towards our dream home with consistent saving. Having him by my side to hold me accountable helped us both contribute monthly to a special home account and buy our first home in 2015. Purchasing a home was a big milestone for me. It amazed me to see what a large amount I could save if I put my heart into it.

Two big influences in my journey towards financial independence have been Dave Ramsey and SugarMamma.TV (Canna Campbell). I came across Canna through YouTube. Dave taught me to hate debt with a passion and to identify common traps in society which prevent everyday people from becoming millionaires. Canna inspired and motivated me to pay off toxic debt through small consistent steps, and to never underestimate the power of small intentional steps like the $100/500/1000 challenge to achieve Big Hairy Audacious Goals (BHAGs). Her videos about The $1000 Project, saving and investments, minimalism and manifesting money have encouraged and guided me towards a world of abundant wealth.

I started budgeting my money, putting everything I had left after essentials towards my financial goals of paying off all debt, building a comfortable nest egg of savings, fully funding my retirement account and proudly paying cash for all my lifestyle wants. Any salary increases and bonuses go towards achieving my financial goals and building my wealth. Going to nice restaurants, buying designer goods and vacations are regular occurrences which are planned, budgeted and paid cash for.

I paid off my student loan debt in 2014. We paid cash for our wedding overseas in 2016. I paid off my car loan in 2017. Today we have no debt except our mortgage including no monthly car payments. We save and pay cash for any home improvements, big ticket items, splurges for ourselves or vacations. If we ever need a second car, we plan to shop for a two-to-four-year-old car and save and pay cash for it.

I am now working with my husband to pay off our home in five years and to build my personal investment portfolio. I use my daily commute to work to watch SugarMamma YouTube videos as a constant motivator to achieve my goals. On days when my goal to pay off my mortgage appears never-ending and too big, I watch SugarMamma's videos on mortgage payoff in a loop.

CHAPTER SEVENTEEN

Feeling Mindful About Money

'Real wealth has nothing to do with how much you earn, but rather what you do with what you earn.' Me, *The $1000 Project*

As you've been reading through this book, adding crib notes, highlighting certain paragraphs and, most importantly, completing the workbook sections, I hope that you're feeling a stronger awareness and exciting potential awaken within you as you become more mindful about money.

To ensure that you keep growing your mindful money, not just financially but emotionally and spiritually as well, I recommend keeping this book close by. You should refer back to it regularly, reminding yourself what your next step is, getting inspiration for new passive-income-building ideas and learning how to increase your freedom further and with more strength and stability. And remember to update any new goals along your journey to success.

Keep this book safely on your bedside table so you can reassure yourself as to what you're proactively building in your future before drifting off to sleep; then you can refer to it to springboard you out of bed in the morning, with each day providing you with new opportunities and energy.

As I said at the start of this book, my approach isn't all trading software programs, get-rich-quick schemes, taking dangerous risks or selling products to you, but more about presenting you with a philosophy.

By doing the initial groundwork first, through writing out your budget, reprogramming your money mindset, fixing your super/retirement investments and personal insurances for protection, and best of all, setting your number in how much passive income you want to earn, the hard work is behind you.

And this becomes so easy and enjoyable to manage, because as you manage your money you are actually building it, witnessing it mindfully grow from strength to strength. **It literally takes a few minutes each month** for you to update your worksheets, tracking and monitoring the progress and growth of your personal wealth and passive income, and brainstorm new ideas that might help leverage you further and faster. Best of all, each time you see these worksheets, you realise you are one powerful step closer to your number, and making serious progress in the right direction.

In doing this, you start to embrace life to the fullest, with less weight on your shoulders, because you can see and feel the pay-off already from prioritising and proactively taking care of your financial wellbeing. Your financial goals are established and your game plan is in place, bubbling away in the background. And best of all, your money is working for you efficiently and effectively and not taking up your time or energy.

Knowing this, and actually *having* this, frees up your time and energy for more important things like your family, your friends, your health, your community and, best of all, your relationship with yourself. These are the things that make us feel truly happy and connected.

You may be someone who's really blessed and loves your life; it may be that it's already filled with these great aspects, and perhaps you don't need or want to retire. And that's a wonderful position to be in, but consider the additional benefit and comfort of knowing that your financials are well organised, invested and set up in the right way for you; that their management is quick and easy to understand, control and alter as you and your goals naturally change; and that one day you'll have the choice of taking that passive income if and when you want to.

It may simply be to allow you to reduce your working hours to part time, or to help you take a break for a few years while you raise a family, look after a family member or even embark on a new career path or study. Whatever it is, you'll have comfort and choice because you've applied a mindful money approach to your finances.

If you're still feeling nervous or overwhelmed because you worry you don't have enough money, you're starting too late, or you're all on your own in doing this, remember that you already most likely *do* have some money – you can start with your superannuation (or your country's equivalent retirement savings account), as this counts towards your wealth.

Superannuation or your country's version of retirement savings (which you know is really retirement investings) will most likely be one of your biggest sources of passive income, so if you want to, you could just focus all your energy (after paying off toxic debts, of course) into building this up as much as you can. I have plenty of clients who focus 90% of their wealth strategy around their superannuation assets. This makes a lot of sense if they are starting out at a later stage in life with no other assets behind them. We know that they'll be able to access their super soon and we know that this is a really effective and efficient place to quickly build wealth while accessing taxes rates as low as 15% (or even less when those lovely franking credits are applied).

So if you want, just start with your super, even while you are doing other things like paying down debt. Follow these seven simple steps:

1. Set your number as your goal.
2. Play with our calculators.
3. Change your super, if you need to, to a more cost-effective account.
4. Change your investment portfolio within your super so that it matches your long-term goals, using two-dimensional assets such as index ETFs and LICs – remember that these can help cut your fees in half and ensure diversification and can help minimise the ending effect of CGT.
5. Go through your budget and banking ritual, looking for ways to save money so that it can be put towards your super.
6. Start contributing as soon as you can, even if it's only $10 per week, through salary sacrificing or after-tax contributions, or even both. Slowly increase this when you can – you won't miss the money.
7. Update your passive income and wealth creation worksheets every time you do something that increases your super. See and feel the new lightness that comes from being mindful with money.

If, along the way, you surprise yourself with your successes and find yourself back on track with building your number and buying more passive income streams through your super, you can then start to consider investing outside of super. This will mean that you have another structure that provides you with a source of passive income that's always accessible. It will also complement your super strategy and provide an additional safety net for you to rely on.

If you think you're too old to start building passive income and 'have missed the boat' – that's rubbish. Age has nothing to do with this; it's time that makes a difference. And as you are now aware, your retirement is full of time. There's a lot you can achieve once you put your head, heart and mind to it. You can make up for lost time very easily by saving, hustling and earning extra money and proactively putting it towards buying long-term income streams. So don't waste a second – get started today so that you maximise your time.

If you think your budget is already tight and there is no 'extra money lying around' to do this, remember The $1000 Project. At the time of starting this financial challenge, I had just gone through an expensive divorce, taken on a huge amount of debt to get myself and Rocco out of the situation, and was a shell of a human being. My budget was so tight I had no savings to invest, and I had no room in my budget to invest.

But I set myself a small goal to come up with $1000 at a time, doing all sorts of different things to save money and earn extra cash. And the moment I had that money in my hand or in my account (I work in the cashless world), I immediately made it count by transferring it into 'My $1000 Project Account' so there was no temptation to spend it.

The moment the account balance hit $1000, I put that $1000 towards my main financial goal (and passion), which was buying blue chip industrial shares and rebuilding my passive income. And then I went straight back and did it all over again, hustling, saving, creating, earning (working) for my next $1000. And it didn't matter whether it was $2 that I transferred or $200 that I transferred, every dollar counted and was equally respected. It all added up, and added up quickly. In fact, this is the most common thing that I hear from people who message me through Instagram: they're shocked how quickly and easily their balance grows when they're doing their own $1000 Project. It fuels their motivation and desire to keep going and see what they can do next.

Since starting The $1000 Project just over 3.5 years ago, and having just completed its third round, I have saved and invested $94 000 and built a growing passive income from buying industrial dividend-paying shares of over $4556 p.a.[9] growing every year into the long run.

Knowing what you now know about investing and long-term income and growth opportunities that come with two-dimensional assets, imagine where The $1000 Project will be in five, ten or fifteen years' time? Pretty exciting! You can do this too – you are welcome to join in with me at any time.

Now, not a dollar came out of my base salary or from my savings accounts; it came from raising my bar and getting out there and having a really good go. So you too could make The $1000 Project your strategy to build your number. You don't have

---

9   I donate this passive income to various charities each year. These have included The Gidget Foundation, Indonesian orphanage – Pa van der Steur and RizeUp Australia.

to make it as restrictive as I did; you can use some or all of your savings to kickstart the process, and you can take money out of your salary towards buying these shares. You create your own rules and timeframes.

The point is, take one big goal, break it down into bite-sized, manageable and achievable goals, and just do it. Regularly update your worksheets along the way with every step in the right direction, and document your progress and success.

Also, as I said, mindful money is not about strict rules, percentages or deadlines. If you don't want to allocate 10% p.a. from your passive income for future ongoing investing, you don't have to. It will make your required number smaller and more approachable and achievable. And at any stage you are free to change your number as your life naturally evolves through different life stages and your values and needs change. That is perfectly normal and natural.

We have built an extensive library of helpful, easy-to-understand and visually based calculators on SugarMamma.TV for you. Regularly play around with them as you review and consider your goals and dreams. While there may be periods or phases in your life where you can't invest as much as you would like, those times won't last forever, so if you know and can see what potential strategies or game plans lie in your future, as your situation changes and improves, you will know to cease those strategies immediately, to experience the shift and level up in your financial wealth.

And if you want to do this but have a big goal such as buying a home, or want to focus on getting ahead on paying off your home loan further before embarking on this journey of your number, that's completely fine. You can still do this. If you are focusing on saving up for your first home or even your next home, you can focus your energy on saving the biggest deposit possible, without the temptation to increase your budget with it. In the meantime, make sure you fix up your superannuation along the way and include it as part of your source of passive income towards your goal (keeping access in mind). When you've bought your home (or are already in it), and the mortgage is dropping at an efficient speed with the term much shorter than when you started, down to twenty years or less, look to start investing – or even better, consider the debt-recycling strategy that the Howards use in Chapter seven.

If you're doing this financial independence thing as a single person, good on you. Me too! It feels so empowering to know that everything I've created and worked for is off the back of my own determination, resilience, action, sacrifice and hard work. I don't have to justify, compromise or ask permission from anyone. And to say it's empowering knowing that I'm standing on my own two feet, only getting stronger with each step in the right direction, is an understatement. So don't let singlehood hold you back – it's actually a blessing.

And what I love even more is that I can choose to and afford to share my financial successes along the way. Which of course I will do, but there's a great sense of stability, strength and self-respect within myself that I have taken care of myself as a priority and from doing that, I can pour from a full bucket into everyone else's. And that is a beautiful feeling.

So now that you understand what mindful money means, what financial freedom and independence look like, and how quick and easy it is to manage and achieve your goals once you have set everything up correctly, let's have a quick refresher of the steps.

1. Clear your toxic debt once and for all – draw a line in the sand and make it your business to manage your cash flow responsibly and realistically and never repeat history.

2. Build emergency savings – enough to help you out in an emergency should the situation arise. If you ever tap into it, replace it.

3. Work out *your number* – that is, the passive income you want to earn to give you the life and freedom that you want.

4. Adjust your mindset, getting excited about your future. Always be aware of the power and impact of your mind and self-talk – work on it all the time.

5. Build your budget – feel proudly responsible for knowing where your money goes. Review it regularly.

6. Look for ways to save and earn extra cash to put those savings and earnings towards your goal so that they count and don't get accidentally spent.

7. Design your banking ritual instructions – including your financial goal account. Make this a habit like cleaning your teeth, you don't think about it, you just do it.

8. Start buying and building income sources through two-dimensional assets – assets that grow in value and have growing income. Immediately update your worksheets, tracking and monitoring your progress – it just takes a few minutes and feels great and consider your asset ratio.

9. Take care of your superannuation (or your country's retirement investments) and include it in your passive income number if you want.

10. Make sure you have the right type of personal insurances in place – and sleep well at night.

11. Include charity along the way, give what you can, not necessarily money but time, energy, awareness and effort. Be part of something that makes a difference and is meaningful to you.

12. Inspire others – tell people about your exciting goals, your new focus, your big dreams and desires. You can have a profound effect on others and dramatically change and improve other's lives and futures by sharing your story and determination with them.

And finally as you go through this process, please know that you are not alone. Everything that I have recommended in this book **I do for myself. I practise what I preach.**

I have shared my experience, my knowledge, my mistakes, my wisdom and my financial super powers with you, to help you. This book has a bias towards ETFs, LICs and industrial shares and to a limited extent, property. And for a good reason.

It is quick and easy to start building your number and create an inroad towards building your number and your financial freedom. But most importantly, the passive income grows at a faster rate through these type of investment assets. In particular, industrial dividends, which since 1979 have grown on average 6.5% p.a.[10]

I am not interested in chasing capital growth, because the value of an asset can't give me ongoing financial freedom unless I sell the asset and then if I did, I would have to end up spending the proceeds to live off it, eventually leaving me back at square one, no better off once all the money is spent, and potentially too old to start again from zero dollars.

So I choose to chase dividends, dividends from index ETFs, LICs and industrial shares, which grow consistently over time, never touching the capital. I happily love adding and including more

---

10 Statistic provided by Whitefield.

investments in my portfolio as it is only benefiting me in building and working towards *my own number*.

And finally, stay in touch. I'm a regular, everyday person just like you, working on my own financial goals and passive income one step at a time. I love to hear from you, because your stories inspire me right back and give me the boost to keep going as well. When you can share inspiring stories, you become part of an incredible flow-on effect that awakens many other people, serving as their much-needed wake-up call and reinvigorating your own energy and passion for life.

At times you will definitely face frustrations, setbacks, challenges and disheartening moments. This is all part of life and how you get through it depends on how you choose to react.

When this happens (which it does for me as well), take a deep breath, go back to your notes in this book about why you are on this path, what your values and personal definitions are and what you want to create. Look for the lesson that is trying to be taught, and then the blessing in disguise, the benefit, insight or new knowledge that you are going to come out with at the end of this, after whatever challenge you are facing has passed. Never stop setting and working on those mini goals around the problem, breaking everything down into bite-size steps and brainstorm as many different ideas and solutions that might help. Sometimes the most ridiculous idea is a stroke of genius.

Neither Canna Campbell nor the SugarMamma.TV brand is leaving you in the lurch. You can watch me on YouTube every Monday for a 'Money Monday' video, where I talk about investing, wealth creation, budgeting, passive income, etc. You can use this as your weekly financial vitamin tablet and it is completely free. Also, every Thursday I publish a 'Lifestyle Love' video, where I share more personal videos inside my life, particularly around my passion for minimalism, the juggle of motherhood in a modern world, and other interests or fun challenges that I like to set for myself. Then if you want more, you can always join the private paid membership group, The $ugar Tribe by heading to my Facebook page.

More books will follow from this one, starting with my determination to educate children and teenagers around the world about financial literacy going forward in a cashless society, followed by a book on relationships and money – how to be a powerful united financial front. So stay tuned, our financial awakening has only just begun.

In the meantime, get ready for your financial future to change forever. Enjoy the new lightness that comes with facing your financial fears and challenges head on, turning them into goals and successes, growing both personally and financially along the way and amazing yourself with what you can achieve with your newfound mindful money approach.

CHEAT TIP FROM CC:

If you would like my encouragement and support in your own wealth creation journey, make sure whenever you do something for your financial wellbeing or for your $1000 Project, that you follow me on Instagram @SugarMammaTV, and tag #mymindfulmoneynumber and #the1000dollarproject – I can then regularly check in on your progress and cheerlead you along the way. We also have an Instagrammer of the week, as your pictures, quotes and actions are a powerful inspiration and help others with their own financial journey.

---

xCC

WHERE TO FROM HERE?

Just like we always need to work on our physical fitness, it is so important to continuously feed and build our financial wellbeing and knowledge. We are constantly surrounded by new opportunities, new rules and regulations. In addition to regularly referring to this book and your handwritten notes in the workbook, updating them as you discover and learn more, see below for some excellent resources that I recommend to keep on hand.

1. *Motivated Money* by Peter Thornhill
Easy to read and understand, this is a book on investing in shares. Peter also runs seminars around Australia in-between travelling the world and spending time with his beautiful family. You can read more on his website www.motivatedmoney.com. au. Every single person that I have recommended watch Peter speak has called me immediately after to share with me their awakening. This is one of the best investments that you will ever make – his information and advice applies to everyone around the world.

2. Oliver's Insights

I am super strict about newsletters I sign up to, but this one is essential, plus it is free. Shane Oliver has a wonderful way of explaining financial news and how it impacts you. He always takes a calm rational approach, focusing on the big picture and blessings and opportunities that exist for you. He gets straight to the point but backs everything up with facts and figures.

3. The $ugar Tribe

If you want to be a part of our private membership group, you can find all the details on the SugarMamma.TV website. While the advice is general advice only, I create additional educational content around money, beyond my YouTube channel, including vlogs of me doing The $1000 Project. This is a highly engaged audience where the members have direct access to me and we support each other as a team while working on our individual financial goals.

4. *The $1000 Project*

My first book. One of the great things about The $1000 Project is that you can get started straightaway. You can also use it to speed-read through all the recommendations in this book. From getting out of debt, to building emergency money, and of course to building passive income and preparing for retirement. It has helped thousands of people around the world. The one thing that stands out is that once you start your own $1000 Project, you stick to it because it works and helps make a big difference. You can pick and choose what you use it for. It has helped its readers pay for IVF (including my own baby, Apple), save family pets, fund weddings and school fees as well as other financial accomplishments.

5. SugarMamma Financial Library

If you subscribe to our website, you can see the growing list of books that we recommend reading, beyond personal finances. Also, by being subscribed to our website, you can access our budget templates, ebooks and worksheets, plus you are always up to date on our financial videos and blogs. We also run regular competitions on a monthly basis, with the average monthly prize value over $1000. This includes self-care packs and financial coaching sessions with me, as well as other helpful prizes.

6. Lars Kroijer – Books & YouTube Channel

I highly recommend watching any of Lars's videos on YouTube and then checking out his books, *Money Mavericks: Confessions of a Hedge Fund Manager* and *Investing Demystified*. Like Peter Thornhill, he lets you see the trees through the woods and shows you what risks are worth taking and how to recognise when you need to delegate to a fund manager. A huge fan of international index ETFs for full diversification and long-term passive income. Slow and steady wins this race.

ACKNOWLEDGEMENTS

Thank you, Tom Simpson. I don't think I have ever met a more passionate and loving person who can make as many people laugh like you do in any situation. It is an honour to call you my partner and such an incredible role model to Rocco and myself. You are always challenging us to go deeper, find more, understand more and at the same time so protective of us. You encourage us to raise our bar, and believe in us with complete faith. No two days are ever the same with you and no two days are more special. Rocco's and my lives have never been more fun and meaningful since the day we met and I cannot wait to see what more adventurers and little people await ahead of us.

To Mum and Dad, thank you for teaching me how to be mindful with money, how to respect it, honour it, nurture it and share it. There is no way I would be where I am today without the wisdom, patience and generosity you both installed in me and I hope to be able to share with others for them to experience the freedom themselves.

Georgie Abay and The Abay Family. When people ask me how I juggle things, it is because I have a Georgie Abay breathing oxygen into me, keeping me focused, inspired, sane and still laughing. You and your family are everything to me and my family. Tom, Rocco and baby Apple.

One of the most wholesome, fun and down to earth families I know is the Simpson family. Thank you! You truly know the value of what is important in life. You have all been so kind, warm and welcoming to Rocco and me into your family and I have learnt so much. Mike and Vicki, who have raised three incredible boys in a small country town, who have each gone on to build their own individual successes and picked amazingly beautiful partners, both inside and out, with happy healthy and big personality children. This is what real wealth is.

Thank you, Peter Thornhill, for inspiring me over fifteen years ago when I first watched you speak. The gift you give people with how to work through all the intimidating numbers and jargon and see the simple truth. You have changed so many people's lives, including mine and you have been so gracious in the time, guidance and advice passed on to me. I can't thank you enough.

Thank you to the $ugar Tribe, the closed group that I run on Facebook with a group of amazingly kind, motivated and driven people from all over the world. They are all working hard to improve their own financial wellbeing, but are also always supporting and encouraging each other along the way, and raising each other up. It is an honour to help each of you work on your goals and watch you go from strength to strength, as well as be a form of support for me. Thank you to all the tribe members.

Thank you, Chloe Morello. This is the person who pushed me to launch SugarMamma.TV. None of this would have ever happened if it wasn't for you. You told me I need to use my knowledge, experience and voice to help people around the world create a better life for themselves. Your support, encouragement and warmth are just some of the many things that make you such a special person and someone who is so authentic.

Discover a
new favourite